THE PUBLICATION OF THIS WORK HAS BEEN AIDED
BY A GRANT FROM
THE ANDREW W. MELLON FOUNDATION

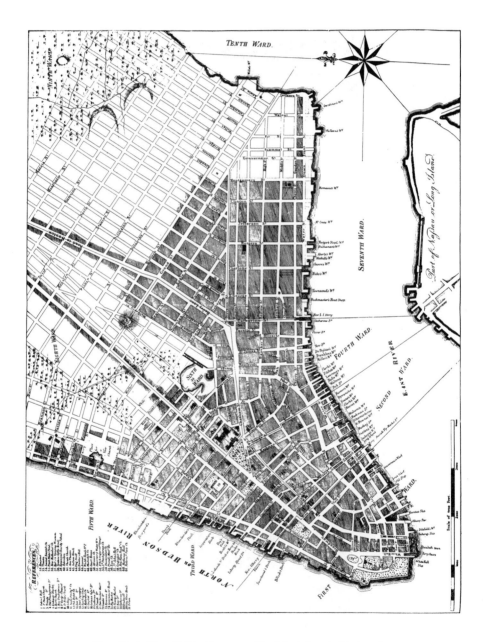

New York City, 1808. Courtesy, Florida Atlantic University.

Artisans of the New Republic

The Tradesmen of New York City in the Age of Jefferson

Howard B. Rock

New York University Press
New York *and* London
1984

127404

First paperbound edition 1984

Copyright © 1979 by New York University

Library of Congress Cataloging in Publication Data

Rock, Howard B., 1944-
   Artisans of the New Republic.

   Bibliography: p.
   1. Artisans—New York (City)—History.
2. New York (City)—Social conditions. I. Title.
HD2346.U52N5524   301.44′42   78-55570
ISBN 0-8147-7378-8
ISBN 0-8147-7388-5 pbk.

Manufactured in the United States of America

For My Father and in Memory of My Mother
And for Ellen and David

PREFACE

Important studies have been published on the artisans (or mechanics, as they were more commonly known) in the revolutionary and Jacksonian eras. Suprisingly little, however, is known about craftsmen in the intervening Jeffersonian period. This is regrettable, for this period was one of considerable significance for American workingmen. Politically aware, mechanics composed a decisive electoral bloc in the nation's major seaport, playing a major role in the development of partisan politics. In the marketplace, too, artisans were influential as active entrepreneurs and, most critically, as adversaries in serious and sometimes protracted labor disputes, conflicts that would have a lasting effect on American working-class history.

This study is an attempt to fill this gap in our understanding of the historical sojourn of American craftsmen. Emphasizing the social, political, and economic lives of the bulk of the city's population, it is, at least in part, a segment of the new social history now being written about the lives of heretofore forgotten Americans. It is not, however, intended as a presentation of definitive explanations about the mechanics' behavior. Rather, because it covers a period in labor history previously overlooked, it is intended to open paths for further work. It is my hope that others will pursue in their own way some of the questions discussed in this book.

As used in this study, the term "Jeffersonian era" is roughly meant to comprehend the first two decades of the nineteenth century. In politics, paralleling the research of Edmund P. Willis, it deals primarily with the period from the inauguration of Jefferson in 1801 to the end of the War of 1812. The chapters on artisan endeavors in the marketplace include these years as well as the economic problems encountered from the end of the war through the panic of 1819.

It gives me the greatest pleasure to be able to acknowledge the individuals and institutions that have assisted me over the years. Parts of this study have appeared in somewhat different format in *New York History* and in *Labor History,* and I appreciate the journals' permission to use that material in this context. The American Council of Learned Societies provided an important grant that allowed time for the writing of a substantial portion of this manuscript, while the Florida International University Foundation gave further assistance toward its publication.

Also generous in their assistance were the staffs of the New York Public Library, the Winterthur Library, the General Society of Mechanics and Tradesmen, the New York City Municipal Archives, the Historical Documents Collection (Queens College, CUNY), and the New York Historical Society. At the Historical Documents Center James Owre was most helpful in showing me new sources, while at the New York Historical Society, where I was for many months a common and, I hope, welcome sight, Roger Mohovich, John Lovari, and Tom Dunnings provided guidance to the immense resources of this outstanding institution.

During the early part of this research, Drs. Paul O. Weinbaum and Brian J. Danforth gave me valuable criticism and advice. Professor Patricia U. Bonomi tendered important aid in conceptualizing major themes. Too, fellow faculty members at Florida International University offered hepful ideas in faculty colloquia. Also at Florida International, Judy Green, Diana Richardson, Al Granado and Jesus Pedré-Crespo put in many patient hours in the typing and preparation of this manuscript. Most of all, I am indebted to two scholars who gave selflessly of their time to the improvement of this work. No words of thanks can adequately repay Professor Alfred F. Young of Northern Illinois University for his detailed, meticulous, and perceptive critiques of this study at different stages of its development. So, too, I am grateful to Professor Carl E. Prince of New York University for both the personal and the professional counsel he gave me during the growth of this project from a seminar paper under his direction to its current publication. I find myself doubly fortunate to have him as both an adviser and a friend. Finally, I wish to acknowledge my wife, Ellen, whose critical suggestions, faith, and confidence have been essential to the completion of this work.

CONTENTS

III. THE NEW MARKETPLACE 235

LIST OF ILLUSTRATIONS

LIST OF
TABLES AND MAPS

INTRODUCTION

Early-nineteenth-century New York was characterized by a significant degree of social and economic divergence. Imagine a
visitor traveling Gotham's streets around 1810. Arriving in the
fashionable lower area of the city, and likely wandering along
Broadway and Pearl streets, he would be impressed by the seaport's elegant stores, offering at wholesale and retail both the finest
of imports from England, France, and the Orient, and the better
local manufactures. Entering one of these establishments, he might
be startled by the unsubtle, sartorial statements of the elite mercantile proprietors, sporting their expensive blue waistcoats, long
hair, short buckled breeches, and ruffled shirts. If he were fortunate
enough to have a letter of introduction or other means of entry into
the circle of the city's gentry, he would be invited to the home of
one of these merchants. There he would find a graceful two- or
three-story brick townhouse, staffed by respectful servants and
slaves and decorated in the "tasteful magnificence of modern
style," with furniture from the shops of Duncan Phyfe and other
American and European cabinetmakers. At midafternoon he
would partake of a sumptuous multicourse dinner, symbolic of a
life-style that one Englishman described as "more luxurious than
that of the same description of people found in England."[1]

If our tourist proved curious the next day, and left behind the Fraunces Tavern, Trinity Church, Tontine Coffee House, and Bank of New York to venture out into the outer wards which enclosed the metropolis, he would see a very different scene. First of all, his footing would grow perilous as paved thoroughfares gave way to unregulated dirt streets made all the more hazardous by recklessly driven carts and unchecked rambling pigs. Walking carefully along these roads, he would immediately notice that the luxurious stores of the lower wards were replaced by all manner of workshops, including blacksmith, shoemaking, tailoring, and printing operations and bakeries and numerous small groceries and taverns. Most of these enterprises were of modest size, but a number of sizable establishments could also be sighted; the tanneries of the Fourth Ward were unmistakable for their odors as were the glue and candle manufactories, turpentine distilleries, and slaughterhouses. So, too, the major shipyards along the waterfront were large-scale operations.

Had he risen early, around six in the morning, he would have found the streets filled with men walking to work. Traversing the roads on their way to the docks, coopers, riggers, shipwrights, caulkers, and sailmakers would come into view. In the Sixth Ward, home of many cartmen, he would spot drivers saddling their horses and heading off in all directions to carry the city's many wares. Equally apparent were the masons and carpenters working on the latest construction sites, uptown and downtown, that were constantly going up in the rapidly growing city. Too, he would meet butchers, cabinetmakers, goldsmiths, hatters, and the rest of the city's large artisan population on their way to their jobs or businesses. Tradesmen's wives, as well, were no less visible, either walking to the city's markets to get the best pick of the meat and vegetables, just arrived from the country, or else themselves going to work.

These were the mechanic wards, the modest but respectable home and workplace for the majority of the city's artisan community. And while it may have been apparent to our traveler that these vibrant, civic-minded wards were not slums, the contrast between them and the fashionable lower wards was striking. In place of the breeches and waistcoats worn by the merchants, most mechanics dressed in leather aprons and trousers and caps. Instead of retiring for a leisurely supper, most craftsmen did not return home until sundown (though there were a number of work breaks). "Home" sometimes consisted of wooden shops and workrooms with living quarters in the back. Most artisans, however, lived in rented dwellings in these outer wards. Commonly a number of families, totaling twenty-five to thirty members, lived in four- or five-room dwellings. Young unmarried journeymen lived in crowded boarding houses close to the waterfront.[2]

Perhaps the starkest example of the meaning of the variance in economic standing occurred during the yellow fever epidemics that ravaged New York and other American seaports during the late eighteenth and early nineteenth centuries. To avoid this fearsome threat, the wealthier, living in the lower wards (1–3), moved during the dangerous summer season to the suburb of Greenwich Village or even farther into the country, leaving behind the mechanics and laborers in the outer wards. From 1801 to 1803, for example, the population of the elite first and second wards declined during the summer from 4,320 to 1,370 and 5,167 to 549, respectively. These were decreases of seven and nine out of ten. In the mechanic sixth and seventh wards, however, the population lessened only from 13,076 to 10,076 and from 18,394 to 15,394, or differences of two and one out of ten, respectively. Although occasional newspaper articles condemned this inequity, little was done to assist the tradesmen.[3]

Little attempt was made in early national America to hide the differences in status. As Jackson T. Main has found, it was generally accepted that men could be ranked and that class differences and antagonisms were inevitable. An editorial in the *Commercial Advertiser* declared that "the warfare between the different classes of people began and will end only with man." And, while the boundaries of social ranking were not necessarily defined by occupation—a few prominent and ambitious mechanics did reach upper-class standing—most tradesmen fell into the lower middling "inferior orders of people." This was well beneath the "great merchants [who] like their prototypes in Venice, were the leaders of society in all its phases," and still below that of smaller merchants, government officials, clergy, and lesser attorneys. As skilled wage-earners and shopkeepers, the craftsmen were, however, above day laborers, Irish immigrants, free blacks, and slaves. In sum, as traveler Lambert remarked: "Those who expect to see a *pure republican equality* existing will find themselves greatly deceived." [4]

The "pervasive sense of social separateness, which apparently grew stronger than weaker after the Revolution," was based on an English heritage that saw artisans as men of inferior status and lesser ability. This legacy is clearly revealed by an analysis of the contemporary meaning of the word "mechanic," the most common and inclusive name for artisans and tradesmen.[5] Definitions taken from the *Oxford English Dictionary* and Samuel Johnson's noted *Dictionary of the English Language* reveal the pejorative meaning of the word. The *Oxford* defines "mechanic" as "belonging to or characteristic of the lower orders; vulgar, base"; Johnson describes a mechanic as "mean, servile; of mean occupation." Quotations drawn from English literature illustrate this prejudice: [6]

Suffering Mechanick, Ignorant fellows to preach and expound the Scripture.

(1662, Charles I, *Decl. Works* II, 170)

The Tontine Coffee House in the heart of the mercantile district. Notice the lavish dress of the gentry. Courtesy, New York Historical Society, New York City.

I am glad you have taught me at what distance to keep such mechanics for the future.

> (1733, Fielding, *Intrigues of a Chambermaid*)

This fellow is a wretched mechanic.

> (1828, Scott, *F.M. Perth*)

Other studies also reveal this prejudice. Colonial printers, for example, like their counterparts in England, "had to face the hard, discouraging fact that" despite their intellectual ability, "in the eyes of their neighbors they were by training mechanics, without full legitimacy as men of independent intellect and creed." So, too, a recent biographer of Alexander McDougall, a man who rose from a New York City milkman and apprentice sailor to be a noted major general in the Continental army, notes that the influence of a "deference-based society" had considerable influence on his personality and ambition as he doggedly pursued his career, ever sensitive to attacks on his character.[7]

In early national New York, the most significant example of this heritage were the deferential expectations held by the local gentry, particularly merchants, lawyers, and landowners. To these men, mechanics were base and contemptuous, neither worthy or capable of aspiring to political or economic leadership, nor of full participation in the life of the community; rather, they were expected to accede to the wisdom and guidance of the wealthier, better educated, and better bred. Three writers perceptively depict this attitude. First, Thurlow Weed, who began his career as a New York printer, recalling his experience in Albany attempting to secure a charter for a local typographical society, described the effect of these expectations on both himself and his social betters:

> I remember with what deference I then ventured into the presence of distinguished members of the Legislature, and how sharply I was rebuked by two gentlemen, who were shocked at the idea of incorporating journeymen mechanics.[8]

Second is the account of Tammany historian M. R. Werner, who quotes an early-nineteenth-century observer on artisans' difficulty

Two scenes from the Fifth Ward. Most of the buildings would house a number of families. Notice the increased density in the lower illustration, made around 1820, as compared to the above, drawn in 1809. Top: Museum of the City of New York. Bottom: Courtesy, New York Historical Society, New York City.

in gaining access to banking privileges: "A mechanic never ven-
tured to ask for a discount in those days without some merchant as
a patron and friend, and then the loan was obtained as a special
favor." [9]

The third telling statement is an artisan satire on the attitudes of
the upper class toward tradesmen. The article describes a dialogue
purported to have taken place among a group of New York's finer
young women:

"Who is that?"
"Why don't you know him! Why not John W—? oh fie."
"What, the cooper's son?"

"Yes, and what is he now? He is still the son of a cooper; I
mean he is not a lawyer, or a priest or some other professional
gentleman. No, no, he is what I said he was, a cooper's son,
the son of a cooper."

"But then I have heard it said, that he is a young gentleman of good abilities, and bids fair to prove a shining
ornament in society. I am inclined to think also, that he is a
worthy young man, from the little acquaintance I have with
him."

"Nonsense! Still you think that he is a cooper's son, and
nothing more than the son of a cooper."

"Why my dear, what if he be the son of a cooper, may not
the son of a cooper be a worthy man; and is not even a
cooper, a character that is generally respected; and notwithstanding, he is the son of a mechanic, he will no doubt be of
as much consequence in society as the son of a nabob. Is it not
reasonable to believe, that he will ever be considered by the
wiser part of mankind no less deserving esteem on account of
his origin?" [10]

The conversation continues at some length with the cooper's son's
advocate finally declaring that she would even consent to be John's
"partner in life," in preference to a man who, though he possessed
"titles and empty dignities," had an inferior moral character.

Despite the ridicule with which the narrator derides the values
of these young ladies, the sense of inferiority against which mechanics had to struggle is clearly present. In these incidents, and

many more to be found within the narrative, craftsmen were repeatedly reminded that they occupied a lower rung on the social ladder.

This legacy of inferiority and deference was, however, only part of the American craftsman's heritage. During the colonial era the availability of land and a labor intensive economy gave artisans greater opportunity and wealth than their counterparts in the old country. Lower suffrage requirements, moreover, particularly in the city and county of New York, allowed mechanics at least a say in which elite group would assume political power in the city and colony. And with the coming of the American Revolution, mechanics assumed an active role in the resistance to Great Britain's policies and in the ranks of the Continental army. For the artisan, the Revolution catalyzed previous economic and political gains into a new prideful sense of being participants in the creation of a new republic, while giving them greater hope that they could and ought to more fully share in the growing economic bounty.

It is the conflict between the legacy of second-class citizenship and deferential expectation and the recent heritage of economic, political, and revolutionary roles that is at the heart of the story of the New York mechanic during the Jeffersonian era. That the only major newspaper directed at the tradesmen community was entitled the *Independent Mechanic* is symbolic of this. The artisan, having helped gain his country's independence, was now striving for his own freedom. His aspiration was to be respected as a man of independent mind, as an honorable journeyman, a self-sufficient entrepreneur, an active leader and participant in the nation's politics and government, and as a proud family man of high moral standards.

This study explores mechanics' efforts to achieve the sense of independence and esteem they so greatly desired. It describes their specific political and economic goals, relating them to the aspirations and conflicts of different sectors of the mechanic population. Politically, tradesmen were an active and decisive factor on the New York scene. All parties had to be cognizant of, and sensitive to, mechanics' social and economic needs. Consequently, partisan politics allowed craftsmen to continue their revolutionary era struggle for greater stature. Through their roles as officeholders, candidates, and voters, they both asserted their place in the body politic and punished those who opposed them. However, their position as voting blocs subordinate to national parties and state and local party figures made them dependent on political leaders with other interests to speak to their needs. While this solution was generally successful, especially with the additional prestige afforded by the various patriotic activities of the artisans' benevolent and trade societies, it did not solve the specific problems of the journeymen, nor did it protect tradesmen from political manipulation. That is, participation is party politics proved to be a partial but not totally satisfactory means to greater standing and influence in the community.

In the marketplace, mechanics sought to improve their station by taking advantage of the buoyant economy of the nation's leading seaport. Many were successful, although their endeavors against the remnants of mercantilistic controls and their ventures into the new area of commercial banking often placed them in vulnerable positions. Furthermore, a number of major mechanic crafts came under the influence of capitalist-oriented production, leading to a serious threat to the welfare and status of the journeymen and precipitating major labor conflict. Finally, the growth of the modern marketplace, together with the influence of the Revolution, brought the beginning of significant changes in the work culture and moral outlooks of the mechanic population.

Prior to commencing this analysis, it is helpful to understand what is meant by the terms "mechanic" and "mechanic community." A mechanic was a skilled handicraftsman, owning his own tools, who worked either for himself or as a foreman for a contractor or merchant, in which case he was a master craftsman, or else for a daily or weekly wage, in which case he was a journeyman.[11] He may have labored in any one of a large number of trades, providing the city with needed services such as breadmaking, carting, or blacksmithing, or else with manufactured goods such as shoes, furniture, and fine clothing.

Many of the mechanic crafts required intricate skills and long periods of training. Shoemaking, for example, involved many procedures. Having cut the leather to size, a craftsman had to hammer it on a lapstone, size it on a last, and sew on the heel. He then carefully fastened the shoe by stitching and the use of a

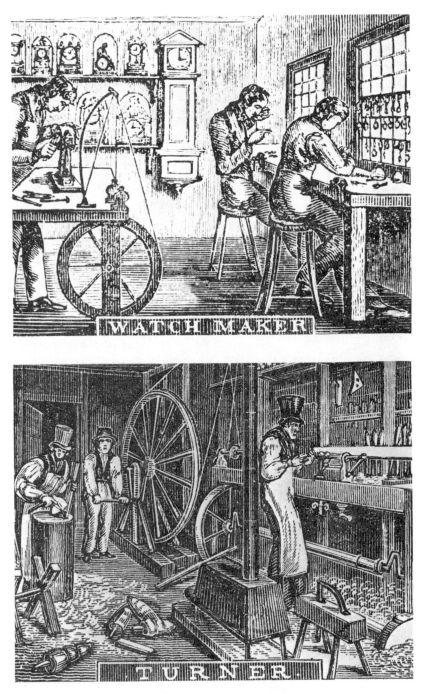

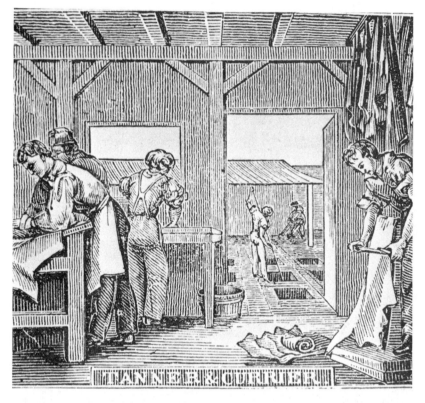

Four scenes of mechanics at work. Artisan skills ranged from the intricate craft of a watchmaker and turner to the more strenuous tasks of the blacksmith and tanner. Such trades were at the heart of the preindustrial urban economy. Other than the blacksmith these scenes are taken from woodcuts in Edward Hazen, *The Panorama of Professions and Trades* (Philadelphia, 1837), reprinted (1970) as *Encyclopedia of Early American Trades* by Century House Publishers, Watkins Glen, New York, 14891. Watchmaker and turner: Courtesy, New York Historical Society, New York City. Blacksmith: Courtesy, New York Public Library. Tanner: Courtesy, Century House. Watkins Glen, New York.

leather "welt" and, finally, trimmed and polished it. Cabinetmaking, perhaps the most refined of the mechanic branches, required knowledge of drawing, proportion, current styles, wood texture and adaptability, as well as expert skill in such processes as veneering, gluing, varnishing, and joint construction. The fine work of such men as Duncan Phyfe and Charles Lannuier is yet tribute to the artistic talent of these craftsmen, and many antique books recount details of mechanic achievement.[12] Equally renowned is the cooperative work of the many artisan trades responsible for the construction of the fine sailing ships of the early nineteenth century or for such buildings as New York's elegant City Hall.

The mechanic population of New York (Table 1) formed a community, a social group with a common heritage and common interests and characteristics; it perceived itself and was perceived as being distinct in some respects from the rest of society. That this was so is indicated by a number of factors. The primary determinant was unquestionably professional skills. It was their association with skilled manual labor that allowed poor tradesmen to differentiate themselves from unskilled laborers, while the same association with artisan production separated the more prominent mechanics from the merchant classes. Other characteristics such as common dress and housing and place of residence reinforced this identity. So, too, continuing historic traditions, such as the period of apprenticeship to learn the "mystery" of a trade and continuing recourse to fraternal craft-oriented societies for social and recreational outlets, fostered a sense of commonality. Politics also had been an important forum for separate community involvement, particularly in the Revolutionary era. This legacy continued, nowhere more evident than in the fact that mechanics were without question the single group to whom most election appeals were addressed. No ethnic or religious group rivaled them on this score. Finally, the legacy of inferiority and deference, while not a proud inheritance, was a strong common bond among mechanics of all ranks and professions.

What distinguished the mechanic community of the Jeffersonian era from that of earlier periods was the size, complexity, and division within its ranks. While the percentage of the city's population composed of mechanics remained at between 50 and 60 percent throughout the era, the increase in numbers was sizable.

TABLE 1

NEW YORK CITY MECHANICS (3886)*

Construction Crafts

Carpenters (370)
Masons (149)
Painters (87)
Sawyers (36)
Stone Cutters (36)
Glaziers (24)
Coachmakers (18)
Wheelwrights (15)
Dock-builders (6)
Nailers (4)

Clothing Crafts

Tailors (195)
Mantua makers (59)
Hairdressers (56)
Hatters (47)
Seamstresses (31)
Dyers (8)
Starchmakers (4)

Leather Crafts

Tanners and Curriers (24)
Shoemakers (291)
Saddlers (27)
Harnessmakers (8)
Morocco Manufacturers (8)
Skinners (8)

Shipbuilding Crafts

Shipwrights (116)
Riggers (59)
Sailmakers (40)
Ropemakers (34)
Caulkers (3)
Block-makers (17)

Food and Tobacco

Butchers (124)
Bakers (97)
Tobacconists (34)
Distiller (13)
Brewers (19)
Segar-makers (13)
Millwrights (7)
Sugar-refiners (13)

Furniture

Chair and Cabinet-
Makers (75)
Carvers and Gilders (15)
Upholsterers (23)
Whipmakers (4)

Forging Crafts

Blacksmiths (104)
Brass-founders (12)
Tinmers (20)
Coppersmiths (15)

Printing and Paper

Printers (41)
Bookbinders (24)
Engravers (11)

Comb-Crafts

Brushmakers (7)
Combmakers (6)

Transportation

Cartmen (1200)
Porters (41)

Boiling Crafts

Tallow Chandlers (14)

Container Crafts

Coopers (101)

Clock and Jewelry

Watchmakers (30)
Gold and Silversmiths (27)
Jewelers (16)

*The numbers in parentheses are provided only to give a picture of the concentration of artisans in
the different trades. They are taken from the General Trade Directory of the 1805-1806 *Longworth's
New York Directory*. This guide listed about two-fifths of the mechanic population except for the
cartmen who, licensed, were all included. This format is adapted from that of Charles S. Olton,
Artisans for Independence: Philadelphia Mechanics and the American Revolution. (Syracuse, 1975),
pp. 4-5. Only crafts with at least three entries are included in this table.

New York grew from a port town with a population of 33,031 in 1790 and with about 4,000 working tradesmen to a city of 60,489 in 1800 with perhaps 7,000 active mechanics. By 1810 New York was a metropolis of 96,373 with approximately 10,000 tradesmen, and in 1820, as the nation's largest urban center, numbering 123,706 inhabitants, it contained about 14,000 craftsmen. While the increase in mechanics during the thirty years from 1760 to 1790 had been little over 2,000, the next thirty years saw the artisan sector grow by 10,000.[13]

Not surprisingly, a number of different subcommunities arose within this expanding population. Mechanics divided into separate groupings according to individual craft, political affiliation, neighborhood residence, ethnic background, and most importantly, journeyman or master craftsman standing. This last division saw significant resentment and strife over conflicting economic aspirations and increased disparities in income and assets.

Because of this complexity and division, the story of the mechanic is an intricate one, following a number of different paths. Yet, within this diversity, craftsmen's mutual heritage and common goals must be kept in mind. With few exceptions, the members of the different subcommunities remained within the mechanic orbit in this era, identifying as artisans. All were angered by aspersions against mechanics, and all fought for greater self-respect and community position. The means to this common end, particularly when economic interests collided, could differ radically, as in the case of the journeymen and masters. But throughout the period, the mechanic population remained an identifiable community, working toward improved social and economic standing, sometimes in harmony and sometimes not.

NOTES

Unless otherwise noted, all newspaper citations refer to newspapers published in New York City.

1. John Lambert, *Travels Through Canada and the United States* (London, 1814), pp. 82, 91, 102-03. See also Franklin Scott, ed., *Baron Klinköwstrom's America: 1818-1820* (Evanston, 1952), chap. 13.

2. Paul Zankovich, "The Craftsmen of Colonial New York," Ph. D.

diss. (New York University School of Education, 1956), p. 399; M. R. Werner, *Tammany Hall* (New York, 1928), p. 21; D. R. Fox and J. A. Krout, *The Completion of Independence* (New York, 1944), pp. 29-40.

3. Lambert, *Travels Through Canada and the United States,* p. 84; *Morning Chronicle,* October 29, 1803; *American Citizen,* July 19, 1802, August 24, 1803, October 27, 1803.

4. Jackson T. Main, *The Social Structure of Revolutionary America* (Princeton, 1965), p. 228; *Commercial Advertiser,* March 7, 1801; "New York City in the Nineteenth Century," *American History Magazine,* 32 (1906), 203; Lambert, *Travels Through Canada and the United States,* p. 103.

5. Staughton Lynd and Alfred Young, "After Carl Becker: The Mechanics and New York City Politics," *Labor History,* 5 (1964) 215-224. Though the terms "craftsman," "mechanic," "artisan," and "tradesman" may have originally had separate meanings, I use the words interchangeably as they were used in the early nineteenth century. If anything, the word *mechanic* was taking on a more proletarian meaning. See Richard B. Morris, *The American Revolution Reconsidered* (New York, 1967), p. 131. For their earlier meanings see Charles S. Olton, "Philadelphia Artisans and the American Revolution," Ph. D. diss. (Berkeley, 1967), pp. 3-16.

6. *The Compact Edition of the Oxford English Dictionary* (New York, 1971), p. 1756. Samuel Johnson, comp., *A Dictionary of the English Language* (London, 1730).

7. Stephen Botein, " 'Meer Mechanics' and an Open Press: The Business and Political Strategies of Colonial American Printers," *Perspectives in American History,* 9 (1975), 136, 157-158, 222. Roger J. Champagne, *Alexnder McDougall and the American Revolution in New York* (Syracuse, 1975), p. 136 and passim. See also, for other examples, Robert A. Gross, *The Minutemen and Their World* (New York, 1976), pp. 64-65, and Edmund S. Morgan, *American Freedom, American Slavery: The Ordeal of Colonial Virginia* (New York, 1975), p. 255.

8. Quoted in George A. Stevens, *Typographical Union Number Six* (Albany, 1912), p. 98.

9. Werner, *Tammany Hall,* p. 21

10. *Independent Mechanic,* August 11, 1811, May 30, 1812.

11. This definition is partially adapted from that of Eric Foner in *Tom Paine and Revolutionary America* (New York, 1976), p. 271, n. 19.

12. An excellent display of these crafts may be found in Charles F. Montgomery, *American Furniture: The Federal Period, 1788-1825* (New York, 1966).

13. For general population figures for New York see David T. Gilchrist, ed., *The Growth of the Seaport Cities, 1790-1825* (Charlottesville, 1967), pp. 34-35, 41. The figures for the percentage of mechanics in the city are

derived from four different sources. A study based on the 1796 directory finds a mechanic population of 52.6 percent, while one based on the 1806 directory (p. 87) finds a working population composed of 50.5 percent mechanics. These directory-based studies tend to underestimate the mechanic population by at least 5 percent and likely by as much as 10 percent because many journeymen are not listed. Two other figures are derived from the New York City Jury Lists from a sample including the second, fifth, eighth, and tenth wards for 1816 and 1819. These lists included every household in the ward though they did omit a number of aliens and journeymen (p. 265). In 1816 the jury lists indicate that 54.5 percent (4,797) of the sample was composed of mechanics, while in 1819 the figure was 58.9 percent (4,589). In contrast, the figures for merchants in 1796 and 1806 were 13.0 and 13.2 percent, respectively, and for 1816 and 1819 were 10.5 (924) and 8.9 percent (697); the percentages for unskilled laborers were 9.9 and 8.2 percent in 1796 and 1806, respectively, and 13.8 (1,144) and 10.3 percent (802) in 1816 and 1819, respectively. The data for 1796 are taken from Carl F. Kaestle, *The Evolution of an Urban School System: New York City, 1750-1850* (Cambridge, 1973), pp. 31-32. For 1806 they are derived from *Longworth's New York Directory* (New York, 1806); the 1816 and 1819 data are from the New York City Jury Lists, second, fifth, eighth, and tenth wards, 1816 and 1819, Historical Documents Collection, Queens College, City University of New York. The four lists are compiled according to individual trades in James Owre, "Effects of Immigration on New York City, 1800-1819," M.A. diss. (Queens College, 1970), Appendix.

Part I

POLITICS *of the skilled working people of NY*

Chapter 1

THE REVOLUTIONARY
HERITAGE

Politics reflected the aspirations of the mechanic community more clearly than any other aspect of their lives. Moreover, it also expressed most directly the meaning of '76 and the continuing expectations held by tradesmen for the complete fulfillment of the Revolution. Indeed, it was in the field of revolutionary politics that mechanics first came into their own, raising their position, influence, and self-esteem. Consequently, prior to examining the role of artisans in Jeffersonian New York politics, it is important to examine craftsmen's entry into the political arena as well as the nature of the political process that had developed by 1800.

The politics of prerevolutionary eighteenth-century New York consisted of a battleground for factions competing for executive power and control of the Provincial Assembly. Whether it was the Albany interest versus the New York City merchants, landed estate holders against an urban-mercantile coalition, or various personality conflicts involving such notables as Governor Cosby, Lewis Morris, and James Delancey, New York was the scene of repeated internal power struggles. In the midst of these contests, leaders could and did switch allegiances when it seemed advantageous to their personal political concerns.[1]

In this world of conflicting factions, the role of the mechanics was that of individual voters rather than of an organized and self-aware sector of the electorate. Workingmen did not shape the paths of partisanship, nor did they compose the core of leadership or formulate the issues over which elections were contested. However, suffrage requirements were not stringent for local assembly elections, and in New York City many tradesmen could and did vote. Furthermore, a number of men from middling ranks held high city office during the colonial era. Thus, although neither their place in society nor their immediate concerns were major factors in the meanderings of factional disputes, mechanics were directly involved in the political process.[2]

With the coming of popular resistance to the Stamp Act in 1765 and then to subsequent British measures, the nature of artisan participation changed markedly. From the beginning, tradesmen were active both in the protests and the more radical organizations. They composed the heart, if not the leadership, of the Sons of Liberty, an extralegal society that provided the coercive power in the enforcement of anti-British measures and that often organized and led popular demonstrations. In the aftermath of the Stamp Act, the "Liberty Boys," including many spirited and angry carpenters, shoemakers, cartmen, blacksmiths, and other craftsmen, together with discontented seamen, forced the resignation of John McEvers, the appointed stamp distributor, and sacked the home of Major James, a British officer who had vowed to enforce the notorious act. They also forced the port to reopen and, to some extent, caused business to continue as usual. Printer John Holt, for example, began printing on unstamped paper after receiving a note from the Sons of Liberty warning him that otherwise his "house, person and effects" would be in "imminent danger."[3]

Following the Stamp Act, mechanics continued at the forefront of resistance to British measures. In 1767, with the implementation of the Townshend Acts—taxes that were particularly burdensome to artisans—tradesmen in the Sons of Liberty pressed hard for a policy of nonimportation. They also protested strongly two years later when one of their leaders, Alexander McDougall, was imprisoned by the Provincial Assembly for attacking that body's decision giving in to the king and financially supporting local

British troops. Large meetings and parades were held in support of this "Wilkes of America." [4]

A significant confrontation occurred in 1770 between mechanics and the local garrison of troops. The soldiers, who not only insulted the artisans' sense of dignity but also hurt them economically by taking part-time jobs, triggered a wave of indignation when a group of them chopped down a liberty pole. A protest meeting "of not less than three thousand" was soon held, which endorsed a Sons of Liberty resolution against the employment of soldiers. This was followed by an angry reaction from a number of soldiers of the regiment who, on their way back to the barracks after posting bills attacking the Sons of Liberty, slashed their way through a hostile crowd, wounding several people and killing one sailor. The next day, a group of sailors and townsmen turned on a number of soldiers and chased them back to the barracks. The "Battle of Golden Hill" ended with the erection of a new liberty pole that remained standing until 1776.[5]

Mechanics were less successful in their determination to maintain a policy of nonimportation. In 1770 the city's merchants, anxious to resume trade, canvassed the city twice on whether or not to commence commerce, and then proclaimed their side to be in the majority—though the second poll gathered only eight hundred signatures. With the passage of the Tea Act in 1773, however, the Sons of Liberty once more regained the initiative. First, they called for a boycott against any importer or vendor of tea. Then, they adopted a plan for maintaining correspondence with Sons of Liberty in other cities. Finally, following the example of Boston, they dumped a cargo of tea into the depths of New York Harbor.[6]

As resistance grew in intensity with the passage of the hated "Intolerable Acts," mechanics became a truly "independent and organized force in New York politics." While the more conservative Livingston and Delancey factions controlled the first ad-hoc governing body, the Committee of Fifty-One, an opposition group, the Committee of Mechanics led by Alexander McDougall, exerted considerable pressure, forcing the endorsement of a call for a Continental Congress. After the Congress was indeed organized, craftsmen, disillusioned by the delaying measures of the mercantile community, decided to put up their own slate of delegates to go to Philadelphia. Consequently, the merchants, in order to gain support for their joint slate, had to accede to artisans' demands that the New York delegation request the Congress to implement a nonintercourse policy toward Britain. In joint governing committees organized in the next few years, mechanics continued to share power; if they did not have the final say, they watched carefully that the merchants directed their efforts in support of the rebel cause.[7]

While the mechanics generally cooperated with these governing committees, they also took independent political action. As Gouverneur Morris noted, tradesmen took very seriously the gentry's discussion of constitutional principles and individual rights. So, too, they attentively read and listened to the writings of Tom Paine, a former staymaker. The fruits of this learning were eloquent memorials whose egalitarian and republican message would continue to echo in Fourth of July orations through the Federalist and Jeffersonian eras. One petition to the Provisional Assembly called for the popular ratification of the new state constitution then being drafted. Declaring that it was the "birthright of every man" to pass on the laws under which he was to live, and that the "people's free assent" was the only valid criterion for "true lawfulness and legality," the mechanics asked for the submission of the charter to the populace. Another compelling address urged that instructions be given New York's delegates to the Continental Congress to vote for independence. In personal statements, individual artisans also argued that men should be allowed the vote without property restrictions.[8]

While little political activity was possible in New York during the Revolution because of the British occupation, when civil rule resumed in 1783 the mechanics continued to play an active role in city and state politics. Through the Committee of Mechanics (no longer tied to the defunct Sons of Liberty) they nominated their own assembly tickets; in various memorials to Albany they pressed for the payment of state debts, a stronger national government, protective tariffs, free public education, relaxed naturalization procedures, and restrictions on the activities of Loyalists. In their advocacy of a strong federal government, mechanics and merchants found themselves in agreement; however, they differed over the question of protective duties, which merchants opposed, and over the incorporation by the state legislature of the General Society of Mechanics and Tradesmen, which the mercantile community feared might allow mechanics to increase their wages and even gain "governmental power." 9

In postwar New York politics the mechanics played a substantial but subordinate role. While the Mechanics Committee did nominate its own assembly slates, the tickets were composed mainly of merchants and lawyers. Moreover, despite the size of New York's tradesmen population, these slates were not always successful at the polls. Yet if electoral authority was out of reach, and a continuing force of deference remained, by 1785 the mechanics, influenced by active military service and their part in the creation of a new republic, had come to a new awareness of their political strength and a desire to use that strength for greater respect and recognition.10

With the ratification of the Constitution in 1789 and the subsequent emergence of a strong federal union, the nature of New York politics changed significantly. Local leaders and factions now found it necessary to seek national as well as state and local ties, and to affiliate with one of the emerging national parties. These organizations, to be victorious, had to seek strength from all constituent groups: farmers, lawyers, professionals, merchants, and mechanics. In New York the two major parties were the Federalists and the Clintonians (later the Democratic-Republicans).

The Federalists had led the fight for ratification of the Constitution; two of the writers of the famed *Federalist,* John Jay and Alexander Hamilton, resided in New York State. In New York City, the Federalists, led by the city's prominent merchants and attorneys, formed a powerful electoral coalition that included the mechanic community. Artisans were anxious to see the new nation have the power and respect it deserved. Moreover, with the merchants, they supported a strong national government that would protect commerce and pay its debts, thus insuring good business conditions for all. Since New York was a major port of entry, the future of all classes rested on the fortunes of foreign and domestic commerce.

The Federalists expected the deferential support of the mechanics as a matter of course. They assumed that craftsmen would recognize the mercantile community as the city's natural leaders. As Hamilton wrote in the *Federalist No. 35:* "Mechanics and Manufacturers will always be inclined, with few exceptions, to give their votes to merchants in preference to persons of their own professions and trades." Even so, cognizant of the mechanics' growing political awareness, the party would usually nominate an artisan or two for its slate. In 1789 the ticket was put together at a joint meeting of the Mechanics Committee and the Merchants Committee chaired by Hamilton. Harmony between merchants and tradesmen was in evidence as the Federalists swept New York in the assembly elections by a tally of 2,342 to 373 votes. The triumphant parade of craftsmen bearing the model ship *Alexander Hamilton* was further proof of this accord. The anti-Federalists and Clintonians had virtually no artisan support.[11]

Yet, as strong as the Federalists' hold on the mechanic constituency was in 1789, within six years they were unable to enlist a majority of artisans within their ranks. This erosion of support was the collective result of a number of events. Basic to each encounter was the Federalists' inability to recognize the stature with which mechanics held themselves as a consequence of the Revolution, and to align themselves with the revolutionary ideals that most artisans saw as central to 1776.

During the first Washington administration, mechanics generally continued to support the Federalists. The Federalist-controlled Congress did pass some mildly protective tariffs in support of artisan trades, while Hamilton remained a popular and heroic local and national figure. Nor did the embryonic Republican coalition of Clinton, Livingston, and upstate farmers have any history of concern for the needs of the urban tradesmen. There were, however, signs of disenchantment. The rejection of the bid of the General Society of Mechanics and Tradesmen for incorporation in 1791 stirred considerable anger and spurred craftsmen to offer a separate assembly slate that year. (The charter passed quickly in 1792.) So, too, the failure of the banking schemes of William Duer, a friend of Hamilton's, brought financial ruin to a number of speculative artisans and caused antagonism to the Hamiltonian system.[12]

It was during Washington's second term that the most serious breaches in the mechanic-Federalist alignment took place. The first was over the French Revolution. Most mechanics greeted the news from Paris with jubilation, marching in the streets, learning French songs, and toasting the success of the new republic. To them it was a continuation of the egalitarian movement they had begun in the states but a few decades earlier. Democratic societies with significant mechanic memberships were formed to give support to France. So, too, the French Revolution gave the inspiration for Fourth of July celebrations and orations where the spirit of '76 was loudly proclaimed.[13]

The Federalist leaders, an Anglophile gentry in spirit, taste, and mercantile interest, were openly hostile to the French Revolution. They saw it as a threat to their financial concerns and to the very order of society. Perhaps some even feared they might share the fate of Louis XVI. In any case, their criticism of the Revolution, and their use of such terms as "rabble" and "swinish multitude" to depict its supporters, was directly contrary to the ideals and direction of most tradesmen.

The situation was not improved by the attitude of Federalists toward the British during the war between England and France. Most mechanics were enraged by the impressment of American sailors and the seizure of neutral American ships. Major demonstrations filled New York City's streets in denunciation of these British acts. The Federalists, while deploring the breakdown in relations, sought and achieved reconciliation through a mission of John Jay to London. The resulting Jay's Treaty of 1794, while committing the British to a withdrawal from the northern forts and to certain commercial agreements, did not "recognize the traditional principle that free ships make free goods," nor include any statement that the British would cease impressment. While the Federalists defended this as avoiding war, mechanics considered it an insult to their pride as citizens. Once again bonfires marked the city's thoroughfares, as artisans, together with other enraged citizens, gathered in large protest meetings to condemn the treaty and its Federalist backers.[14]

The "Keteltas Affair" was a third major cause for the alienation of mechanics from the Federalist camp. In 1796 Federalist Gabriel Furman had two Irish ferrymen arrested and tried for "insulting an alderman" when the boatmen, Thomas Burk and Timothy Crady, were allegedly insolent while taking him from Brooklyn to

New York. The two men were convicted without counsel and without being allowed to speak in their own behalf. Both were sentenced to two months' imprisonment, with Crady also getting twenty-five lashes. Soon after this incident, a Republican lawyer, William Keteltas, brought the case before the state assembly, demanding that the alderman and court officers be removed from office. When an investigating committee absolved the officials, Keteltas condemned the assembly for "the most flagrant abuse of rights." Summoned before the legislature, he refused to apologize and soon found himself taken away to jail—in the arms of an encouraging crowd that included many poor craftsmen. The arrogant treatment of two workingmen and the denial of rights helped to separate the Federalists from their mechanic followers, especially those of poorer means.[15]

Reaping the benefits of the failure of the Federalists to support mechanic aspirations were the Democratic-Republicans. This growing party, aligning with the national movement led by Jefferson and Madison and marked by egalitarian and civil libertarian ideals, was responsive to craftsmen's needs and sentiments. It responded warmly to the French Revolution while evincing a decided coolness to the British cause. The Jeffersonians, too, expressed concern for all classes, including the growing ranks of the poor, founding an assistance society to aid new immigrants and a Humane Society to help the destitute. Responsive to craftsmen's complaints about British imports, they supported the mechanics' quest for protective tariffs. They also gave assistance to individual trades, such as the tallow chandlers, whose enterprises the Federalists wanted removed from the city limits because of supposedly noxious fumes. Finally, Republican ranks were open to the middling classes, especially through the Tammany and Democratic societies where mechanics, composing more than half the memberships, mingled as peers with fellow Republicans of equal or higher occupational standing.[16]

With these advantages, together with a sophisticated political organization that maintained lists of voters; data on their temperament, health, and habits; information on the effort necessary to get supporters to the polls; and house-to-house campaign solicitations, the Republicans soon outdistanced the Federalists in the mechanic wards. And with the help of the pluralities gained there, with the exception of 1799, they did not lose one assembly election in the city between 1796 and 1810.[17]

The Democratic-Republicans did not, however, win over the votes of all mechanics. The Federalists retained a loyal contingent. And, while it is difficult to know with any certainty who voted for whom, Alfred Young has put forward a reasonable hypothesis for the 1790s. In the Federalist camp were craftsmen not in need of tariff protection (building trades), some poorer mechanics connected with merchant services and loyal to their employers, the few artisans with Loyalist backgrounds, some well-to-do tradesmen, and newly arrived English tradesmen anxious to disassociate themselves from their more radical Irish and French counterparts. The Republicans, meanwhile, found support among mechanics in need of protective duties (tanners and hatters) and in need of legislative support (tallow chandlers and shoemakers); and among the cartmen (who were alienated by an arrogant Federalist mayor), new Irish and French immigrants, the many veterans of the Revolutionary war, and many poorer craftsmen.[18]

These mechanic constituencies represented a part, but only one part, of large countywide, statewide and nationwide parties. Political leaders, such as Aaron Burr, Henry Rutgers, and De Witt Clinton, were not mechanics, and while they were willing to listen to the needs and attitudes of tradesmen, they had the interests of their party closest to heart. On the other hand, the close rivalry between the two parties insured that the electorally potent artisan community would not be ignored. Both parties entered the nineteenth century believing that their organization was in greatest harmony with mechanics' interests, although clearly the Republican party, an optimistic, ambitious group of self-made men, held the advantage.[19]

The next fifteen years constituted a period of Democratic-Republican triumph nationally. Locally, during the first decade of the nineteenth century, the Jeffersonians vigorously presented the mechanic constituency with an ideology that placed tradesmen on an equal footing with other citizens, proclaimed their importance to the body politic, and continued the revolutionary campaign against Toryism and the influence of an aristocracy. This proved most successful in assembly elections against the elitist and Anglophile outlook of the Federalists. However, from the inception of the embargo through the War of 1812, a period of severe economic dislocation stemming from Republican foreign policy, mechanic support proved less certain and, consequently, so did Democratic-Republican majorities. In the local charter elections, where the Federalists retained ascendancy through the 1790s because of suffrage restrictions, control shifted repeatedly during the next decade and a half, partly from eased voting requirements, and partly because of a welter of local and factional issues.

It is helpful at this point to take an overview, first of the offices contested, then of those citizens eligible to cast ballots, and, finally, of the specific election results. From 1801 to 1815 New York polls were open twice yearly: for three days beginning on the last Tuesday in April, and on the third Tuesday in November. The spring elections included all contests for state and national office. Among these, assemblymen were selected each year, governors every three years, congressmen every two years, and state senators at different intervals. City assembly slates consisted of thirteen men in 1801, nine from 1802 to 1807, and eleven from 1808 to 1815. These tickets were chosen at large to represent the whole city. The state senate district included part of Westchester and Long Island as well as the metropolis, while the congressional district constituted the city itself.

The assembly elections were of major significance to both the Democratic-Republicans and the Federalists. Besides choosing presidential electors and U.S. senators, the assembly in conjunction with the state senate could pass laws affecting many matters of importance to metropolitan residents. Such legislation ranged from the authorization of taxes to the enactment of measures regulating the city's commercial life. In all, the legislature's authority encompassed such affairs as ferry rates, street and road construction, poor relief and charities, the watch, prison regulation, and wharfage supervision.[20] Control of the assembly also gave a party the power to dominate the Council of Appointment, which was responsible for appointments to all major state offices, including New York City's mayor, recorder (chief legal officer), common clerk, sheriff, justices of the peace, police justices, the commissioner of liquor excise, the health commissioners, and the local district attorney.

The council consisted of the governor and four state senators, one each elected by the assembly from the four districts of the state.[21]

The governor's executive and veto powers as well as his conjunc- ~Mayor~ tive appointment authority were of major importance to New York City life and politics. Nowhere was his jurisdiction—along with that of the assembly—more pronounced than in the appointment of the mayor. The city's chief magistrate had, besides his duties as head of the Mayor's Court, a great deal of patronage to dispense. He alone appointed the city's chief constable and forty deputies and submarshals. The markers and sealers of weights and the measurers along with the city's cullers owed their jobs to his pleasure, as did the cartmen, whose licenses were issued by the mayor. By 1801 the latter trade included 1,050 individuals. Finally, the mayor received large sums of money from cartmen's fees, marshals' licenses, and an annual stipend in lieu of the excise taxes and market fees that had once been a part of his perquisites.[22]

Elections were held in the fall in each ward for the municipal ~City Council~ positions of alderman, assistant alderman, collector, assessor (two), and constable (two).The alderman and assistant alderman both sat on the Common Council along with the recorder and the mayor. The council was responsible for local legislation that did not fall under the jurisdiction of the legislature. It also supervised the public markets and other public conveniences and let city contracts. Like the mayor, the council had considerable patronage to > dispense. It appointed a city treasurer, corporate attorney, superintendents of scavengers, election inspectors, public weighmasters, measurers, and inspectors. Mechanics were deeply affected by the council's decisions. Whether it was a petition for a butcher's stall, an application for inspector of hay or potash or lumber, a request to be appointed a fireman, or a desire to supply wood or bread to the city's almshouse, the influence of the municipal legislative body on working people was immense.[23] The elected alderman also had considerable power in his own ward, where he acted as chief judicial officer.

The tax assessors were of enormous importance to the many inhabitants who paid taxes, as of course was the collector, who could authorize delays in the payments of a man's assessment. Constables were not paid any salary, but received fees according to *constable*

a scale established by the state legislature. They were charged with keeping order in the ward, arresting criminals and vagabonds, enforcing all laws and ordinances including Sabbath observance, antigambling restrictions, and licensing requirements, and with implementing and serving court orders and warrants.[24]

Suffrage requirements varied according to the office. Elections for assemblymen and congressmen had the least stringent requirements. One could qualify to vote for candidates for these posts with either a twenty-pound (fifty-dollar) freehold (real estate), or by paying at least forty shillings (five dollars) per year in rent. According to calculations made by Edmund P. Willis, this made about 62 percent of the adult male population eligible to vote in 1801. Renters outnumbered freeholders by 2.5 to 1 in 1801, by 3 to 1 in 1807, and by 3.5 to 1 in 1810 and 1814. Thus, the rent proviso was essential in giving the franchise to a majority of New York's citizenry. Still, 38 percent of the adult male population remained ineligible to vote in 1801, and close to 25 percent in 1810 and 1814. These percentages must have included recent immigrants, day laborers, many blacks, the very poor who paid minimal rents, and transients.[25]

In 1801 suffrage requirements for gubernatorial, senatorial, and charter (municipal) elections did not include a provision allowing renters to vote. Rather, freeholders alone held the franchise, and in municipal elections they could exercise their right in every ward in which they held the requisite amount of property. This requirement limited the percentage of adult white males eligible to vote to 23 percent in 1801. In 1804, after a long and heated struggle, the implications of which will be discussed below, the law governing municipal elections was changed to allow those paying rents of twenty-five dollars per year the right to vote, and eliminating any individual from voting in more than one ward. While this was a slightly higher rent than was required in assembly canvasses, it eventually proved to be a negligible difference, since inflation drove the cost of housing up. By 1814 the ratio of assembly voters to charter voters had dropped to 1.1 to 1, down from a ratio of 3.4 to 1 in 1804.[26] The suffrage requirements for gubernatorial and senatorial contests, limiting the vote to property owners, remained in effect until 1822.

It is difficult to determine the number of mechanics who voted in these elections. In 1807, the midpoint of our study, workingmen made up approximately 60 percent of those inhabitants who were listed with a trade in the local city *Directory.*[27] However, more mechanics than other professions were likely to fall in the category of ineligible voters for both assembly and charter elections. In any case, an experienced political leader, Matthew Davis, an ex-printer who was once an officer of the General Society of Mechanics, estimated that in 1810 the number of "mechanics and laborers" who voted was 4,000.[28] This would make up about 38 percent of those voting that year. Obviously some mechanics were not eligible, and others did not choose to vote. Yet 38 percent is a higher percentage than any other group was likely to achieve: and, if coupled with the votes of the grocers, who were fairly close to the mechanics in social status and economic standing, probably equaled half of all the ballots cast. Unquestionably the mechanics' electoral strength was significant.

During the fifteen years covered by this study, polling for assembly slates was by secret ballot. For municipal elections, however, it was conducted *viva voce* until 1804, and after that also by secret ballot. Voice voting, of course, allowed election inspectors and other observers a means of intimidation, an obstacle Republicans managed to remove in the legislation that eased the suffrage requirements for charter elections. Until 1813, when printed tickets were allowed, assembly ballots had to be written out by the voters themselves, a requirement favoring the more educated and committed.[29]

In the elections held from 1801 through 1815, the Democratic-Republicans remained the dominant party through 1809. In the assembly elections (Table 1.1), they received majorities ranging from 61.6 percent in 1801 (3,660 votes) to 50.6 percent in 1809 (5,035 votes). The Federalists began making serious inroads on the Republicans after 1808 due to economic and diplomatic difficulties. From 1810 on they managed to win a majority of the city's electorate each year but 1814. Looking at the analysis of three wards (Table 1.1-B), as well as at the political map (Map 1.1), the heart of Republican strength is clearly seen to be in the poorer outer mechanic wards where most craftsmen lived (wards five to eight and ten; the Ninth Ward contained the suburban homes of the wealthy). These wards, such as the seventh, gave Republican majorities nearly every year. Before Madisonian policy began hurting the city's economy, these pluralities were often well over 60 percent. After 1809, however, the differences between the parties were quite slim, often less than 10 percent. In contrast, the wealthy, lower merchant wards (one to three) went consistently Federalist by strong majorities. The relatively small populations of these districts, however, limited their value to the Federalists. The Fourth Ward, a swing district that voted Republican seven times and Federalist eight, was composed of a mixture of all classes. It is a good barometer of the direction of the electorate, as the shift to the Federalists there after 1808 is reflected in the consecutive, though narrow, majorities for that party from 1809 through 1815.

The aldermanic council elections (Table 1.2) reveal similar trends, although because local issues were of considerable importance within the different wards, there is a considerable shifting of votes within the wards from year to year. Once the suffrage requirements were changed in 1803, the Republicans, with the exception of 1806, won a council majority until 1809. They were never able to capture a majority after that, although they did manage a 10 to 10 tie in 1813. The ward and map analyses demonstrate that the Republicans were again successful in the outer mechanic wards and the Federalists dominant in the lower merchant wards. The minority party often did not even run candidates in the wards in which they lacked support. The swing Fourth Ward went Republican once the new suffrage laws went into effect and remained so from 1804 until 1808 with the exception of 1806. It voted Federalist after that, but often by very slim margins.

Balloting during these years was often close, particularly after 1805. Neither party could take its success for granted in either the aldermanic or the assembly contests; a shift of only 2 or 3 percent of the vote could easily swing an election. And in an assembly race where the entire delegation ran at-large, this shift of a few hundred voters could mean the difference of eleven important seats in Albany.[30]

The results of the congressional elections in the city follow the assembly polls, since the balloting was held at the same time and suffrage requirements were the same. Consequently, with the help

Table 1.1: ASSEMBLY ELECTIONS 1801-1815

A. TOTAL VOTE		1801	1802	1803	1804	1805	1806*	1807	1808
REP.	No.	3660	1755	3453	3505	1082	3738	4894	5646
	%	61.6	--	55.4	55.3	--	50.2	52.2	55.5
FED.	No.	2282	--	2779	2834	--	3561	4482	4527
	%	38.4	--	45.6	44.7	--	47.6	47.8	44.5
Total Vote:		5942	1755	6332	6339	1082	7449	9376	10173
% of Electorate Voting:		71.9						75.5	

		1809	1810+	1811	1812	1813	1814	1815
REP.	No.	5035	5304	3914	3400	4923	5270	4643
	%	50.6	49.9	42.5	36.5	49.3	49.8	49.5
FED.	No.	4917	5325	5295	4885	5062	5180	4788
	%	49.4	50.1	57.5	52.5	50.7	48.9	50.5
Total Vote:		9952	10629	9209	9305	9985	10595	9481
% of Electorate Voting:			67.8				75.7	

B. WARD VOTING		1801	1802	1803	1804	1805	1806	1807	1808
Ward 1	Party	Fed.	Rep.	Fed.	Fed.	Rep.	Fed.	Fed.	Fed.
	Total Vote	431	161	485	847	106	888	976	932
	%	51.3		57.3	65.9		64.8	65.3	62.7
4	Party	Rep.	Rep.	Fed.	Rep.	Rep.	Rep.	Rep.	Rep.
	Total Vote	701	149	737	856	136	921	1200	1202
	%	60.8		50.2	59.4		51.8	52.3	52.6
7	Party	Rep.	Rep.	Rep.	Rep.	Rep.	Rep.	Rep.	Rep.
	Total Vote	1406	458	1554	994	208	1263	1621	1310
	%	75.0		63.8	69.6		64.8	62.3	65.4

		1809	1810	1811	1812	1813	1814*	1815
1	Party	Fed.	Fed.	Fed.	Fed.	Fed.	Fed.	Fed.
	Total Vote	919	1000	877	909	931	946	806
	%	62.9	63.9	67.0	65.4	63.6	58.7	63.2
4	Party	Fed.	Fed.	Fed.	Fed.	Fed.	Fed.	Fed.
	Total Vote	1144	1189	1007	1038	1114	1058	1050
	%	51.4	51.3	61.3	54.8	51.4	55.4	51.1
7	Party	Rep.	Rep.	Fed.	Fed.	Rep.	Rep.	Rep.
	Total Vote	1227	1266	1183	1121	1153	1124	1005
	%	57.9	55.0	55.6	46.6	51.2	53.2	54.5

Source: Edmund P. Willis,"Social Origins and Political Leadership in New York City
from the Revolution to 1815," Ph.D. diss.(Berkeley,1967), pp.53,72,75,77.
*Indicates a divided Republican vote due to factionalism. The number given is
the vote for the faction receiving the most votes.
+In 1810 six Federalists and 5 Republicans were elected.

Table 1.2:   COUNCIL ELECTIONS   1801-1815

A. TOTAL VOTE

		1801	1802	1803	1804	1805	1806	1807	1808
REP.	Seats	6	4	7	14	15	6	13	12
	No.				2770		3360	3074	4082
	%				61.0		49.5	63.5	52.6
FED.	Seats	8	10	11	4	3	12	5	8
	No.				1771		3428	1767	3679
	%				39.0		50.5	36.5	47.3
Total Vote					4541		6788	4841	7761

		1809	1810	1811	1812	1813	1814	1815
REP.	Seats	4	8	8	7	10	8	8
	No.	3480		2210	2637	4662		4585
	%	46.9		44.0	42.7	53.0		49.4
FED.	Seats	16	12	12	13	10	12	12
	No.	3941		3812	3534	4134		4697
	%	53.1		56.0	57.3	47.0		50.6
Total Vote		7421		5022	6176	8796		9281

B. TOTAL VOTE

Ward		1801	1802	1803	1804	1805	1806	1807	1808
1	Party	Fed.	Fed.	Fed.	Fed.	Fed.	Fed.	Fed.	Fed.
	Total vote				653		410	562	609
	%				83.9		--	61.9	64.0
4	Party	Fed.	Fed.	Fed.	Rep.	Rep.	Fed.	Rep.	Rep.
	Total vote				789		985	878	1024
	%				58.1		51.8	63.9	50.6
7	Party	Rep.	Rep.	Rep.	Rep.	Rep.	Rep.	Rep.	Rep.
	Total vote				239		1098	502	772
	%				--		66.5	--	67.2

Ward		1809*	1810	1811	1812	1813	1814	1815
1	Party	Fed.	Fed.	Fed.	Fed.	Fed.	Fed.	Fed.
	Total vote	390		344	257	730		767
	%	--		--	--	58.9		63.9
4	Party	Fed.	Fed.	Fed.	Fed.	Fed.	Fed.	Fed.
	Total vote	1039		791	855	1109		1038
	%	50.6		62.5	53.6	50.1		51.8
7	Party	Fed.*	Rep.	Rep.	Rep.	Rep.	Rep.	Rep.
	Total vote	873	--	--	832	1092		993
	%	36.4			52.1	54.5		54.2

Source: Edmund P. Willis, "Social Origins and Political Leadership in New York City from the Revolution to 1815," Ph.D diss. (Berkeley,1967) pp. 70,74,76.

*Republican vote divided by two factions.   Blank spaces indicate no information available.

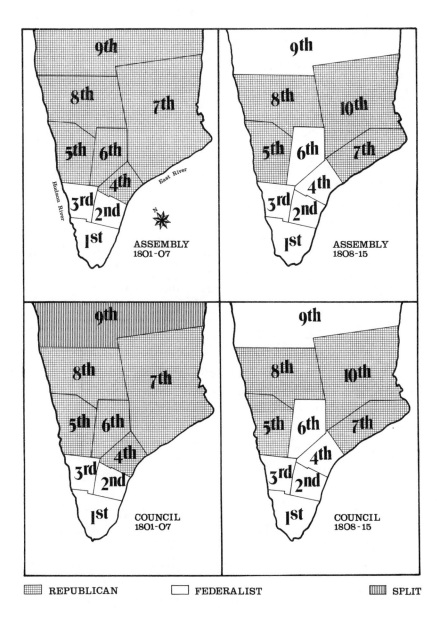

Map 1.1. Political preferences of New York City wards, 1801-1815.

of the outer wards, the Republicans won all congressional elections except those of 1810 and 1812. In the gubernatorial and state senate contests, however, in which a voter was required to own real property worth 100 pounds (250 dollars), the Federalists carried each election in the city except for 1801. The average difference between the Republican vote for congressman and for governor or state senator was a significant 5.6 percent.[31] Like the other elections, these races, too, were often very close.

In the 1790s, the entry of the mechanics into politics, together with the growth of the two-party system and the presence of vital, far-reaching, and polarizing issues about the nature of society and the role of the artisan within it, had great impact upon electoral contests, turning elections into large-scale efforts to arouse and bring to the polls a major proportion of the male citizenry. In the Jeffersonian era, the party system continued in full force, and the eligible electorate grew considerably, to a great extent from the rapidly increasing mechanic sector of the population. Furthermore, issues of critical concern to craftsmen, involving their right to freely participate in the political process, the presence of aristocratic, antirepublican policies and officeholders, and the perplexing problem of economic travail versus patriotic sacrifice remained central in New York's elections. Consequently, the popularization of politics continued at an even higher pitch as parties sought to reach their constituents, to get them to the polls, and to quickly and decisively persuade them to vote their tickets.

Newspapers were the most common and most critical way of convincing voters, particularly mechanics. A Connecticut newspaper noted that craftsmen "had no way so cheaply and so eligibly to communicate their ideas to each other" except through the daily and weekly press.[32] These early newspapers, often ragged single sheets folded into four large pages, acted for each party as "the conduit between its leaders and philosophers and the masses."[33] As the Peacham, Vermont, *Green Mountain Patriot* stated, the availability of the public press meant that "all ranks of men read, study and endeavor to comprehend" the problems of the day.[34] According to an 1800 magazine, Americans had become a "nation of newspaper readers."[35] Novelist Charles Brockden Brown observed that papers were read more commonly in America "than in any other part of the world," while Pierre DuPont de Nemours commented in 1800 that "a large part of the nation reads the Bible, all of it assiduously peruse the newspapers." [36]

Wherever people gathered, and especially in the local taverns, newspapers were visible. Philip Freneau's character, Robert Slender, slipped out to a local pub "where now and then a few neighbors meet to spit, smoke segars, drink apple whiskey . . . and *read the news.*"[37] A Federalist complained that the Republicans left their papers "gratis in every grog shop in our city." [38] For those who did not frequent the taverns, shared subscriptions were an alternative. There was, in all, a "seemingly insatiable American appetite for political intelligence" that engrossed many literate tradesmen of the city.[39]

The Republican party was the greater beneficiary of the widespread dissemination of political newspapers. An historian of partisan newspapers in the 1790s, Donald H. Stewart, has called their influence "decisive" for the Republicans. As Jefferson stated, "our citizens may be deceived, but so long as the presses can be protected, we may trust to them for light." Although they had fewer journals than the Federalists, Republican publications were by far the more vigorous, the more able to speak to workingmen in a style and about interests with which they could relate.[40]

The Federalists complained bitterly about the scurrilous public prints, but found that in spite of their reproaches, the people "do read them, and thousands who read them, read nothing else." [41] When they tried to eliminate the most offensive papers through the notorious Alien and Sedition Acts, the party of Adams and Hamilton saw its popularity fall that much more as Republicans lionized the persecuted publishers.[42] Particularly with the mechanics, the Federalists lagged in establishing effective electioneering organs, giving the Jeffersonians a considerable advantage.

Finally, along with newspapers, handbills were particularly effective in communicating with mechanic voters. These could be quickly printed in large, dramatic type that included a generous use of italics, capital letters, and exclamation points. And, unlike newspapers, which still devoted most of their space to advertisements, handbills were quick attention grabbers lacking extraneous material. During election days these could be found in large numbers around the outer-ward polling stations.

In reaching voters, newspapers and handbills devoted a great deal of space to specific voting blocs. Germans were solicited in German language leaflets; Republicans courted Catholic voters with Federalist-attributed anti-Catholic statements; Quakers and blacks were enticed with words addressed to their particular concerns. The Federalists found a positive response within the black community because of their antislavery sentiment. Most of all, however, the votes of the mechanics were sought by direct appeal as craftsmen were addressed as a self-aware community.[43]

The popularization of politics and especially the increasing participation of the less articulate meant strenuous efforts to get out the vote. The detailed Republican voting lists, mentioned previously, played an important part in the crucial Republican victory in 1800. Such maneuvering and strategy continued in following years. During one election a Democratic-Republican victory was attributed to "carriages, chairs and wagons, constantly going and coming, bringing to the poll every man in their interest who could be found within twelve miles." The Federalists had their coaches, too, parading in the streets. One in 1807 was plastered with signs on all four sides as well as on the driver's hat proclaiming the "American ticket." [44]

On election days political organizers would rise well before dawn to begin their electioneering. Robert Troup wrote that during a canvass he was so involved in overseeing the election and getting out the vote that he did not sit down once from seven in the morning to seven in the evening, nor did he eat dinner for the three days that the polls were open.[45] At the polls a voter could hear the leaders of both parties debating the issues. Washington Irving, an active Federalist in 1807, describing with some distaste his electioneering experience that year, declared that he "got fairly down into the vortex . . . as deep in mud and politics as ever a moderate gentleman would wish to be." To his great displeasure Irving "drank beer with the multitude, . . . talked handbill fashion with the demagogues and . . . shook hands with the mob." Forced to wander in "such filthy nooks and filthy corners," he afterward asserted that he would not "be able to bear the smell of beer or tobacco for a month to come." [46] Indeed, handbills and newpapers were numerous and were given out to all interested and probably many uninterested citizens. Nor did the liquor stop flowing from the opening to the closing of the polling stations.

The counting of ballots had to be closely watched by the election inspectors and party representatives. It was not unusual to hear accusations that invalid ballots were being distributed by one's opponents, or that tickets containing the names of one party's candidates were being handed out under the other party's label.[47] Furthermore, sharp election inspectors could create a "pernicious delay" in the balloting by challenging without cause the tickets of their opposition.[48]

The coming of popular politics also affected the nominating process. Assembly slates were chosen by a general committee of each party composed of delegates selected by each ward at local party meetings.[49] Charter candidates were selected and approved at local ward meetings held three to four weeks before the election. These gatherings were open to all interested party members in the ward. While it is no doubt true that the candidates nominated were often chosen by party leaders prior to the meetings and that most nominees selected for the higher offices were from the elite of New York society,[50] it is also apparent that in order to garner enthusiasm for the election, local leaders placed much emphasis on the popular endorsement of the tickets at ward meetings. Moreover, later rallies to generate political support were common and very much a part of the spirit of the time. Irving described the "orators" at such meetings as men of "profound and perplexed eloquence" who were the "oracles of barbers' shops, market places and porter houses." After climbing onto a chair, table, or anything else available, they would "thunder away their combustible sentiments at the heads of the audience, who are generally so busily employed in smoking, drinking and hearing themselves talk that they seldom hear a word spoken on the matter."[51] Indeed, unlike politics in the 1790s, Jeffersonian campaigns included a great deal of popular oration by candidates, political leaders, and local citizenry.

A final and very important result of popular, strongly contested elections was the heightening of political passions to intense emotional peaks. A letter to the Federalist *Washington Republican,* a weekly intended for mechanics, illustrates this point. The author claimed that the *Republican* would have a larger circulation in the Fifth Ward, where there were "many if not more of the poorer classes," than in any other part of the city, if that ward were not "so completely infested with a set of infernal jacobins." The situation there was so bad that "a poor Federalist dare not open his mouth for fear of being knocked down, or his life threatened." Indeed, it would not be surprising if the Republicans met in caucus and swore an oath not to allow any Federalist to reside in the ward unless he pledged allegiance to "democracy and Bonaparte." One Republican opponent, in fact, was overheard saying that "sooner than see the Federalist Washington Society walk again in procession, he would see Bonaparte enter the city with ten thousand troops." [52] Tempers ran high over the issues of the day. Citizens, including tradesmen, took their politics very seriously.

It was the "practical objective of winning" that led to heated emotions, large political gatherings, and the general democratization of politics.[53] For mechanics, specifically, this meant that their votes were eagerly sought and that their participation in the political process was encouraged. As Irving observed, it was common to see "bread and butter politicians . . . engaged in dreadful wordy debate with old cartmen, cobblers and tailors."[54] With the coming of the mechanics into the thick of political argument, the stage was set for the questioning of their role in society, and of the relationships of class and status within the entire community.

NOTES

1. Patricia U. Bonomi, *A Factious People: Politics and Society in Colonial New York* (New York, 1971); Milton Klein, "Democracy and Politics in Colonial New York," *New York History*, 40 (1959), 221-246. These works modify Carl Becker's noted study, *The History of Political Parties in the State of New York* (Madison, 1909), which saw a stricter class division in the colony.

2. Bruce J. Wilkenfeld, "The New York City Common Council, 1689-1800," *New York History*, 52 (1971), 252-266 and passim; Bonomi, *A Factious People*, pp. 178-223, does see mechanic participation in heated elections but finds no separate role for the mechanics before 1765.

3. Philip S. Foner, *Labor and the American Revolution* (Westport, Conn.,

1976), chaps. 2, 3. Roger J. Champagne, "The Liberty Boys and the Mechanics of New York City," *Labor History*, 8 (1967), 119, 130-135, emphasizes the control of the Sons of Liberty by the Livingston and Delancey factions, though there is little doubt that a great deal of politicization took place among tradesmen, whether or not they were guided by artisan leaders.

4. Foner, *Labor and the American Revolution*, pp. 81-87; Roger J. Champagne, *Alexander McDougall and the American Revolution* (Syracuse, 1975), chap. 3.

5. Ibid., pp. 88-95; Lee R. Boyer, "Lobster Backs, Liberty Boys, and Laborers in the Streets: New York's Golden Hill and Nassau Street Riots," *New York Historical Society Quarterly*, 57 (1973), 281-307.

6. Foner, *Labor and the American Revolution*, pp. 104-107, 117-121; Champagne, *Alexander McDougall*, pp. 44-51.

7. Foner, *Labor and the American Revolution*, pp. 127-134, 140, 142; Champagne, *Alexander McDougall*, chap. 5. Michael Wallace, "Party and Democracy in Jacksonian America," Ph.D. diss. (Columbia University, 1973), p. 40. Staughton Lynd, "The Mechanics in New York City Politics, 1774-1785," *Labor History*, 5 (1964), 225-229. Bruce Bliven, Jr., *Under the Guns, New York: 1775-1776* (New York, 1972), p. 93, describes the Mechanics Committee as a group of artisans, clerks, and workingmen, many of whom were unable to vote. In *The Road to Independence: The Revolutionary Movement in New York, 1773-1777* (Lexington, 1966), pp. 27-66, Bernard Mason notes that the formation of the Mechanics Committee in 1774, if it was not the creation of two local activists, "was an important declaration of political independence by the craftsmen who heretofore were content to align themselves with one of the factions or to accept the leadership of a Sears and McDougall."

8. Foner, *Labor and the American Revolution*, pp. 154-155, 158-165; Lynd, "Mechanics in Politics," 229, 231; Mason, *Road to Independence*, pp. 155-160. The Provincial Congress refused to print the memorial calling for independence, though it normally printed all petitions. Bliven, *Under the Guns*, pp. 198, 199, notes that the Mechanics Committee was also capable of taking direct action. When the committee found that a bookseller had pamphlets attacking Thomas Paine's ideas, it burned the books (*The Deceiver Unmasked*) on the commons to prevent possible dissemination of these unwanted tracts.

9. Lynd, "Mechanics in Politics," 235-228; in 1784 the Mechanics ticket won by a four to one margin.

10. In 1786 the two mechanics on the ballot were not elected. Ibid., pp. 239-241.

11. *The Federalist*, Mead Earle, ed. (New York, 1937), p. 213; Alfred F.

Young, *The Democratic Republicans of New York: The Origins, 1763-1797* (Durham, 1967), pp. 100-102; Alfred F. Young, "The Mechanics and the Jeffersonians: New York, 1789-1801," *Labor History*, 5 (1964), 247-249.

12. Young, "Mechanics and Jeffersonians," 252-256; Young, *Democratic Republicans of New York*, pp. 207-230.

13. Young, "Mechanics and Jeffersonians," 256-262; Young, *Democratic Republicans of New York*, chaps. 16, 17, 18. Eugene Perry Link, *The Democratic Societies, 1790-1800* (New York, 1942), pp. 71-99, states that workingmen outnumbered all other occupation groups; for Philadelphia he found that the membership contained 37.8 percent craftsmen; see also pp. 108-123, 125-265. Alfred Bernstein, "The Rise of the Democratic Party in New York City," Ph.D. diss. (Columbia University, 1964), p. 401, found that 121 of the 162 members whom he could identify in the New York Society were mechanics (75 percent); Young, "Mechanics and Jeffersonians," found that of the 30 men whose occupations he could identify, 12 were craftsmen (40 percent).

14. Young, *Democratic Republicans of New York*, chap. 21.

15. Ibid., chap.17.

16. Young, "Mechanics and Jeffersonians," 264; Bernstein, "Rise of the Democratic Party," 401-406; W. Bruce Wheeler, "Urban Politics in Nature's Republic: The Development of Political Parties in the Seaport Cities in the Federalist Era," Ph.D. diss. (University of Virginia, 1967), p. 303. Jerome Mushkat, *Tammany: The Evolution of a Political Machine, 1789-1865* (Syracuse, 1971), pp. 24-25, found that from 1797 to 1801 the Tammany Society had of its 112 identified members, 57 artisans, 7 cartmen, and 6 printers, or 70 (62.5 percent) mechanics. See also Peter Paulson, "The Tammany Society and the Jeffersonian Movement in New York City, 1795-1800," *New York History*, 34 (1953), 72-84.

17. Edmund P. Willis, "Social Origins and Political Leadership in New York City from the Revolution to 1815," Ph.D. diss. (Berkeley, 1967), pp. 72, 75, 77.

18. Young, "Mechanics and Jeffersonians," pp. 269-270.

19. Ibid., pp. 270-272.

20. Sidney I. Pomerantz, *New York: An American City, 1783-1803* (New York, 1938), p. 54.

21. Ibid., p. 503.

22. Ibid., pp. 39, 503-504.

23. Ibid., p. 504.

24. James F. Richardson, *The New York Police: Colonial Times to 1901* (New York, 1970), pp. 17-19.

25. Willis, "Social Origins," p. 53.

26. Ibid., pp. 51, 93.

27. See Table 3.1.

28. Matthew Davis to William P. Van Ness, New York, February 13, 1810; William P. Van Ness Papers, Misc. Reel, New York Historical Society.

29. Willis, "Social Origins," p. 53; Broadside, "To the Friends of Peace, Liberty and Commerce," April 16, 1813, New York Historical Society.

30. Michael D'Innocenzo, "The Popularization of Politics in Irving's New York," in Andrew B. Myers, ed., *The Knickerbocker Tradition: Washington Irving's New York* (Tarrytown, 1974), pp. 33-35.

31. Ibid., p. 35.

32. [Litchfield] *Weekly Monitor* quoted in Jackson Turner Main, *The Social Structure of Revolutionary America* (Princeton, 1965), p. 262.

33. Edwin Emery and Henry Ladd Smith, *The Press and America* (Englewood Cliffs, 1954), p. 140, as quoted in Donald H. Stewart, *The Opposition Press in the Federalist Era* (Albany, 1966), p. 13.

34. June 1, 1798, in Stewart, *Opposition Press*, p. 13.

35. *Port Folio*, in ibid., p. 630.

36. *Monthly Magazine*, 1 (1799), in ibid., pp. 13-14; Fred W. Scott, "Newspapers 1775-1860," in William Trent et al., eds., *The Cambridge History of American Literature*, 3 vols. (New York, 1933), vol. 2, p. 248, in ibid., p. 630.

37. [Philadelphia] *Aurora*, September 11, 1799, in ibid., p. 631.

38. *Washington Republican*, July 29, 1809.

39. Stewart, *Opposition Press*, p. 631.

40. Ibid., p. 629; Thomas Jefferson to Archibald Stuart, May 14, 1899, in Paul Leicester Ford, ed., *The Writings of Thomas Jefferson*, 10 vols. (New York, 1895), vol. 7, p. 378, in ibid., p. 631.

41. Cobbett, in *Washington Gazette*, February 4, 1797, in ibid., p. 635.

42. See James Morton Smith, *Freedom's Fetters: The Alien and Sedition Laws and American Civil Liberties* (Ithaca, 1956).

43. D'Innocenzo, "Popularization of Politics," pp. 16-19 and passim.

44. *Gazette and General Advertiser*, May 13, 1800; *American Citizen*, May 2, 1807, in ibid., pp. 16, 23.

45. Ibid., p. 8; David Hackett Fischer, *The Revolution of American Conservatism: The Federalist Party in the Age of Jeffersonian Democracy* (New York, 1965), p. 96.

46. Pierre Irving, *The Life and Letters of Washington Irving* (New York, 1863), vol. 1, pp. 186-187, quoted in D'Innocenzo, "Popularization of Politics", p. 21.

47. *Evening Post*, April 23, 1803, April 24, 1810, in ibid., p. 21.

48. *American Citizen,* April 28, 1807, in ibid., p. 22.
49. Ibid., p. 14, p. 127, n. 12.
50. See Chapter 4.
51. Washington Irving, *Salmagundi* (New York, 1904), p. 235.
52. *Washington Republican,* August 19, 1809.
53. D'Innocenzo, "Popularization of Politics," p. 28.
54. Irving, *Salmagundi,* p. 267.

Chapter 2

THE REPUBLICAN ADVANTAGE, 1801-1807

The Democratic-Republicans were victorious in all New York City congressional and assembly elections from 1801 through 1807 and, once suffrage requirements were eased in 1804, in the municipal charter elections as well (with the exception of 1806). They achieved this remarkable electoral dominance largely through the votes of the mechanic constituency. During this period the populous artisan wards consistently gave the Republicans 60 to 70 percent of their ballots. It is likely that at least three-fourths of the mechanic bloc went to the party of Jefferson.

The Republican success among tradesmen was due in large measure to that party's ability to convince mechanics that, in contrast to the conservative and elitist stance of the Federalists, the party of Jefferson afforded artisans the esteemed and responsible position in society that they sought. The large volume of political debate aimed at mechanics centered on the place of the mechanic in the community, covering three basic issues: whether mechanics as discriminating American citizens could fully participate in the political process; whether the United States was to be an aristocratic society in which craftsmen occupied a lesser and the wealthy a greater role; and whether mechanics could gain political support for their marketplace needs and aspirations.

The local scene dominated this political discussion during these years.[1] This does not mean that New York's concerns were unrelated to national issues, or, more properly, to the national debate over the ultimate outcome of the Revolution. Rather, local contests were very much related to the conflicting ideals of Jefferson and Hamilton over the nature of American government and society, and between Madison and his Federalist opponents over the meaning and direction of American foreign policy.[2] However, more common than discussion of Louisiana, patronage, slavery, and even protective tariffs were the issues of suffrage requirements, the revolutionary war background and personality of candidates, and the willingness of politicians to assist artisans in their trades. For it was at this most vital and most apparent level that craftsmen saw their place in the community and their chapter in the national contest over the shape of American society at stake.

Central to the battle for artisan ballots was the Federalist view of their ideal society and of the place of the mechanic within it. Nowhere were the Federalists more candid with their opinions than in the controversy over municipal suffrage reform. The law in 1801, it will be remembered, limited the vote in the November aldermanic elections to freemen and those with a freehold (property) worth twenty pounds. Freemen were tradesmen who had been granted a certificate or license allowing them to practice their trade in the city. Technically no one without such a certificate could carry on his business, but in practice the granting procedure—which by the 1790s had become a pro forma matter— was disregarded by the Federalist-controlled Common Council in order to keep new Republican artisan followers from access to the ballot. By thus limiting the percentage of eligible male voters to 23 percent, the Federalists managed to maintain majorities in six of the seven wards until 1800.[3] In 1801 the Republicans captured a second district and had majorities in the largely mechanic sixth and seventh wards. Still, they remained two short of the needed majority. An obvious solution was a change in the suffrage requirements, a goal they sought strenuously.

In presenting their case, the Federalists maintained first that property ownership was a sound guarantee of good civic behavior. This was a reiteration of the venerable "stake-in-society" theory.

Only those with a visible stake in the community should be allowed to govern or to select the governors as they were the "sole depository of the public will." Moreover, with the "weakness of human nature and the present state of society and manners" considered, "independence of circumstance" was no bad security for responsible public behavior. Not to require property limitations would only excite "irreconcilable enmity between the rich and the poor of the same society." [4] In other words, were the many mechanic renters, not to mention the laborers, to be given the franchise, not only were irresponsible aldermen likely to be elected but this disruption of the natural order would threaten the balance and comity of society.

Second, the Federalists argued that a select body was more capable of making sound decisions than the mass of citizenry. Most members of society lacked the requisite experience needed for the calm deliberation of legislative bodies. The unpropertied were likely to be persuaded more by "suggestions of immediate feeling and party prejudice" than by "considerations of sound and lasting policy." [5]

Finally, the Federalists pointed out the dangers in precipitously altering long-standing institutions such as the charter of New York, written in the reign of George II. Society, Alderman Caleb Riggs asserted, would be in perilous condition if "Constitutions, laws and charters" could be amended at the whim of ambition or party advantage.[6] To give the franchise to "every democrat, both native and imported within five years" would be to give authority to men who "will with equal readiness bawl out for the erection of a guillotine in the park and endeavor to show the possibility of perpetual motion in the action of the knife." [7] Federalist logic maintained that loss of deference—as maintained by the charter—would result in an anarchic society, perhaps dominated by hordes of ignorant Irish immigrants.

Federalists elaborated on their views about the role of the workingman on a number of other occasions. In a letter Alexander Hamilton claimed that mechanics ought to willingly defer to the views of the merchant who was their "natural patron and friend." Tradesmen were, he believed, "sensible that their habits in life have not been such as to give them those acquired endowments, without which in a deliberative assembly, rights and natural abilities, are for the most part useless." [8] So, too, a communiqué in the *People's Friend* raged against a recently circulated handbill charging that Federalist merchants were exploiting the labor of tradesmen in order to make ungainly profits. In truth, this Federalist writer declared, the Republicans were only stirring up trouble among the mechanic community to enhance their personal ambitions. A correct understanding of the matter made it clear that the "field of honest industry" was open to workingmen, as it had been to the merchants and their fathers before them. A man's position in society depended upon his own skill and ambition. A mechanic with ability could rise, and if and when he did, the tradesmen were told, "you will then have your laborers, and your porters and your cartmen who will thank you for wages as you will pay them for your work." [9] Society had a natural order, and there was little room for "Jacobins" who would attempt to upset this harmony.

For the mechanic who was having difficulty ascending the ladder to success, but was also having trouble accepting his place in society as a mere craftsman or laborer, the Federalists also had an answer. In a poem printed in the *Washington Republican,* a Federalist newspaper intended for mechanics, a story was told of a Republican "Friend of Humanity" who ran into a lowly knife grinder clad in torn and ragged clothing and sitting by the side of the road. The democrat lamented the poor man's plight:

> Weary knife grinder!—little think
> the proud ones
> Who in their coaches roll along the road,
> What hard work 'tis crying all day
> "Knives and scissors grind O."

With "drops of compassion" trembling on his eyelids, he asked the unfortunate soul what sad tale he had to relate, and whether he had yet read Paine's *Rights of Man*. Alas, the knife grinder had no story to tell other than a night of drinking in the local tavern where his clothes were torn in a scuffle, after which he was arrested by the constable. He said, however, that he would be glad to drink to his benefactor's health if the man would lend him sixpence, but that as far as the *Rights of Man* was concerned, he preferred not to meddle in politics. At this inappreciative response the concerned democrat flew into a rage, called the poor grinder a "sordid, unfeeling reprobate, degraded, sportless outcast," and kicked him to the ground, knocking over his wheel. This "Friend of Humanity" then turned and "exited in a transport of republican enthusiasm and universal philanthropy."

In case the reader had missed the point of this story, the editor patiently explained the moral: "The idea that the laboring part of society are the most miserable is as prevalent as it is unjust." It was the knife grinder who lived the happy, carefree life and the merchant whose days were full of worry: "The former hears the winds whistle about him, whilst the latter slumbers in the rock of anxiety, fearing that his speculations may be thwarted, his ships buried on the ocean, or his riches swallowed by flames." [10] Despite the author's good intentions, one must wonder how well such advice went over with the members of the considerably ambitious mechanic community, many of whom would have liked at least an opportunity to feel that "rock of anxiety" beneath their heads.[11]

The Federalist outlook was incompatible with the aspirations of most of the city's artisan community. Mechanics' ideology, shared in large part with the Republicans and reflected in the Fourth of July orations (Chapter 5), called for a nondeferential, egalitarian, meritocratic, and libertarian society in which artisans played a central role, befitting the important tasks they performed. Tradesmen demanded acceptance of themselves and all taxpaying citizens as qualified and independent examiners of national and local policies, as intelligent voters fully capable of selecting competent leaders, and as responsible officeholders making judicious executive and legislative decisions. The right of complete participation in the political process was a major issue drawing artisans to the Democratic-Republicans.

Access to the ballot was a prerequisite to mechanics' full entry into politics and, consequently, the struggle for suffrage reform remained a central issue throughout this era. The most noted example of this movement was the fight for an alteration of the city charter that would enable renters to vote in municipal elections. Led by James Cheetham, Jacobin editor of the *American Citizen*, himself a former hatter and the author of *A Dissertation Concerning Political Equality and the Corporation of New York*,[12] Republicans and tradesmen attacked the Federalists in a number of ways. The first method was to use somewhat devious tactics to gain electoral majorities. This included the purchase of small parcels of land in different wards so as to have multiple or "faggot" votes in the charter elections (each freeholder could vote in each ward in which he held property), and the loose and expeditious naturalization of Irish immigrants.[13]

The second and more lasting procedure was to attack the "consummate and unbearing haughtiness" of the Federalists by securing a legislative alteration of the charter.[14] Beginning in 1801, such an effort was made each year until the goal was achieved in 1804. Many petitions and memorials were sent to Albany during this campaign. One signed by mechanics hopeful of receiving the vote stated that each citizen of lawful age who had a fixed residence in the city and who paid taxes "ought to be duly represented in the government of the city." [15] This was not a call for universal suffrage, and it was far from a Jacobin's cry for an American "reign of terror." Indigent transients and the very poor were to be excluded from the franchise. Mechanics did not voice objections to such restrictions, for they had no desire to be equated with the lowest orders in society. They too did not want the right of suffrage "indiscriminately conferred." But neither did they wish it dependent on the ownership of real property. Asking the legislature whether "the dirt on which we tread [is] represented?" they denied that land was the proper basis of determining a man's qualifications, even invoking Rousseau's *Social Contract* to prove their contention. The Republican and mechanic viewpoint was that "suffrage is the first right of a free people." All who had a stake in society, if only through their skills, should have an equal opportunity to decide who their leaders would be.[16]

The debate intensified when Alderman John Bogert, a Federalist, was sent a petition by three hundred cartmen asking that they be made freemen. Bogert replied that it was not "expedient" to take such action because it might encourage three thousand others to request the same privilege. Such an act would be especially dangerous, since it would mean that "so large a body of people were possessed of an equal right." Labeling this "the language of tyrants to their miserable slaves," [17] Republicans rejoined that it was imperative that men be elected to municipal office who would "enable the industrious mechanic and honest citizen to participate, as far as may be possible, in every right and privilege." [18]

Suffrage reform was finally secured in 1804 by an act allowing all citizens paying twenty-five dollars in rent to vote in charter elections. Cheetham hailed this new law as a "Second Declaration of Independence to the Citizens of New York." [19] However, possession of the right to vote in itself was, unfortunately, no assurance that tradesmen could freely exercise that privilege. Attempts at denial of the freedom to vote one's conscience were not uncommon. Such acts were extremely offensive to mechanics' sense of pride and responsibility and consequently became as prominent a political issue as access to the polls.

One method of coercion was the use of scare tactics. The Republicans in 1801 reported a strategy meeting in which a young Federalist described his invention to keep Republican voters in the artisan Sixth Ward away from the polling booths: a "submarine" that would "blow up" in the ward on election day "so as to astonish the natives and immobilize them with fright." Six years later the Federalists were said to have appointed a "Committee of Interruption" to disturb the Seventh Ward canvass.[20] Not only did these tactics play on mechanic fears that the elite were attempting to prevent them from carrying out the prerogatives of citizenship, but such implications of simpleminded gullibility also cast aspersions on their status in the community as intelligent members of the body politic.

A more serious threat to a mechanic's unfettered balloting rights were cases of economic coercion. The Republicans constantly raised allegations of Federalist blackmail and bribery. Especially vulnerable to the former threat were the cartmen, who carried on their trade at the pleasure of the mayor. In 1801 the *American Citizen* claimed that Mayor Richard Varick had in 1798 revoked for three-quarters of a year the licenses of many cartmen who espoused the Republican cause. A subsequent article by "Leonidas" claimed that "so thoroughly convinced" were the cartmen that their permits had been removed because of Republican activity that "many of them have since lived, and even now do live, in fear and trembling." [21]

The cartmen's problems went beyond that of securing certificates. Often their merchant employers tried to influence the
votes of their employees. The most blatant action took place in
1799 when, according to "Cartman," his fellow workers were
"threatened with ruin" if they refused to cast Federalist ballots. In
order to "deceive" the cartmen of the "free choice" which "election
by ballot" offered, they were brought to the polls by the "Federal
merchants," told that to "preserve the constitution" they would
have to vote for the "Tories whom they have nominated," and
then formed into lines. Each man was given a red or blue ticket
which the "bullies" required him to deliver to the election inspectors. The only alternative was to "lose all employment." [22] This
was a far cry from the days of the early 1790s when the cartmen
had met voluntarily to endorse the Federalist ticket.[23]

In 1807 Mr. Kane, a Federalist employer of "Tory family," was
accused of discharging Mr. Cuypers, a Republican driver, stating
that "we Federalists will employ none but Federalists." [24] Furthermore, indignation arose among both Republicans and workingmen
when a former cartman, Moses Coddington, was fired from his
municipal job because he would not vote Federalist. In this instance the Federalists were warned that the cartmen were a
"shrewd and discerning body of men" who would never forget
"federal intolerance." [25]

Imputations of coercion were also made about mechanics in
other trades. During the middle of a hotly contested assembly
election, a strongly worded handbill found its way onto the streets
of New York. Boldly entitled, "EXPOSURE OF FEDERAL MEANNESS AND
DESPOTISM," its tone was urgent:

> *Fellow citizens*—LET us support our independence! If we are
> Mechanics, Labourers and Artizans—Why should we sur-
> render our opinions and our rights to the arbitrary mandate
> of a Tory Employer, and that employer, perhaps a foreign
> emissary! . . .
>
> Now, bribery and denunciation are threatened! No man
> who dares to oppose Federal men is to be employed by them!!
> *Look at the following affidavit?* Read! Consider! Then determine
> for yourselves. Is it possible there can exist one Republican in

this city who will sell his principles *for all the federal party can offer?* Is there *ONE?* [26]

The affidavit told of one Garret Van Horne, Jr., a carpenter, who swore that William Bridges, a master builder, had told him at the Fifth Ward poll that although work would be "dull" after May, Bridges would have two or three houses to build and Van Horne could have the work if he voted for the Federalist ticket. This allegation, plus another that Bridges had offered a black man a dollar to vote Federalist, were both denied ten days later in an affidavit of two cabinetmakers and a mason. However, this took place long after the election was over, an election the Federalists lost. This was the second year in a row that such a controversy had arisen. The year before a Federalist merchant was accused by a Republican ropemaker of refusing to deal with him if he voted Republican. A similar affidavit of denial appeared in the newspapers after the election.[27]

Bribery, too, was an insult to the self-respect and integrity of a mechanic, seriously impairing his right of suffrage. In 1806, the *Citizen* reported that Federalist landlords had visited their various lessees in May, the month in which houses were let for the year, offering them a lower rent than usual "on the express condition that the tenants should vote for the Federalists and the quids." [28] The following year two cartmen claimed that Federalists had offered a two-dollar bribe for food and drink.[29] This was a slight variation of a common charge. In 1800 the Federalists had been accused of forcing ballots into the palms of cartmen after they had plied them with a "strong glass of grog." Seizing their hands, they led them "handcuffed like" to the polls "without quitting their hold, or allowing them to look at or examine their ticket."[30]

Although they could not match the Republicans, the Federalists did manage a few countercharges of their own. In one instance of unethical favoritism, the *Evening Post* exposed the Republican-controlled Common Council's offer of advantageous stalls to certain Republican butchers. This became a major issue in the ensuing charter election in which the Federalists—at a meat handlers' meeting—protested the "disregard" of the "rights and welfare of butchers not among the favorite number." [31] While this controversy did help the Federalists regain a majority on the Common

EXPOSURE

OF FEDERAL MEANNESS

AND DESPOTISM.

Fellow Citizens—LET us support our Independence? If we are Mechanics Labourers and Artizans—Why should we surrender our opinions and our rights to the arbitrary mandate of a Tory Employer, and that employer, perhaps a foreign emissary! A few years ago the worthy Mr. Coddington was insulted and *whipped* by a son of the same Neilson, who *invited the British Fleet* to protect our Commerce, and became instrumental to the death of PIERCE. Remember this! Mark them!

Now, Bribery, and denunciation are threatened! No man who dares to oppose Federal Men is to be employed by them!! *Look at the following Affidavit?* Read! Consider! Then determine for yourselves. Is it possible there can exist one republican in this city who will sell his principles *for all the federal party could offer?* Is there *ONE?*

AFFIDAVIT.

City of New York, *ss.* Garret Van Horne, Junior, of the city of New York, Carpenter, being duly sworn, doth depose and say, that this day, the 27th April, at the Fifth Ward Poll, William Bridges of the same place, Architect and Surveyor, did tell him this Deponent, "That after May, work would be *dull* and that he the said William " Bridges had Two or Three Houses to build, and that if he, this Deponent would vote " for the Federal Ticket, he Mr. William Bridges would give him this deponent a JOB ;" or words to that effect, and further this Deponent saith not.

Garret Vanhorne, Jun.

Sworn before me this 27th april, 1808.
DAVID M. ROSS, *Notary Public* for the State of *New York*

Broadside from 1808 Assembly campaign. Courtesy, New York Historical Society, New York City.

Council, the wrongdoing involved only a political payoff to mechanics high in Republican ranks. Such an act carried no lasting stigma of disrespect or condescension and did not appear to hurt the Republicans beyond that single election.

Of the more compelling charges of coercion, the Federalists could muster only a few examples. In 1807 Henry Rutgers, an eminent Republican merchant, was said to have stood at the polls, "looking every one of his poor tenants in the eye" to insure that they voted for him.[32] The final instance of alleged Republican intimidation is significant for what it tells of the expectations of wealthy employers. In 1803 John D. Miller, a leading Republican merchant, was quoted speaking angrily about some of his employees. Upon learning from a clerk that a number of his cartmen had complained that "it was too much trouble" to vote, he replied that "we did not think it too much trouble to search the city for them, to give them the preference of our business," and that in the future it would become "too much trouble to give them our carting." [33] Clearly the deferential expectations of Federalist merchants touched their Republican colleagues. This statement, moreover, reveals that some workingmen did not find their interests and those of the major parties compatible.

A final political right sacred to citizens of a republic was that of running for and holding responsible offices. As we shall see in a detailed analysis of candidacies in Chapter 4, the Federalists held a marked bias against mechanic nominees. Craftsmen were aware of this attitude and the danger that it posed to their standing in society. Evidence of this lingering prejudice appeared in a handbill distributed in the fall of 1804 during a special election to fill the city's seat in the House of Representatives. In it "Elector" complained that the reason for the low voter turnout was that George Warner, a well-known sailmaker mechanic and the "most suitable candidate," had not been given the Republican nomination because "certain of the leading men" of New York had decided upon a merchant, Gordon Mumford. At the nominating meeting, the "combined interests of the lawyers and the merchants" overpowered the mechanic representation, who favored Warner. "Elector" concluded with a plea for party unity, questioning whether "the best interests of our country can be supported by any particular class.[34] Bias against mechanic candidates among Republican leaders posed a serious threat to that party's welfare.

Their own particular elitism, however, did not prevent Republicans from attacking the even greater Federalist disinclination to offer artisan candidates. Taking note of the absence of craftsmen from the assembly ticket in the spring of 1806, the *Citizen* pondered that "it must be either that no mechanic would serve the managers of the party or," it concluded, "they hold a mechanic in too much contempt to nominate even one of that numerous and respectable class of citizens." [35]

Prejudice against the artisan's capacity for office was deep-rooted. On the surface there was a rational argument against it, yet that argument only masked the contempt and arrogance that the artisan so feared and resented. An article by "Paddy" in the *Citizen* in 1810 (when that paper was leaning toward the Federalists) makes this clear. "Paddy" questioned the propriety of three Republican mechanic nominees for alderman, George Buckmaster, a boatbuilder, William Burtis, a coachmaker, and John Pell, a well-to-do butcher. His argument against their candidacies was that the position of alderman was a judicial post requiring legal ability; without such skill an official could readily become "a mere tool or instrument in the hands of the more knowing who make use of him when the occasion requires." This may have been an arguable point, except that this logic was not equally applied to merchants. Moreover, Paddy's language exposed an inherent disdain. He asserted that though Mr. Pell could "stick a pig as well as any man," he would have "no pigs to stick" on the Common Council. The same was true for Mr. Burtis, who may have known that wheels make coaches go, but that, too, was not enough. Mechanics, even the most skilled and most prominent, were considered limited men, contained politically by the boundaries of their trade. Their leaders were not given credit for breadth of knowledge and experience.[36]

In sum, the question of mechanics' full capability and participation in the political process was a major and forceful political issue. What had once been a largely deferential mechanic class had since the American Revolution taken on new electoral power, self-esteem, and self-consciousness. These gains continued during the years of Jefferson's presidency as the mechanics gained even greater access to the ballot and greater recognition of the importance of their votes. There were, however, still doubts about whether their ability as intelligent citizens was accepted by the leadership of the Federalists and even, on occasion, by the Republican power brokers.

As crucial as the issue of political capability and participation was the question of aristocracy and democracy: the nature of the new American society and the place of the artisan within it. As in the question of suffrage and coercion of ballots, Federalist attitudes and personalities set the stage for debate. That party's conception of a static, ordered community in which prominent, well-educated merchants and lawyers occupied the higher positions made the Federalists vulnerable to the accusation that they considered the rich superior to the poor and middling classes. That is, when Federalist personalities were condemned as aristocrats, they were pilloried for an outlook that placed mechanics as men of inferior political capabilities, whose duty it was to adhere to the decisions of their social betters.[37] This attitude, and the word "aristocrat" itself, was also directly associated with the meaning of the Revolution. Many tradesmen identified the Federalists, who generally defended the British cause in the diplomatic quarrels of the day, with the hated British enemy of '76. With wartime antagonisms still very much alive, this connection proved most effective.

Republicans touched a sensitive area with the assertion that artisans were as able as any class of men to determine the direction of the nation. Answering his counterpart, "Bit of a Cartman," "Mechanic" explained that while a man "brought up to a mechanical employment" might not be capable of writing as "learnedly and elegantly" as those among the higher professions, when it came to the "true policy and real interests of our . . . country, plain common sense" was a better guide than the "over refined speculations of your very learned men."[38] Similarly, "Shoemaker," replying to a Federalist who had argued that the Republicans were trying to deceive that trade, asserted that the cordwainers were "capable of thinking and acting for ourselves . . . from principle; . . . from conviction of the justice and utility of the cause."[39]

Indeed, the independent mind of the artisan was deemed superior to that of the haughty. In battle against the Federalists, it was crucial that mechanics understand this strength. As the *American Citizen* pointed out in 1801: "to the fascinating and powerful eloquence of a tyrant, and his courtiers, has been opposed the powerful, plain, honest and unadorned language of the American yeomanry." The Federalists were trying to "ROB the mechanics and laborers of their independence of mind" and, as "Mechanic" warned his fellow craftsmen, attempting to "wantonly and basely take away your rights." [40] Any "friend to his country" who cared for the "liberties of his fellow men" would vote the Republican ticket. It stood for the "simplicity of liberty" rather than the "imaginary pomp of royalty." [41]

Along with harboring contempt for the minds of artisans, a second Republican claim was that the Federalists were rich men who cared only for their wealth and position and were attempting to institute a monarchical, aristocratic system at the expense of the less affluent tradesmen. This was a prominent theme in the 1801 gubernatorial election between Federalist Stephen Van Rensselaer, the "social leader of the state," and George Clinton, the Republican leader. A Federalist newspaper, the *Commercial Advertiser,* complained that the election was made to look like "a contest between the Rich and the Poor" in which Governor Clinton was pictured as the "friend of the Poor" and Van Rensselaer as "a rich man and a friend to the rich man." [42] The editor tried to counter these charges by explaining that Van Rensselaer paid more in taxes. Such reasoning, however, could not hide the sharply different levels of wealth separating the Federalist candidate and the vast majority of New York mechanics. Tradesmen were more likely to respond to the Republican appeal: "If, fellow citizens, you love liberty and republicanism, you will vote for your true friend, Clinton." [43] The question was whether the state was to be governed by "a purse proud Aristocracy, or by the will of the sovereign people." [44] Although George Clinton was anything but a pauper, these Republican allegations remained telling.

The movement for suffrage reform gave the Republicans further opportunity to accuse the Federalists of "aristocratic indolence and excessive abuse." [45] Taking the side of the disfranchised mechanics, they claimed that the forthcoming fall election was a "contest between aristocrats and republicans ... whether this aristocracy can be removed from the metropolis of our state," [46]

Jeffersonians also saw in the behavior of leading Federalists evidence of aristocratic manner and leanings. Mayor Richard

Varick was a favorite Republican target; his treatment of the ferrymen and cartmen has already been mentioned. In 1801 he aroused mechanic wrath anew when he chose Federalist residents from other districts to be election inspectors in the mechanic wards. This action was quickly interpreted either as meaning that he did not consider the local inhabitants adequately responsible to impartially oversee the counting of votes, or that he desired Federalist influence in the tabulation of ballots. "X. Y." delivered a sharp rebuke to the mayor, informing the wards' inhabitants on how they might get rid of their chief magistrate:

> This man hates you; from his own soul he hates you and was determined by this appointment to let the world see how he despises you. Rouse, my fellow citizens, exert yourselves to the utmost; watch these election inspectors closely; do your duty and you will have nothing to fear. Yet three months, . . . and you will get rid of a mayor who acts as if he thought a poor man had no more right than a horse.[47]

The individual most singled out for Republican barbs was Alexander Hamilton. This was likely because, until his untimely death in 1804, he was the most formidable Federalist campaigner within the artisan constituency. In the late 1780s and early 1790s he had been a hero in the mechanic community for his support of the Constitution. And while his reputation fell precipitously in the late 1790s, he was one of the few Federalists with an appreciation of craftsmen's sensitivities and with a willingness to go out and speak directly to tradesmen. In the famous election of 1800, in the hopes of capturing the mechanic vote, he arranged a Federalist ticket composed almost entirely of artisans. He could still be seen at the polls engaged in debate, or attending political rallies, including those specifically designed to attract artisan support.[48]

Hamilton was the object of much personal vitriol. For his proposals at the Philadelphia convention, he was accused of attempting to "institute monarchical government" in America. And, for his adulterous role in the notorious Reynolds affair, he was condemned in the eyes of the moralistic mechanic community as having "violated the honor of his bed, though in the marriage contract he called God to witness . . . that he would 'cleave to his wife.' " Even more effective were accounts of the Federalist leader's arrogant, aristocratic demeanor, a bearing he was unable to suppress. One anecdote became current following Hamilton's attendance at a meeting of cartmen. In the account, a cartman accosts him on the street:

> "Well, General, since you have come to be a cartman, you ought to put on your frock and trowsers and mount your cart.—I wish you would lend me a hand, I have a job of riding timber, and if you will help we'll go snack on the profit." The General treated the offer with contempt. The value that will be set upon the conduct and character of such a brother cartman, the fraternity are best able to judge.[49]

Hamilton had come to the meeting hoping to persuade cartmen to return to the Federalist camp. He was far more successful, however, in subjecting himself to ridicule. An address, "To Every Cartman," claimed that the drivers would not be "such fools as to frizz their hair on their forehead two stories high," although occasionally they would find a little "dust in their heads." In that same article a stranger asks whether all the men at the meeting were cartmen, and is given a reply: "Cartmen! Yes, to be sure they are—but new made cartmen. They will cart you to the polls and dump you down." [50]

Aside from being labeled aristocrats, Federalist personalities were often accused of Loyalist leanings. Because more Federalist leaders were thought to have Tory backgrounds and more Republicans patriot pasts, the charge of "Tory" was a forceful Republican arrow that found its mark whether or not the allegation was true. As Stephen Allen, the mayor of New York who began his career as a sailmaker around the turn of the century, recalled, his decision to follow the Republican banner was influenced by the fact that he saw "all the old Royalists and Tories whom I had known while yet a boy attaching themselves to the Federalists, while . . . many of the Old Whigs who had ever been friends of the Revolution were joining the Republicans." [51]

A barrage of accusations continually kept the Federalists defending their nominees and leaders against charges of disloyalty. In 1801 candidate Van Rensselaer was depicted as a representative of money and British influence.[52] Earlier that year, William Coleman, editor of the Federalist *Evening Post,* fended off allegations that many Federalists were either Tories who had retreated behind British lines or else ambitious men who had used the war to further their personal careers. Included in the latter category were John Jay, John Adams, and Alexander Hamilton.[53] President Adams, with his haughty bearing, was a favorite target of the mechanics:

> In Adams' administration
>> From which many evils have flow'd
> Of the hardships impos'd on the nation,
>> Mechanics have bore a great load.
> When to Congress he'd make his fine speeches
>> Not a word to their comfort did say
> While he suffer'd the English leeches
>> To draw all their substance away.[54]

Particularly important to craftsmen was the case of house carpenter, Stephen Rudd. An active political organizer among the tradesmen, Rudd had delivered a biting attack on Republicans in the *Evening Post,* calling them the "Jacobin" party of "assassination, crime and plunder" that was ready to bring on "revolution and counter-revolution." [55] The *Citizen* replied that Rudd had been a British soldier during the Revolution who was paid by the "King of England" to "destroy every American subject." [56] In a public affidavit Rudd replied that he had indeed been in the British army but that he had tried to escape, had been caught and put in irons, and finally had served as a carpenter's mate on board a British ship. He also swore that he had never fired a gun during his term of service. In allegations such as this the passions of war remained alive and burning in the hearts of veteran artisans.[57]

The Federalists mustered little defense against the pro-British, Tory, and aristocratic labels thrust upon them by the Republicans. Decrying these attacks as "political calumny ... beyond the bounds of political difference," they claimed that the Democrats were using such charges to "get power and place." The party of Washington and Hamilton did try a few counterallegations, reproaching the chairman of a Republican political meeting in the (cartmen's) Sixth Ward, Leonard Lispenard, as an "excellent Re-

The finifhing
STROKE.
Every Shot's a Vote,
and every Vote
KILLS A TORY!
DO YOUR DUTY, REPUBLICANS,
Let your exertions this day
Put down the Kings
AND TYRANTS OF BRITAIN.
LAST DAY.
April, 1807.

Broadside from 1807 Assembly campaign. Courtesy, New York Historical Society, New York City.

publican TORY," and the speaker at that meeting, a Doctor Smith, as "another excellent monarchical Tory." [58] But such incriminations could not blunt the force of a similar Republican assault. The Federalists did tend to favor British policies, did have more leaders with Tory backgrounds, did have more wealth among their followers, and, in general, did believe more strongly in a society in which the workingman graciously and willingly deferred to his social and economic betters. And, to many mechanics, a vote for them was a vote against everything they had fought for from 1776 on, as well as a retreat to the position of second-class citizenship prevalent in the days of British rule.

Marketplace issues were a third area of appeal to mechanic constituents. Politically oriented and organized crafts, such as the shoemakers and cartmen, could form significant voting blocs. Speaker of the Assembly Samuel Osgood stated that it was the vote of New York City's shoemakers that gave the Republicans the victory in the assembly election of 1800 when New York's legislatively cast electoral votes were crucial to Jefferson's election. Another newspaper, meanwhile, estimated that six to seven hundred votes were included in that craft.[59]

Concerted attempts to secure the votes of the cordwainers continued after the election of Jefferson. In 1801, with the Federalists in control of Albany, shoemakers were both angry and fearful over what they considered an excessive production of shoes for public sale at the state prison located in the city. The shoemakers sought legislation that would prevent the sale of prison-made shoes below the going market prices. Such a bill was introduced, but after considerable debate it failed to pass, and each party blamed the other for this failure.

"Brutus," the Federalist apologist, charged that the Republicans had contrived to allow the bill to pass the assembly, which they controlled, only because they knew that it had no chance of passing in the Federalist-controlled senate. Thus the shoemakers had allowed themselves to become "tools in the hands of fellow citizens to serve their own purpose": to continue in control of the assembly in 1801 with the help of the cordwainers' votes.

By appealing to class pride and dignity, "Brutus" attempted to turn the issue against the Republicans. His main target was Aaron Burr, still a popular New York figure and a state senator early in 1801. According to the Federalist spokesman, Burr approved the bill only because he feared that otherwise poor people would be tempted to commit crimes and enter prison in order to learn the shoemaker's trade. Carrying this twisted logic to its conclusion, "Brutus" claimed that Burr not only thought that a "convict shoemaker" would not disgrace the trade, but that "common crimes" would no longer carry any disgrace "provided the convict was made a shoemaker." Such an attitude represented the "most extraordinary reflection on the poorer and more industrious class of citizens of anything that was ever uttered in a public assembly." [60]

Having defended the status and independence of the shoemakers from alleged Republican contempt, "Brutus" then told the cordwainers that if they wanted any remedial legislation, they would have to support and elect Federalists—not because they were better advocates of the shoemakers' cause—but because they controlled the Senate and could block any bill that they did not want to pass.[61] The Federalists' expectations of deference from the artisan community and their insensitive attitude to the shoemakers' genuine market fears almost precluded any true advocacy of that craft's cause. Their argument that the shoemakers had better vote Federalist or they would get nothing gave no support to the mechanic's sense of dignity and independence. It was in strong contrast to the Republican attempts to pass legislation. Furthermore, since very few journeymen shoemakers could meet the restrictive suffrage requirements for the state senatorial contests, their sense of helplessness and anger at the Federalists was no doubt intense.

While the Federalists, in their contradictory and ambivalent manner, tried to cajole, persuade, and finally coerce the shoemakers, the Republicans stuck to their story of support for the bill only to meet defeat at the hands of the Federalists in the state senate. Moreover, they backed the cordwainers' charges that the Federalist-controlled state prison was endangering their financial security by selling shoes under market prices and in "vast quantity," all in accordance with the "hostile spirit" of the Federalist administration.[62] Although the Federalists claimed that since shoes had to be imported to meet the demand, there was plenty of room in the New York market, this convinced few shoemakers as the journeymen met as a group and endorsed the Democratic-Republican ticket.[63] Evidently believing the Republicans, a spokesman, "Shoemaker," asserted that "the majority of the Federal party have uniformly for their object the suppression of liberty and the promotion of tyranny." [64]

The shoemakers' endorsement spurred "Brutus" to continue his appeals, but in a new vein: he portrayed the Republican master shoemakers and leathermakers both as men hostile toward journeymen's organizations and scornful of the status of journeymen. "Brutus" claimed that a few years ago when the shoemakers "turned out almost to a man" in an effort to get wages equal to those of other crafts, the master shoemakers, rather than heeding these just demands, banded together under the leadership of three tanners. One of these men, Democrat Philip Arcularius, was on the assembly slate the shoemakers had just endorsed. Yet he had been part of this cabal that had agreed not to sell "one ounce of leather" to the journeymen until they gave up their wage demands.

Nor was this the only such incident. But a short time before the 1801 election, some Democratic master cordwainers came to a common agreement that sought better regulation of their journeymen. The "Bausses" decided that henceforth they would not hire any journeyman unless he possessed a "discharge in writing" from his previous employer. Pushing his effort to arouse indignation over class pride and self-respect, "Brutus" declared that this rule would have put the journeymen "upon the same footing with a hired Negro wench that must have a recommendation to get a place." As a final insult, two of these plotting shoemakers, Mills and Vanderbilt, were constantly selling in their shops ten pairs of out-of-state shoes to every one made in New York, thus further depressing the journeymen's financial plight.[65]

The shoemaker issue continued to draw fire long after 1801. In 1804 the Republicans managed to pass a law in Albany limiting the number of inmates who might work as cordwainers to one-tenth of the population of the state prison.[66] In 1807, with the Republicans in power, a new debate broke out, with the Federalists claiming that more convict shoemakers were employed in the state prison than during the days when the Federalists had run the prison. Armed with its own tables, each side argued on.

A second significant labor dispute that became embroiled in politics was the "Workshop" proposal, a public rehabilitation project of Republican Mayor Edward Livingston. This was an attempt to aid new immigrants, the sick and handicapped, orphans, and ex-convicts by helping them learn mechanic trades through municipally owned and operated workshops.[67] Despite the charitable intention of the plan's supporters, craftsmen perceived this proposal as a serious monopolistic threat to their economic security. With equal alarm, they also saw it as a threat to their social status because it would identify artisans with the rabble of the city. As mechanic opposition grew, almost all of the signers of the proposal—community leaders of both parties—withdrew their support. Soon the different party newspapers were denouncing the plan while criticizing each other as responsible for it. It quickly became a major issue in the assembly and state senate elections of April 1803.

Because the plan was instigated by a Republican mayor and because prominent Republican candidates, including merchant John Broome, the candidate for state senator, was himself a petition signer, the Federalists were in a strong position. Attempting to split the Republicans from their mechanic supporters, the *Evening Post* reminded the tradesmen that Samuel Osgood, a supporter of the shoemakers' struggles in Albany, had signed the hated petition. Another spokesman, "Mechanic," urged the artisans and tradesmen to unite in their own interest and not elect any merchants (Broome) who had signed their "death warrant." They should carefully ponder how in their hour of need their beloved Republicans "incautiously forsook them." [68]

In this explosive incident, the Federalists were not alone in attempting to split the mechanics from Republicans. The newly dissident Burrite faction was also seeking to sunder the union between artisans and their Jeffersonian allies. Led by Matthew Davis, a former printer and officer in the General Society of Mechanics and Tradesmen, it anonymously announced a general meeting of mechanics at which seven hundred workingmen assembled. This was an extraordinary congregation, as it represented a large political assembly of tradesmen outside the governance of a major party. That such a number of mechanics could come together at a political caucus is an important indication of both tradesmen's ability to respond to common interests and of their political awareness. Still, this mobilization, called as it was against the wishes of the Republican leaders, must have been a very tense gathering. The anti-Burrite *Citizen* reported that at first no one was willing to take the chair and identify himself as a dissident leader. Then a man in the hall raised the question of who had called the meeting. Again there was no response. Finally, Davis rose and gave a vigorous speech denouncing Broome. By calling for a mechanic to represent the artisan class, the printer-turned-politician hoped to split the mechanics from the regular Republican party. His words are worth recording at some length both for their content and as an example of political rhetoric directed at workingmen:

> I trust sir, that I never have done, and never shall do anything that I am ashamed to avow. I trust, sir, that my conduct will bear the test of scrutiny. This meeting, sir, may, if the gentlemen pleases, be ascribed to me ... I say sir, that the mechanics ought to have a senator of their own. I say sir, that I pledged myself to 1,500 of my fellow mechanics, not to vote for a man who signed the memorial for the workshop? And pray sir, what was the design of that memorial? ... To reduce the mechanics of this city to the degraded state of those of England. ... Yes sir, I say to a state of vassalage. And I am called upon to vote for a man who signed the memorial.

Davis had hoped that Ezekiel Robins, a Burrite hatter, would be put on the ticket in Broome's stead. He even went so far as to threaten to work for the election of Jacob Sherred, a Federalist mechanic, if Robins was not nominated.[69]

Davis's speech was answered by George Warner, a loyal Republican sailmaker. Warner spoke out against the notion that mechanics were entitled to have their own candidate. Such a measure, he cautioned, would set "one class against another." That the mechanics had a "due influence" in elections was correct and accepted by society, but it would be "highly improper" for them to "arrogate to themselves an *exclusive* nomination." [70] It was essential for the Republicans that Warner stave off any sizable mechanic defection. The Federalists had not survived such a loss, and neither could the Republicans. Any kind of move for an exclusive ticket was dangerous to the party's coalition. And, fortunately for the Jeffersonians, none materialized from this incident. Though their margin of victory dropped by about half from the last contested election, the Republicans remained victorious in the 1803 assembly elections. In the state senate race, Broome, who was opposed by both a Federalist and a Burrite, lost New York City by seventy-four votes. However, with the help of the rest of the district he was able to win the seat.[71] The Workshop issue damaged the alliance between mechanics and Republicans, but it did not render permanent injury.

This issue was typical of the controversies that dominated political literature directed at mechanics. Like bribes, blackmail, arrogance, Toryism, and British aristocracy, the workshop struck directly at the self-esteem and position of the workingman in American society. What was unusual about this case was that for perhaps the first time before the embargo the Republicans were on the defensive, hard pressed to keep the trust and support of the mechanic community. Yet while the Republicans lost some ground, the Federalists' liabilities were far too great to be overcome by this controversy.

In the controversies over prison-made shoes and Livingston's proposal, tradesmen were generally united in their stand. However, it must be noted that in the marketplace the mechanic community was not always of the same mind. The early nineteenth century saw a serious deterioration in the relations between journeymen and master craftsmen, causing journeymen to form their own trade associations and to engage in a number of bitter strikes and boycotts, as we shall see in Chapter 10. This was particularly true in the construction, printing, tailoring, and shoemaking trades, crafts that tended to support the Republicans. The difficulty that the situation presented to the Jeffersonians was twofold. First, many of the master craftsmen were Republican, including important members of the party's leadership. However, many journeymen were also part of the party's electoral supporters. Second, Democratic-Republican ideology was opposed to any coercive action taken by journeymen trade associations, such as the requirement that all men working in a shop belong to an association. Such a stance was considered contrary to the "tacit compact" of all professions to work harmoniously toward a good society.[72]

The division within the mechanic community thus posed a significant problem to the Republicans, who could not support one group without alienating the other. Fortunately for that party, however, the Federalists were equally vulnerable, for they too were employers and so threatened by concerted action among workingmen. Moreover, their ideological position was also opposed to trade organizations, societies they saw easily becoming Jacobin mobs.[73] Consequently, other than Brutus' single foray, the Federalists did not make labor strife a political issue. What this meant was that journeymen-master disputes, despite their considerable significance during this era, never entered the political arena. In fact, the newspapers completely ignored the famous 1809 trial of twenty-five journeymen shoemakers for conspiracy (enforcing a closed shop through their trade society) in which both the prosecutor and defense attorneys were notable Republicans. Both parties had a great deal to lose by bringing this subject into electoral politics.

The group that was most hurt by this position of silence was, of course, the journeymen. They had no political ally in their struggles in the marketplace. A number of them were probably of similar mind with the cartmen who Republican merchant William Miller condemned for declaring it "too much trouble" to vote. The majority of journeymen, however, likely did remain within the Republican camp. The Jeffersonians were certainly more palatable than the contemptuous Federalists. Their patriotic, egalitarian appeal, coupled with the judicious silence about labor conflict, generally proved effective. So, too, at least in periods of labor quiet, masters running on the Republican ticket generally retained journeymen's loyalty. Against an adversary unwilling to put artisans on the ballot and scornful of the abilities of nearly all tradesmen, their candidacies still represented the aspiration of the entire mechanic class for social recognition.

Taken as a whole, the Republican campaign within the mechanic community constituted a direct attack upon the Federalist view of society and, beyond that, on the idea that mechanics were any less capable of civic responsibility than men of higher breeding or profession. This assault very nearly overwhelmed the Federalists. The minority of artisans to whom their appeals could yet be attractive were most likely craftsmen of pro-British or anti-immigrant inclinations; workingmen yet untouched by Republican zeal who still regarded their genteel employers as patrons; the more prominent tradesmen who like the Federalists believed in a stable, property-based society and deeply distrusted change of any kind; or else voters who were alienated by the increasing factionalism that began to plague the ranks of New York Democratic-Republicans from 1804 on.

The Federalist view of what was happening was a sad one indeed. Not trusting political parties and factions, they deplored the "scandal and abuse" that they produced. The Republicans were hypocrites who on the one hand expounded "on every corner" that "*all men are free and equal,*" yet on the other hand, when meeting a man who differed from them, attempted to "knock out his eye for a damned rascal." [74] "Brutus" declared that he had never before seen such "PERSECUTION . . . with murderous hand" singling out the "good and virtuous" for its victims. As a result "RUIN" was overtaking the community, and the "welfare of society, itself," was at stake.[75]

After his experience as an active Federalist politico in 1807, Washington Irving gave a colorful account of Federalist disgust with the Republican onslaught. Appalled by the "scenes of confusion" and "licentious disorganization," he saw the entire city "given up to the tongue and the pen; to the puffers, the bawlers, the babblers and the slangwhangers." Gotham's population was "convulsed with a civil war." Good men were "verbally massacred," while families were "annihilated by the whole sheerfuls." The "slangwhangers," particularly, made merry as they went on "coolly bathing their pens in ink and rioting in the slaughter of their thousands." The picture was pitiful:

> I have seen . . . that awful despot, the people, in the moment of unlimited power, wielding newspapers in one hand, and with the other scattering mud and filth about, like some desperate lunatic relieved from the restraints of his strait waistcoat. . . . I have seen liberty! I have seen equality! I have seen fraternity! I have seen that great political puppet show— an election.[76]

In a more reasonable mood, Alexander Hamilton, too, bemoaned the fact that the political process was reaching all classes. For the former secretary of the treasury the problem was that in human nature "the vicious are far more active than the good passions." In order to move the "vicious passions" to the Federalist side, the party had to "renounce our principles and our objects, and unite in corrupting public opinion until it becomes nothing but mischief." [77]

Although a number of Federalists did come to learn the use of modern political techniques such as barbecues and electioneering newspapers, it appeared unlikely that they could recapture the mechanic constituency. First, until the embargo the Federalists were seriously handicapped by the lack of a persuasive issue to take to the tradesmen.[78] Occasionally they attempted to respond in kind to Republican charges, but their efforts were weak and ineffectual. Second, the Federalists, frightened by the French Revolution, feared and distrusted craftsmen as either potential "Jacobins" or as a potential "swinish multitude." [79] One of Irving's *Salmagundi* characters evinced these sentiments when he declared it "better to trust to providence, or even to chance, for governors, than resort to the discriminating powers of an ignorant mob." [80] Finally, and most important, the Federalists could not grant mechanics the sense of equality and independence the artisans sought. Instead, they continued to insist on deference to their role both as benevolent employers and as the elite segment of society. As General Hamilton said of some Federalist merchants who were incensed over the Republican allegiances of their cartmen: "no gentlemen of the old school could bear it with patience." [81]

Artisans resented being likened to a mob. They, too, respected property rights and wholeheartedly endeavored to succeed in the marketplace, often with the goal of purchasing property. But they also advocated a society that allowed them the liberty to participate in the body politic as citizens with rights equal to men of higher social or economic standing. They did not advocate the violent overthrow of the government, but neither did they fear a peaceful reordering of society, accomplished through the political process, that raised their stature.

The Republicans, also an upwardly mobile group and with a more egalitarian outlook and less entrenched elitism than their opponents, were able to accept craftsmen's goals and to assist in their fulfillment by providing offices and recognition. Accordingly, they fashioned a powerful political alliance which afforded electoral majorities year after year for over a decade.

NOTES

1. Jerome Mushkat, *Tammany: The Evolution of a Political Machine, 1789-1865* (Syracuse, 1971), p. 26.

2. For examples of debate over national and philosophical issues see *American Citizen,* January 5, 1801, April 6, 1801, April 23, 1802, September 26, 1802; *Commercial Advertiser,* January 1, 1801, April 25, 1801, May 6, 1801, July 15, 1801, October 1, 2, 1801, November 6, 1801; *Evening Post,* April 17, 1802, March 20, 1803; Richard Buel, Jr., *Securing the Revolution: Ideology in American Politics, 1789-1815* (Ithaca, 1972); and Robert E. Shalhope, "Toward a Republican Synthesis: The Emergence of an Understanding of Republicanism in American Historiography," *William and Mary Quarterly,* 29 (1972), 49-80. For discussions of deference in politics see John B. Kirby, "Early American Politics—The Search for Ideology: An Historical Analysis and Critique of the Concept of Deference," *Journal of Politics,* 32 (1970), 808-838, and Ronald Formisano, "Deferential-Participant Politics: The Early Republic's Political Culture, 1789-1840," *American Political Science Review,* 68 (1974), 473-487.

3. Edmund P. Willis, "Social Origins and Political Leadership in New York City from the Revolution to 1815," Ph.D. diss. (Berkeley, 1967), p. 54.

4. *Evening Post,* November 16, 1801. This Federalist view was predominantly that of the "old school." Influence of younger Federalists was felt after 1807. See Chapter 3.

5. *Evening Post,* April 13, 1803.

6. *Minutes of the Common Council of the City of New York, 1784-1831,* 21 vols. (New York, 1917-1930), vol. 3, pp. 192-193 (January 19, 1803).

7. *Evening Post,* November 16, 1801. The Federalist fear of the French Revolution, largely responsible for the increasingly conservative stance of the Federalist party and for the loss of many of their mechanic constituents, is well documented in Alan Blau, "New York City and the French Revolution, 1789-1797: A Study in French Revolutionary Influence," Ph.D. diss. (City University of New York, 1973).

8. Quoted in Michael Wallace, "Party and Democracy in Jacksonian America," Ph.D. diss. (Columbia University, 1973), p. 58.

9. *People's Friend,* April 20, 1807.

10. *Washington Republican,* August 5, 1809.

11. For an understanding of how the Federalist outlook towards mechanics fit into the overall Federalist ideology see David Hackett Fischer, *The Revolution of American Conservatism: The Federalist Party in the Era of*

Jeffersonian Democracy, (New York, 1965), pp 1-49; and Linda K. Kerber, *Federalists in Dissent, Imagery and Ideology in Jeffersonian America* (Ithaca, 1970), entire book, but especially pp. 173-216. Fischer's study reveals that the class-conscious attitude of the Federalists' statements was part of a "habit of subordination" expected by Federalist leaders. This applied most emphatically to the older guard; but the younger leaders, though willing to use democratic means to achieve political victory, still expressed elitist aims and views. Kerber's study puts the generally static Federalist view of society, as depicted above, into an overall picture of men greatly fearing the precariousness of revolution and the danger of democracy disintegrating into violence and chaos. She finds that the Federalists equated the decline of deferential behavior with social decay. A fear of the French Revolution and of the mob—though the mob was not defined by any one social or economic class—permeated Federalist thought. Furthermore, the leaders of this party saw a grave threat in the developing proletarian work force. For other insights into Federalist thought during the 1790s see Donald T. Stewart, *The Opposition Press in the Federalist Era* (Albany, 1969), pp. 371-418, and Buel, *Securing the Revolution.*

12. New York, 1801.

13. Mushkat, *Tammany,* p. 27, Sidney I. Pomerantz, *New York: An American City, 1783-1803* (New York, 1938), pp. 134-138; *American Citizen,* November 17, 1801, January 18, 1807; *Evening Post,* May 3, 1801.

14. Pomerantz, *New York: An American City,* pp. 132-145; *American Citizen,* November 16, 1801.

15. *American Citizen,* January 10, 1803.

16. Ibid., March 2, 31, 1801.

17. Ibid., October 29, 1801.

18. Ibid.

19. Ibid., March 24, 1804.

20. Ibid., April 27, 1807; Michael D'Innocenzo, "The Popularization of Politics in Irving's New York," in Andrew B. Myers, ed., *The Knickerbocker Tradition: Washington Irving's New York* (Tarrytown, 1974), p. 21.

21. *American Citizen,* April 27, 1801.

22. *Republican Watchtower,* April 30, 1800, in Alfred Bernstein, "The Rise of the Democratic Party in New York City," Ph.D. diss. (Columbia University, 1964), p. 404.

23. Blau, "New York City and the French Revolution," p. 323.

24. *American Citizen,* April 27, 1807.

25. Ibid., April 27, 1807, April 22, 1808.

26. Broadside, "EXPOSURE OF FEDERAL MEANNESS AND DESPOTISM," April 27, 1808, Misc. Coll., New York Historical Society.

27. *Evening Post,* May 9, 1808, April 27, 1807.

28. *American Citizen*, November 21, 1806.

29. *Gazette*, April 30, 1799; *American Citizen*, April 29, 1800, in D'Innocenzo, "Popularization of Politics," p. 21.

30. *American Citizen*, May 2, 1807.

31. *Evening Post*, July 24, 1806, August 1, 13, 1806, September 30, 1806; *American Citizen*, August 4, 7, 11, 13, 21, 1806, December 2, 18, 1806.

32. *Evening Post*, April 18, 1807.

33. *Evening Post*, May 5, 10, 1803.

34. Broadside, "To the Mechanics," September 13, 1804, Misc. Coll., New York Public Library.

35. *American Citizen*, April 21, 1806.

36. Ibid., November 7, 1810.

37. This definition of aristocracy is generally in accord with that of Alfred F. Young in his book, *The Democratic Republicans of New York: The Origins, 1763-1797* (Durham, 1967), p. 574.

38. *Morning Chronicle*, April 12, 1803; see also Richard Hofstadter, *Anti-Intellectualism in American Life* (New York, 1962), for an overall perspective on this attitude in American politics.

39. *American Citizen*, April 23, 1801.

40. Ibid., March 11, 1801, April 13, 1801.

41. Ibid., April 13, 1801; "Mechanic" also noted that though he was poor, the common language of his works still bore thoughts worth consideration.

42. Ibid., March 21, 1803; *Daily Advertiser*, April 13, 1801; Dixon Ryan Fox, *The Decline of the Aristocracy in the Politics of New York* (New York, 1919), p. 4.

43. *American Citizen*, March 28, 1801.

44. Ibid., April 30, 1801.

45. Ibid., November 16, 1801.

46. Ibid., October 29, 1801.

47. Ibid., April 20, 1801.

48. Broadus Mitchell, *Alexander Hamilton: The National Adventure, 1788-1804* (New York, 1968), p. 472; Fischer, *Revolution of American Conservatism*, p. 95.

49. *American Citizen*, April 27, 1801.

50. Ibid., April 23, 1801. So strong was the hostility aroused by Hamilton that when the Common Council voted to defray the cost of his funeral with municipal funds, the alderman in the working-class Fifth Ward came under political fire for his ballot in support of this measure. *Evening Post*, November 10, 1804.

51. Willis, "Social Origins," pp. 285-286, finds the following percentages for elite officeholders:

	Patriot	*Loyalist*
Republican:	40.7	5.6
Federalist:	26.7	9.2

James C. Travis, ed., "The Memoirs of Stephen Allen, 1767-1852; Sometimes Mayor of New York City, Chairman of the Croton Water Commission, etc." (New York, 1927), p. 50 (typescript at New York Historical Society).

52. *American Citizen,* March 28, 1801.

53. *Evening Post,* February 19, 1802.

54. *American Citizen,* February 20, 1801.

55. *Evening Post,* April 22, 1807.

56. *American Citizen,* April 27, 1807.

57. *Evening Post,* April 28, 1807.

58. *Commercial Advertiser* April 28, 1801. They also claimed that a deputy marshal appointed for the Sixth Ward had deserted to the British during the war. Ibid., April 20, 1801.

59. Ibid.; *Evening Post,* April 25, 27, 1807, in D'Innocenzo, "Popularization of Politics," p. 18. This estimate may be somewhat exaggerated since *Longworth's New York Directory* in 1806 listed only 291 shoemakers. However, since a number of journeymen were not listed, the disparity may not be that great.

60. *Commercial Advertiser,* April 17, 1801.

61. Ibid.

62. *American Citizen,* April 18, 22, 1801.

63. *Commercial Advertiser,* February 18, 1801, April 20, 1801; also, in a show of support for artisans, the "Republican electors" of the Fifth Ward met and resolved that they approved of the action of the state legislature to "equalize the several mechanical branches in the state prison which has relieved the cordwainers of this city, heretofore oppressed by the arrangements of that institution." *American Citizen,* April 21, 1804.

64. Ibid., April 23, 1801.

65. *Commercial Advertiser,* April 20, 1801.

66. *American Citizen,* March 21, 1804.

67. See Chapter 7, pp. 197-199, 287-288.

68. *American Citizen,* March 25, 1803, April 13, 1803; *Morning Chronicle,* March 21, 1803; *Evening Post,* March 19, 1803; also ibid., April 25, 1803, in Raymond Mohl, *Poverty in New York, 1783-1825* (New York, 1971), p. 235.

69. *American Citizen,* April 11, 14, 1803.

70. Ibid., April 16, 1803.

71. Ibid., April 30, 1803.

72. See Chapter 10, p. 285.

73. Kerber, *Federalists in Dissent,* pp. 173-216.

74. *Commercial Advertiser,* April 20, 1801.

75. Ibid., April 7, 1801.

76. Washington Irving, *Salmagundi* (New York, 1904), pp. 151-152.

77. Alexander Hamilton to Senator Bayard, April 18, 1802, in Henry Cabot Lodge, ed., *Works of Alexander Hamilton* (New York, 1904), vol. 6, pp. 540-543.

78. See Chapter 8. Fischer claims that the Federalists never found an issue that could carry them to victory. This was true, perhaps, on the national level, but in New York City among the mechanic constituency, they did find an issue that garnered enough votes to forge a citywide majority for five of the six years from 1810 to 1815. Fischer, *Revolution of American Conservatism,* p. 180.

79. *Commercial Advertiser,* April 28, 1801; *American Citizen,* April 25, 1801.

80. Irving, *Salmagundi,* p. 214.

81. *American Citizen,* February 24, 1802; Fischer, *Revolution of American Conservatism,* chaps. 3-7.

Chapter 3

A Conflict of Interests:
The Mechanics, the Embargo,
and the War of 1812

The succession of electoral defeats at the beginning of the nineteenth century seriously discouraged New York's Federalists, causing them to talk of withdrawal from politics. For example, after the Federalists had lost majority control of the Common Council in 1804, Federalist editor William Coleman advised "men of character, of sense, and of property" to "sit down quietly and let the torrent rage" rather than make useless efforts in "mock elections." [1] The Democratic-Republicans, in large measure through capturing tradesmen's votes by fostering both a prospering economy and a sense of personal dignity, were well in command. Quickly, however, the situation changed; Republican supremacy came into doubt as the mechanic constituency abandoned its unquestioned support. Because of major economic and diplomatic upheavals, craftsmen were thrust into the unhappy dilemma of having to choose between their self-esteem and their pocketbook. The story of mechanic participation in New York politics from 1808 to 1815 was shaped by the unusual circumstance of men deciding whether to place principle above economic self-interest.

With the resumption of the Napoleonic wars in 1803, the titanic struggle for supremacy in Europe waged between Britain and

France spilled over into American waters. In an attempt to enforce its blockade and supplement its navy, England subjected American ships to continuous search and seizure, and American sailors to impressment. With the British declaration of a blockade of the entire European continent in 1806, their interference reached a new height. As the Republican administrations sought to preserve American integrity but avoid war by means of the Embargo and Nonintercourse Acts, the nation's commercial life suffered grievously. Each American response became a major political issue as the Republicans appealed for patriotic self-sacrifice and the Federalists warned of the impending death of American enterprise.

Ironically, the first salvos fired against the royal government were launched by the Federalists. In accordance with their long-standing advocacy of a strong American navy, they denounced both America's helplessness and British audacity in the actions of the H.M.S. *Leander,* the British man-of-war cruising just outside New York Harbor. *Evening Post* editor William Coleman told the local tradesmen that Jefferson could have better spent the fifteen million dollars that he wasted on Louisiana in building a stronger navy. He wondered whether mechanics preferred leaders who wished to defend American rights and commerce or those who could "patently submit to insult and injury." When John Pierce, captain of the American sloop *Richard,* was killed by shots fired from the *Leander,* indignation and riot swept New York. Shouting for defense instead of tribute, the Federalists were at the forefront of the demonstrations.[2]

The party of Hamilton was soon to regret its words, however. By inclination pro-British and by profession dependent on Anglo-American trade, it could afford to attack the Royal Navy only as long as the channels of trade remained open. When these lines were cut, the terms of political controversy changed abruptly. In December 1807, President Jefferson and the Republican Congress took the bite out of the Federalist offensive with the implementation of the embargo. This law and subsequent enforcement acts forbade all foreign shipping out of American ports and put heavy restrictions on coastal trade. Suddenly it was the Republicans who were foremost in defending American honor and the Federalists who were placed on the defensive.

On the other hand, the Federalists had a way out. The embargo gave them a potent issue to pursue with mechanics: the ruined economy of the city. There could be no argument about what this act did to the life of the seaport. It is well described in the account of foreign traveler John Lambert, who visited New York just before, and again a few months after, the embargo went into effect. On his first stopover in November 1807, Lambert was impressed with the whirl of commerce. He wrote of a port "filled with shipping . . . the wharfs crowded with commodities of every description." "Noise and bustle" were everywhere. While carters were driving busily about, "the sailors and labourers upon the wharfs, and on board the vessel were moving ponderous burdens from place to place." In the countinghouses merchants and clerks worked energetically: "Everything was in motion. All was life, bustle and activity. The people were scampering in all directions to trade with each other." [3]

On his return to New York the following April, Lambert saw the embargo in full force: "How shall I describe the melancholy dejection that was painted upon the countenances of the people, who seemed to have taken leave of all their former gaiety and cheerfulness?" No longer was the feverish movement on the wharves and slips evident. "Not a box, bale, cask, barrel or package was to be seen." Only a few merchants, clerks, porters, and laborers were around, and they were "walking about with hands in their pockets." In place of the nearly one hundred cartmen usually found at the docks, there were less than a dozen, "and they were unemployed." The streets near the water were almost empty, and "grass had begun to grow upon the wharfs." With over 1,100 men in debtors' prison, more than half for debts of fifteen dollars or less, the "first commercial city in the United States" had lost its heartbeat as the embargo had "completely annihilated its foreign commerce." [4]

With their financial survival as well as their political fortunes at stake, the Federalists hastened to inform mechanics that the laws establishing and implementing the embargo were "visionary maxims and pernicious measures" that failed to promote commerce or protect the city. Furthermore, hoping to revive memories of the merchant-mechanic Federalist coalition of the 1790s, the opponents of Jefferson claimed that they could restore financial tranquility, giving "all classes of our citizens the protection and support which the people have a right to demand from their rulers." [5] Industrious tradesmen could no longer discharge their "honest debts" and, as one pointed out, would soon be "subject to confinement." Pointing to the sorry condition of craftsmen who "stand aghast and stare at the naked bottom of the meal cask," the Federalists found that Republican leadership had led its followers into unnecessary suffering and austerity. It was necessary for workingmen to come forward now and speak out: "When destruction is courted and stripes wantonly inflicted, silence is pusillanimous." [6]

The Republicans, in turn, refused to be put on the defensive. With the embargo in place they countered the Federalist claims of common merchant-mechanic interests by intensifying their anti-British barrage and taking over their opponents' arguments about the importance of national honor and defense. The spring 1808 "Resolutions of the Republican General Meeting" declared it the "duty of every American citizen to submit to all deprivations . . . to redress the violated honor of our country." The embargo was a "substitute for war," and those who opposed it were lacking in "love of country." (One Federalist was even alleged to have asked for British frigates to enter and blockade the port.) Though they sympathized with those who had experienced "inconvenience and in some cases distress," the Republicans asserted that there was "no alternative but a choice of evils." Moreover, as a Fouth Ward meeting resolved, "submission" to the embargo was the "highest proof of magnanimity and patriotism." [7] Finally, the embargo might allow the United States to develop its own manufactures, thus providing tradesmen with work not dependent on British favor.[8]

Republican spokesman, "Mechanic," was quick to expose alleged Federalist hypocrisy. He told his fellow tradesmen that the supposed followers of Washington were indeed men of a strange breed; first anger at inaction, but once important steps were taken and the embargo in place, only hostile opposition. Had they instituted the measure, however, "the hills and valleys would have rung with praises of Federal wisdom." Were the Federalists really concerned with American honor they would have "acquiesced like good citizens." [9]

Along with the appeals to mechanics' strong sense of patriotism, the question of artisans' dignity and respect remained at the center of Republican messages to tradesmen. In April 1808, "Another Mechanic" claimed that the Federalists desired to "lay our independence prostrate at the feet of Great Britain" by means of a humiliating accession to her Orders in Council. He quoted a Federalist merchant who had told a Republican mechanic that the United States should not even ask the British to let the American flag protect American seamen:

> "What," said he, "is the loss of a few thousand sailors compared to the friendship of the English?" To which the Republican replied—"suppose yourself for a moment in the situation of one of those sailors, many of whom have families and friends who if not so wealthy as you, are equally near and dear to them; and suppose you to be dragged on board a British man of war, there to be detained, perhaps for years, without the knowledge of your friends;...." This offended Mr. Federalist as he thought there ought to be no comparison between him and a sailor.[10]

The picture of the poor American sailor, or "Tar," as he was commonly known, made for a sharp contrast with the figure of the rich Federalist entrepreneur concerned only about his speculations. It reinforced the hostility between the mechanic, who was likely to identify with the unfortunate sailors, and the wealthy Federalists.

The Republican spirit (and a united organization) overwhelmed the Federalists at the polls. In the only assembly election held during the embargo (Spring 1808), the Jeffersonians received 56 percent of the total vote (5,646)—their highest total in seven years. Surprised and chagrined, the Federalists could not understand how sailors, for whom work had to be "doled out," and mechanics who "begged for bread," could still vote for the "Embargo Ticket." [11] But the Federalists did not yet fully understand what they, as proponents of Great Britain's position and way of life, symbolized for the artisans and tradesmen. To many a shoemaker, shipwright, and cartman, the embargo was worth the sacrifice of meat for a week, or of a pair of new shoes, or even of his job for a while. Did not patriots make much greater sacrifices not so many years before? Had not the Federalists been lamenting lost American honor? Ought not the brave mechanic to stand by his country once more in its hour of need?

While the embargo ended early in 1809, its vitality as a political issue remained. At the height of patriotic fury it won acceptance among many workingmen. However, as it became apparent that the measure had secured neither peace nor American honor, its memory of economic distress grew increasingly bitter. The Federalists encouraged this distaste, arguing that the Republicans were to blame for bringing forth a law that "carried distress throughout the country, evincing an utter disregard for the public welfare." [12] During the prewar years (1809-11), the party of Hamilton and Washington adopted as its slogan, "PEACE, FREE TRADE, and UNION" and taunted its opponents as the representatives of "WAR, Bloodshed, EMBARGOES, non-Importation Acts and Enforcement Acts." [13]

As the difficulties with England and France continued to provoke more harassment of American trade, the Republicans enacted new enforcement acts. Since these only served to further depress New York's trade (after a brief respite in 1809), the Federalist case appeared more and more convincing. In 1810 the *American Citizen,* which had lately split with the Republicans over foreign policy, published an article by "Mechanic," relating the sad plight of a man putting in a hard day's work only to find himself "losing ground every day." With no money in circulation because of the Nonintercourse Act, a workingman had to wonder how long this state of things could last. Perhaps, "Mechanic" pondered, "until our mechanics become beggars and crowd our jails as prisoners?" [14] Such a life contrasted sharply with that led by Republican "pampered sons of luxury," such as General Wilkinson. According to the *Washington Republican,* while the American yeoman struggled valiantly to make an "extra shilling," the general had ordered 844 bottles of claret, 11,350 "Segars," and 196½ gallons of Madeira wine. This was indeed a "curious bill." [15]

Although their attempt to re-create the mechanic-merchant coalition had failed during the embargo, the Federalists, convinced of the reciprocal relationship between the two kinds of professions (and not concerned about the deferential status implied in such a system), continued to push the idea, addressing such juxtaposed groups as "The Merchant, the Mechanic and the Laborer." [16] At a meeting in the Fifth Ward, they reasserted their "friendship" with, and appreciation of, the importance of merchantry. Stating that the metropolis could not survive without the freedom to trade, they told the district's residents: "With commerce it [the city] has increased and must continue to increase. Without commerce it must moulder into ruin. And in this ruin, every inhabitant of every occupation must partake." [17]

On their side, the Republicans were seriously weakened by internal divisions that saw Republicans loyal to De Witt Clinton opposing the major foreign policy moves of Madison. Thus, Republican mechanics had to choose between the Madisonians or the Clintonians, or else retire from or desert their party. Under such conditions, calls for sacrifice made less sense. Rather, the Republicans, either when offering a united front or when offering opposing slates, pressed issues that had proven successful before: Federalist contempt and pro-British prejudice. Emphasizing the continuing anger at the British, an 1810 communication cautioned artisans that voting for the Federalist ticket was a step toward becoming the "slaves" and "vassals" of the "English nabobs and Federal lords." Another allegation claimed that the Federalists were threatening to throw out of work all cartmen who refused to wear the Federalist symbol, the "black cockade." A third message warned mechanics that the attention Federalists gave them at election time was deceptive, and that once balloting ended these "aristocrats" would only scorn craftsmen with "imperious disdain." Indeed the question continued to be whether tradesmen would demonstrate that they were "as necessary to their would be masters as the Tory lordlings are to them." But the Republicans were not as confident as in recent years. When in 1812 internal divisions blossomed into the attempt by De Witt Clinton to wrest the presidency itself from Madison, the Republicans were also threatened with the loss of their previously secure Irish votes.[18]

In contrast, the Federalists in 1810 were a more potent political force than at any time during the prior ten years. They finally had a powerful and encompassing issue that they could take to the artisan community. Equally significant, a number of party regulars had learned the importance of countering the Republicans' efforts in popular politics. Led by young Gulian Verplanck along with Isaac Sebring and Richard Varick, the Federalists in 1808 formed

their own fraternal organization, the Washington Benevolent Society. Its aim was to make Federalism "palatable" to all classes,
and particularly to the mechanics. The society employed secret
rituals, ceremonies, and mysteries, along with huge holiday parades in which gaily clad members walked along in militarylike
formations. The days of celebration, chosen to mix patriotism with
adulation of Federalism's greatest hero, George Washington, were
the Fourth of July, and the birthday and first inaugural day (April
20) of America's first president. A witness reported that the Independence Day procession in 1810 consisted of "substantial Shopkeepers and Mechanics, of men in the middling class, and of a
considerable number of old Revolutionary officers and soldiers." [19]

After the parade the marchers congregated in a church to listen
to an oration. Speakers there invoked the glory of the American
Revolution with special emphasis on the noble exploits of Washington, Hamilton, and Jay, while at the same time excoriating
France and Napoleon. The mechanics in attendance were warned
that "the distress of our merchants" along with the "general
distress which pervades our community" ought not to be allowed
to "pass for nothing." With national character and public spirit at
stake, it was up to the people to rise once again and rescue the
nation. The Republicans, depicted as drunkards, atheists, cowards,
and immoral men, were certainly not equal to the task.[20]

The Washington Society was a political machine organized by
the Federalists to increase their support among tradesmen. By
associating their party with Washington they hoped to lessen the
monarchical, pro-British stigma that was especially hurtful during
times of strife with England. Moreover, the Federalists were now
offering artisans an organization similar to Tammany in which
they could sit down and socialize with men of a higher social status
"in terms of equality and fraternity." It may not have offered as
much hope for political office as membership in Tammany did,
but the Washington Society had low dues (installation fee, one
dollar; yearly dues, fifty cents) and yet still managed to provide
needy members with loans.[21] Indeed, the Republicans considered
the society a benevolent form of bribery, noting that "the Federalists are very rich, and they are trying to see what money can do." [22]

In 1810 the Federalists captured six of the city's eleven assembly
seats with 5,325 votes or 50.1 percent of the ballots cast. (The

Republican vote was 5,304.) While they failed to capture the governor's chair and the important patronage that went with that position, they were once again the majority party in the city. The following year their margin of victory increased to about 15 percent as they captured 58 percent of the vote cast (5,295) for assemblymen. Fourteen hundred fewer votes were cast in 1811 than in 1810, and this decline probably included quite a few mechanics who, while disenchanted with Republican leadership, were unwilling to vote for the Federalists. Yet, considering that but ten years before the Federalists had been on the short end of a 23 percent plurality, and but two years earlier had a 12 percent deficit, their victory was impressive. Moreover, they did well in the mechanic wards, receiving 51, 60, 56, and 55 percent of the votes in the fifth, sixth, seventh, and eighth wards, respectively.[23]

The Federalists claimed that even when Republican factionalism had been considered, their strong showing meant a change of heart among the electorate. Tradesmen had come to understand the absurdity of the Republican attempt to inflame the lingering class differences and, to a degree, hostilities. To the Federalists, theirs was a banal argument:

that the rich and the poor had separate interests; that the cartmen and the mechanics were held cheap by the merchant; and that the buying and selling part of the community were always opposed, in all things, to the laboring part. That, let what would happen, it would always be the poor only who would suffer, but as to the Federalists, they were all rich.

The artisan recognized that both he and the merchant class had lately been reduced to "idleness and want" because of the Republican administration's opposition to free enterprise, commerce, and a strong navy. The common interests were apparent.[24]

In order to assess the Federalist assertions of mechanic allegiance at this critical point, it is useful to compare the occupational distribution of trades found in the General Trade Directory in *Longworth's New York Directory* with the membership lists of the Washington Benevolent Society. The Washington Society attempted to attract a large membership with a special emphasis on the recruitment of artisans. Thus, its success among the different occupations has merit as an indicator of which professions were the more attracted by the Federalist party in 1810.[25]

Table 3.1 reveals that the percentage of merchants and professionals holding membership in the Washington Society was significantly higher than their percentage in the entire working population. Grocers and public officials were fairly evenly divided while the most prominent sector of the mechanic community, the elite manufacturing mechanics (M. Mech.), who were the proprietors of the most notable artisan enterprises, had a slightly lower figure. Tradesmen mechanics (Mech.), journeymen and independent craftsmen of lesser standing who composed nearly half of the city's jobholders, had the greatest difference, with the Federalist society's proportion of these artisans 15 percent less than the corresponding proportion in the General Trade Directory.

When the trades are examined individually, the poorest mechanic professions show the greatest hesitancy in joining the Washington Society. Shoemakers, tailors, and cartmen, all of whom were among the least affluent craftsmen, had strong percentage differences. The more skilled and prestigious artisans in the building trades, such as cabinetmaker Duncan Phyfe, had a higher percentage of membership than did carpenters, joiners, and turners, men who represented the skilled but less distinguished members of that profession. Furthermore, among the building trades associated with maritime commerce (shipwrights, riggers, sailmakers) the percentage differences, though small, always favored the Federalists. These professions were among those most hurt by the interruption of trade. On the other hand, sailors were involved in maritime trade, but still had lower proportions of membership in the Washington Society as compared to the General Trade Directory. Those who were most hurt by the stoppage of commerce, but also immune from the dangers of impressment, preferred the Federalists. Overall, the mechanics tended to have substantially smaller membership percentages than other professions even in a year when the Federalists' overall electoral strength was equal to, or better than, that of the Republicans.[26]

The Federalist claims of new artisan support were probably exaggerated. Similarly, their statements concerning a new merchant-mechanic coalition similar to the one that garnered 80 percent of the vote in the early 1790s were not valid. On the other

Table 3.1

A COMPARISON OF THE MEMBERSHIP

(1810) OF THE WASHINGTON BENEVOLENT SOCIETY

(FEDERALIST) AND THE GENERAL TRADE DIRECTORY (1806)

TOTAL GROUP

a)

Occupation:		Merch	Grcr	Retl	Prof	Offcl	M.Mech	Mech	Lab	Unk
Trade	No.	1027	1015	317	717	136	414	3507	634	
Directory:	%	13.2	13.1	4.1	9.2	1.8	5.3	45.2	8.2	
Washington	No.	204	150	104	195	37	38	354	44	313
Society:	%	18.1	13.3	9.2	17.3	3.3	3.4	31.4	3.9	

BY OCCUPATION

	Trade Directory		Washington Society		Difference
Trade:	N	%	N	%	%
Merchant:	948	11.9	196	17.4	+5.5
Shipmasters:	197	2.5	74	6.6	+4.1
Attorneys:	141	1.8	61	5.4	+3.6
Tavern,Coffee Houses:	110	1.4	38	3.4	+1.9
Public Officials:	136	1.8	37	3.3	+1.5
Gardeners:	25	0.3	19	1.7	+1.4
Cab. & Chair Makers:	75	0.9	26	2.3	+1.4
Porter House Keepers:	48	0.6	19	1.7	+1.1
Accountant:	62	0.8	21	1.9	+1.0
Physicians:	103	1.3	26	2.3	+1.0
Riggers:	59	0.7	18	1.6	+0.9
Shipwrights:	116	1.5	24	2.1	+0.6
Stonecutters:	36	0.5	11	1.0	+0.5
Butchers:	124	1.6	24	2.1	+0.5
Booksellers:	44	0.6	12	1.1	+0.5
Sailmakers:	40	0.5	10	0.9	+0.4
Watchmakers:	30	0.4	9	0.8	+0.4
Hairdressers:	56	0.7	12	1.1	+0.4
Printers:	41	0.5	9	0.8	+0.3
Curriers:	24	0.3	7	0.6	+0.3
Tallow chandlers:	14	0.2	6	0.5	+0.3
Livery Stablers:	8	0.1	4	0.4	+0.3
Lumber Yards:	6	0.1	4	0.4	+0.3
c) Druggist and Dry Good Stores:	200	2.8	34	3.0	+0.2

Table 3.1 (cont.)

Trade:	Trade Directory		Washington Society		Difference
	N	%	N	%	%
Brassfounders:	12	0.2	5	0.4	+0.2
Brewers:	19	0.2	5	0.4	+0.2
Shipchandlers:	17	0.2	4	0.4	+0.2
Saddlers:	27	0.3	6	0.5	+0.2
Blacksmiths:	104	1.3	16	1.4	+0.1
Blue Manufacturers:	2	0.0	1	0.1	+0.1
Bookbinders:	24	0.3	5	0.4	+0.1
Distillers:	13	0.2	3	0.3	+0.1
Dyers:	8	0.1	2	0.2	+0.1
Tobacconists:	34	0.4	5	0.4	--
Brushmakers:	7	0.1	1	0.1	--
Auctioneers:	29	0.4	5	0.4	--
Engrvr., Gld. and Silver:	38	0.5	6	0.5	--
Jewelers:	16	0.2	2	0.2	--
Masons:	149	1.9	21	1.9	0.0
Ropemakers:	34	0.4	4	0.4	0.0
Carvers and Gilders:	15	0.2	1	0.1	-0.1
Coachmakers:	18	0.2	1	0.1	-0.1
Coppersmiths:	15	0.2	1	0.1	-0.1
Wheelwrights:	15	0.2	1	0.1	-0.1
Painters:	87	1.1	11	1.0	-0.1
Oystermen:	25	0.3	1	0.1	-0.2
Teachers:	102	1.3	12	1.1	-0.2
Ironmongers:	39	0.5	3	0.2	-0.3
Bakers:	97	1.2	9	0.8	-0.4
Hatters:	47	0.6	2	0.2	-0.4
Coopers:	101	1.3	6	0.5	-0 8
Mariners and Boatmen:	221	2.8	22	2.0	-0.8
Boardinghouse Keeper:	141	1.8	11	1.0	-0.8
Carpenters and Joiners:	370	4.6	39	3.4	-1.2
Grocers:	682	8.5	82	7.3	-1.2
Day Laborers:	246	3.1	19	1.7	-1.4
Shoemakers:	291	3.7	25	2.2	-1.5
Tailors:	195	2.4	8	0.7	-1.7
Cartmen:	1200	15.0	70	6.2	-9.0

Table 3.1 (cont.)

b) Trades in Directory but not found among Membership of Washington Society:

Trade:	Trade Directory		Trade:	Trade Directory	
	N	%		N	%
Basketmakers:	2	0.0	Millwrights:	7	0.1
Black ball			Morocco-manu.:	8	0.1
makers:	3	0.0	Musical		
Block-makers:	17	0.2	Instr. Maker:	6	0.1
Brokers:	11	0.1	Musicians:	10	0.1
Builders and			Music Prof.:	6	0.1
Architects:	16	0.2	Nailers:	4	0.1
Caulkers:	3	0.0	Notaries:	37	0.5
Coffee Manu.:	10	0.1	Nurses:	25	0.3
Combmakers:	6	0.1	Pilots:	41	0.5
Comedians:	12	0.2	Porters:	41	0.5
Confectioner:	17	0.2	Sawyers:	36	0.5
Conveyancers:	5	0.1	Seamstresses:	31	0.4
Cooks:	7	0.1	Segar-makers:	13	0.2
Cutters:	4	0.1	Skinners:	8	0.1
Dentists:	6	0.1	Starchmakers:	4	0.1
Dockbuilders:	6	0.1	Sugar Refiner:	13	0.2
Fruiters:	27	0.3	Tinner:	20	0.3
Furriers:	6	0.1	Upholsterers:	23	0.3
Glaziers:	24	0.3	Whipmakers:	4	0.1
Harnessmakers:	8	0.1	Miscellaneous:	200	2.5
Mantua makers:	59	0.7 (women)			
Midwives:	8	0.1			
Milkmen:	23	0.3			
Millstone					
makers:	3	0.0			

a) See Table 4.1 for an explanation of occupations.
b) Most of those listed in the Trade Directory and not in the Washington Society records may be assumed to net have belonged to the society. Most are mechanics. This accounts for the large percentage difference in the overall totals.
c) Interpolated from *Directory*; not specifically listed in trade listings.

hand, the Federalists had made significant gains among the tradesmen—enough to either shift or leave hanging the balance of power in New York politics. While some Republican defections were due to factionalism, the disenchantment with Republican foreign policy and its effects on the city's economy was the major cause. The choice between principle and pocketbook was becoming increasingly less easy. Perhaps, their rhetoric notwithstanding, the Republicans really could not maintain American honor, and were bringing the country to ruin. And, even if the Republicans were sincere, how much longer could a man keep living in financial limbo, paying higher taxes and yet finding his job security and his

ability to support his family hanging in a more and more precarious state?

The coming of the War of 1812 made the mechanics' dilemma
even more perplexing. Anti-British and patriotic feelings, now
magnified by the passions of war, contrasted with a continuation of
hard economic times for much of the city's population.[27] Seeking
craftsmen's electoral support were the Tammany wing of the
Republican party and the Federalists. The former fully supported
Madison's war effort, while the latter protested the effects of the
conflict on local commerce and the nation's welfare.

While the war created severe economic distress, particularly
inflation and shortages of needed goods, it also released the enormous spirit of revolutionary patriotism, still a potent force within
the mechanic community. Working together by trade, artisans
volunteered over 100,000 hours of free labor building fortifications
in Brooklyn. And they did so in a very proud manner. The
butchers, for example, besides forming their own "Fly Artillery"
unit, marched to the fort accompanied by a band, their colors
flying with the slogans "Free Trade and Butchers' Rights, From
Brooklyn's Fields to Harlem's Heights," and "Skin me well and
Dress me neat, And send me on board the Federal Fleet." The
printers, meanwhile, announced their impending service with a
notice declaring:

> Still shall our Country and the Press be free—
> Our Cannon and our Ball defend their liberty.

Similarly, tradesmen were quick to celebrate any military success.
After Commodore Perry's victory on Lake Erie, illuminations went
up in front of New York's City Hall and along the butchers' stalls.
In a spectacle of light, the latter read: "Free Trade and Butchers'
Rights." [28]

However, a martial spirit could not lift the serious financial
distress from the city. Hope for a quick end to the war and a
secure, normal existence remained strong. After the truce was
signed the Mechanics Bank erected a large illumination portraying
the mechanic insignia, a hammer held firmly in hand; an eagle
and a cornucopia, the latter symbolizing plenty, the former, free-

dom; and an outward-bound ship, commerce. The motto read: "Peace, the Mechanic's Friend." [29]

The symbols displayed by the mechanics themselves set the theme for wartime political campaigns for the votes of tradesmen. The Republicans heated up the engines of patriotism while the Federalists continued to point to the sad domestic plight of most workingmen. Once again the mechanics found the hatred of Britain and its aristocratic way of life pitted against their economic interests—this as the city suffered through its sixth consecutive year of conflict and restriction of commerce.

Taking as their slogan "Union of the States, Sailors' Rights and Free Trade," the Republicans attacked the haughtiness of the British. They asserted that the decision for war was a last resort, done "for the protection of the brave American sailors." [30] In a rare political statement, the *Independent Mechanic* came out in support of Madison's decision, declaring that after the many "wrongs and indignities" the British had inflicted on the United States, "none but a cowardly sycophant, or an enemy to the country would be the advocate of further forebearance." [31] The current engagement was a contest for rights that "could not be conceded without the loss of national independence" or the "loss of national honor." In the light of British atrocities, "revenge" had to be the "rallying word." It was a "just and righteous war" requiring the support of each citizen, especially against the Federalist or *"Peace Faction*—or to use a more correct term—the enemy." [32]

Comparing the war to a second American Revolution that would finally and completely "annihilate" British influence in America was an effective approach to the mechanic constituency.[33] Similarly productive was the assertion that the Federalists had reversed their position taken in 1789 and were now advocating the overthrow of the Constitution. Pointing to the Hartford Convention and other dissenting moves, Republicans claimed that the party of Hamilton had been completely "debauched" by British persuasion. Therefore, in order to preserve the union and independence, it was necessary to support the war and the Madisonians, regardless of the sacrifice involved.[34]

Finally, as with the embargo, the war was presented as an opportunity for America to expand its domestic manufactures and become free of its dependence on English products. Nearly all

Masthead and detail of a Republican advertisement, November 1813. Courtesy, New York Historical Society, New York City.

articles could and should be made in the United States. This would create jobs and remove the fear of scarcity that the war created. Pursuing this theme, meetings were called to support and encourage American manufacturers.[35]

The Federalists were equally vigorous in seeking the mechanics' support. The first issue they had to face was whether to support a war even if they opposed the government's policies. Federalist leaders were somewhat divided on the question. John Anthon, Esquire, speaking to artisans and other members of the Washington Benevolent Society in 1812, advised that "this war, we, as good citizens are bound to support, until we can destroy the evil, by removing our unprofitable servants from their trusts." [36] A year later, however, Gouverneur Morris, in an oration before the same group, gave different counsel. He proclaimed that it was the duty of every American to know whether the conflict was just, for "let no man persuade himself that the guilt of war will be imputed, only to the government under which he lives." The present hostilities saw the president assuming dictatorial powers that were endangering the foundations of the republic. The stakes were enormous:

> Are you willing to surrender your liberty, and the liberty of your children, into the hands of a President or an emperor? If you are, assemble no more to celebrate this anniversary; let the name of Washington dwell no longer on your lips; let his remembrance be obliterated from your hearts. But you are not so base. You will not tear to pieces the charter of your rights. And for whom are you called on to make the sacrifice? And what is the boon to be obtained? Everything at the hazard to protect men who abandon their country in the hour of her destruction.[37]

Even if they could persuade a number of workingmen that the war was unjust, a futile conflict pursued only for the selfish interests of Madison and his followers, they still had to contend with the fact that many mechanics were actively fighting as members of the local militia. Attempting to respond to this situation—and in so doing use the Republican tactic of focusing on the workingman's sense of esteem—the *Evening Post* published an angry statement charging that the Republican governor, Daniel Tompkins, was demeaning the integrity of mechanics by giving inmates of the state prison their freedom on the condition that they enlist in the militia. These men, whose only appropriate position was in prison or swinging from the gallows, were not fit to stand side by side with the hardworking yeomanry of the state. Such a condition could not continue:

> Farmers of the State of New York! Industrious Mechanics and Laborers! Ye whose fathers, sons or brothers fill the ranks of our army, and must conquer our foes. . . Are you willing to

become the associates of convicted felons? To have your
moral feelings blunted by an unhallowed connection with
thieves and robbers? To sit down in infamy and rise polluted
by the foul contact . . . ? You will feel it a sacred duty to turn
out at the polls in the Ides of April.[38]

Finally, the most compelling of the Federalists' craftsmen-ori-
ented appeals emphasized the continuing financial hardships that
the Republicans were inflicting on laboring tradesmen. An un-
usually literate newspaper, the *Examiner,* edited by Barent Gardenier, asked the artisan poor to remember old Federalist days
when peace and commerce reigned, when "industrious laborers
had work, and having work they had money; and having money
their wives and children were well clothed and well fed and well
warmed. These were Federal times." "Republican times" had
brought large price increases for sugar, tea, and coffee as well as
other necessities, while earnings continued to decrease. How long
could this situation endure before there arose "a multitude of the
naked to be clothed, of the hungry to feed"? Doubting that it
would be many days, or that there would be enough inexpensive
wood or coal for the coming winter, Gardenier suggested to workingmen that they and their families flee "to the dark and towering
forest" until the election when they might return to vote the
Republicans out of office. The Federalists, who after the Revolution had "made us rich," should be given a new opportunity to
save the country.[39]

The following year, 1814, the *Examiner* published another article complaining about deteriorating economic conditions. This
unusual and interesting piece was penned by an obscure tradesmen, "Poor Mechanic." Likely a disillusioned Jeffersonian, his
message to "The Laboring Mechanics" denounced the wealthy of
both parties as solely intent on "oppressing the poorer classes."
Claiming that despite highly inflated prices, there was no real
scarcity of goods, he drew a picture of the "spirit of monopoly with
which the rich had driven up the prices of necessities. It was this ill
humor, which "pervades almost all ranks of married men," that
allowed these scoundrels to make the war "the harvest of the rich,
and the destruction of the poor."

"Poor Mechanic" saw the wealthy within the ranks of both

parties united "as a band of brothers" against tradesmen. What was the solution to this dilemma? For artisans to vote as a bloc for the Federalists. This was strictly a measure of expendiency because the Federalists had promised to end the war immediately. He explained:

> We must be united! It is, shall the rich oppress the poor? If we, the poor, are true to ourselves, we shall all give federal votes, and thus obtain a peace. But we must act with vigor; for thousands of rich Federalists, having tasted the sweets of monopoly, desirous of continuing to reap its advantages, will give democratic votes ... but as a party they must act consistently—let us then, among ourselves, discard the question, are you a Democrat or a Federalist? Let our question be, are you for THE POOR, PEACE AND COMMERCE, or, THE RICH, WAR AND SPECULATION?[40]

Not surprisingly, editor Gardenier, while defending "Poor Mechanic's" right to be heard, found his logic lacking. Tradesmen, too, he argued, once given the opportunity, would speculate. Nor were merchants creating artificial scarcities; rather, men of commerce were selling wares immediately upon receipt. Where "Mechanic" was correct, however, was in pointing the blame for inflated prices on Republican policy.

The Federalists also charged that a major reason for financial distress was Madison's war taxes. Indeed, assessments on ironware manufacturers as well as on manufacturers of candles, hats, paper, leather goods, furniture, liquor, and other sundries came down heavily on many mechanics. Meetings were held and petitions sent to Washington protesting the effects of these levies and the security bonds and confiscation procedures which were set up to enforce them. Already in difficult straits, the nation's largest urban center and its shopkeepers would feel the heaviest part of these three millions of dollars in new taxes levied by the government. This was, the Federalists claimed, in accordance with Jefferson's philosophy that "great cities were great sores." [41]

Other articles detailed the number of ships then idle in New York Harbor along with a detailed accounting of the taxes that a mere day laborer had to pay in order to finance President Madison's war. As "a Republican of '76" explained, these new levies were as unnecessary as the war. Were not both merchants and mechanics solidly against the bloodshed? Nor could American honor be saved by fighting England when France and Spain had also committed grievous insults. Rather, it was time for working people to act sensibly; to "unite and select men of integrity and wisdom." [42]

Having dealt with the questions of national honor, the self-esteem of the artisan, the principle of opposing bad leadership even in war, and having exposed the disastrous economic plight caused by Republican foreign policy, it remained difficult for the Federalists to understand how workingmen could vote for Republicans. Yet the tally remained close. In 1812 and 1813 the Federalists won the assembly elections with margins of 4 and 1.4 percent, while the Republicans prevailed in the 1814 election by garnering 49.8 percent of the total vote.[43] (Dissenting Republican factions accounted for the lack of a majority.) The mechanic wards on average voted Republican by a 3 to 5 percent margin. It seemed especially strange to editor Gardenier that "John," who had no wood for winter and no shoes for his "poor Nancy," could still favor the men who were waxing rich on war profits while everyone else suffered. Certainly it was an odd set of circumstances when a mechanic felt that "his children can freeze, but he must not let the Tories in." [44]

The Federalists' confusion lay in their consistent blindness to all that the British threat symbolized to the mechanic. For many tradesmen the war only hardened their long held hatred of the English along with a similar loathing of the Federalists, whom they saw as their enemy's supporters. There were artisans, however, who did express their disappointment with economic disaster and what they saw as empty promises about peace and national honor by either voting for the Federalists or abstaining from the ballot box. Consequently, wartime elections remained close, their outcome turning on only a shift of 2 or 3 percent of the electorate. The division was similar to that of the immediate prewar years, except that patriotic ardor may have won back a small but highly significant percentage of the Republican mechanic vote.

There were, of course, other issues in these campaigns. Patronage, apathy, personality and especially Democratic-Republican factionalism all played a part.[45] Yet, when these factors are considered, there is little question that, based on the political literature of the day, the major issue confronting mechanics was that of financial prosperity (or even survival) versus self-esteem and American honor. Arguments based on the sorry condition of trade, prices, employment, and poverty carried weight, but so did appeals grounded on tradesmen's sense of both national and personal independence. The conflicts between the two lines of thought must have caused many an artisan hours of soul-searching before he cast his ballot. Was the mechanic's pride as a respected, antiaristocratic, anti-British Republican more vital to his life than his want of immediate peace and the revival of the seaport's economy? Would he rather accept the more open leadership of the Republicans, or ought he to choose the experienced Federalist merchants and attorneys who, try as they would to deny it, expected the deference of the mechanic community?

NOTES

1. *Evening Post,* November 21, 1804.

2. Ibid., April 30, 1806, April 28, 1805; Marshall Smelser, *The Democratic Republic, 1801-1815* (New York, 1968), p. 157.

3. John Lambert, *Travels Through Canada and the United States, 1806-1808* (London, 1814), pp. 62-63; see also George Daitsman, "Labor and the Welfare State in Early New York," *Labor History,* 4 (1963), 248-256.

4. Lambert, *Travels Through Canada and the United States,* pp. 64-65.

5. *Evening Post,* April 11, 1808.

6. Ibid., April 20, 1808, July 20, 1808, August 16, 1808; one poem lamented the plight of the mechanic without a job *(Evening Post,* January 19, 1808):

> Mechanics in the winter time
> Captive like bears in the northern clime
> Burrow in holes and suck their paws—
> They need not mind the sweeper's [Jefferson's] claws.

7. *American Citizen,* April 14, 23, 1808.

8. Ibid., December 31, 1808; for an opposite view see ibid., August 6, 1808.

9. Ibid., April 25, 1808.

10. Ibid., April 27, 1808.

11. *Evening Post,* April 22, 29, 1808.

12. Ibid., April 18, 24, 1809.

13. Ibid., April 25, 1809.

14. *American Citizen,* April 9, 1810.

15. *Washington Republican,* October 14, 1809.

16. *Evening Post,* March 24, 1810.

17. Ibid., April 20, 1810.

18. *Public Advertiser,* April 9, 12, 17, 19, 1810; *American Citizen,* April 2, 20, 25, 1810; Clinton had won the allegiance of the Irish by friendliness and patronage to the new immigrants. His desertion of the party meant that they, too, might follow him.

19. Peter Jay to John Jay, February 23, 1810, in Henry P. Johnston, ed., *The Correspondence and Public Papers of John Jay* (New York, 1893), vol. 4, p. 326, as quoted in Robert July, *The Essential New Yorker: Gulian C. Verplanck* (New York, 1951), pp. 21-24.

20. Ibid., pp. 18-19; Robert Sedgwick, *An Oration* (New York, 1811), p. 11; Gulian Verplanck, *An Oration* (New York, 1809), p. 19.

21. Tammany's attractiveness as a threshold for political advancement may also have contributed to an elitist membership, one composing only the most prominent Republican mechanics. Willis's study shows that only one member of the Washington Society became an officeholder while half of the mechanics who held office were members of Tammany. Thus, the Washington Society may well have been more oriented toward reaching the lower strata of mechanics than the Tammany Society. (It is true that Willis's study covers many years when the Washington Society was not in existence, but with that taken into consideration, the difference is still very large.) Edmund P. Willis, "Social Origins and Political Leadership in New York City from the Revolution to 1815," Ph.D. diss. (Berkeley, 1967), p. 249.

22. *Public Advertiser,* March 29, 1809.

23. Willis, "Social Origins," p. 77.

24. *Evening Post,* May 3, 1811.

25. Stuart Blumin, in "The Historical Study of Vertical Mobility," *Historical Methods Newsletter,* 4 (1968), 1-12, has pointed out that many variables are involved in behavior along with occupational or class identification. However, judging by the disproportionate amount of literature aimed at the mechanics, there is no question that they were an active voting bloc whose votes were up for grabs. This table cannot be considered definitive, but it does have important value as an aid in determining workingmen's political allegiances.

26. Although most of the unknown entries in the membership rolls of the Washington Benevolent Society may be presumed to be tradesmen, this is more than compensated for by the fact that, aside from cartmen, the General Trade Directory omitted a large number of tradesmen, particularly journeymen. (Only about 40 percent of the mechanic population were listed.)

27. Rocellus Guernsey, "New York City in the War of 1812," Address delivered before the New York Historical Society, March 6, 1888, p. 44. New York Historical Society.

28. *Evening Post,* August 15, 17, 18, 22, 23, 24, 1814; *Columbian,* August 13, 1814, October 14, 1814; Thomas De Voe, *The Market Book* (New York, 1862), pp. 415, 431-433; *Evening Post,* August 26, 1814.

29. *Columbian,* March 14, 1815; *Evening Post,* October 25, 1813.

30. *National Advocate,* April 13, 1813.

31. *Independent Mechanic,* April 12, 1813.

32. *National Advocate,* November 16, 1813.

33. "Warren" also declared that because of New York's position as the country's first metropolis, in the forthcoming election "the eyes of the nation are fixed upon the city." He further announced that the Federalists represented a faction "upholding the pretensions of the enemy." In the heat of war politics reached a bitter and emotional tone similar to that of the Revolution. *National Advocate,* November 16, 1813.

34. *Military Monitor,* April 29, 1813; *National Advocate,* March 29, 1814.

35. *National Advocate,* February 11, 1814, April 20, 1814, May 3, 1814; *Columbian,* October 17, 1815; *Evening Post,* February 10, 1815. See pp. 176-177.

36. John Anthon, *An Oration* (New York, 1812), p. 18.

37. Gouverneur Morris, *An Oration* (New York, 1813), pp. 22-23.

38. *Evening Post,* January 29, 1813.

39. *Examiner,* November 8, 1813.

40. Ibid., January 1, 1814.

41. Victor Clark, *History of Manufactures in the United States,* 2 vols. (New York, 1949), vol. 1, p. 274; *Columbian,* March 7, 1815, May 25, 1814, April 6, 25, 1814; *Evening Post,* October 4, 10, 25, 1815, April 14, 27, 1814, May 15, 19, 1815, April 21, 1815; *Examiner,* December 25, 1813. See p. 176.

42. *Evening Post,* November 16, 1813, September 30, 1812. The details of these tables revealed that in 1806, the last year of relative peace, employment and commerce was plentiful compared with the distress caused by 140 ships standing idle in the harbor in 1813. The table on taxes described how the yearly taxes for a common laborer had increased from thirteen to sixteen dollars per year because of the war. For skilled mechanics the increase was even greater.

43. Willis, "Social Origins," pp. 23-24.

44. *Examiner,* October 22, 1814.

45. In 1814 the Federalists blamed their defeat on patronage scandals in the Council of Appointment; yet with the war on, it would seem that problems of the economy and patriotism must have dominated the minds of most mechanic voters.

Chapter 4

GETTING ON THE
BALLOT

Along with the study of campaign issues and language, a comprehensive analysis of the mechanics' role in New York politics requires an awareness of tradesmen's opportunities to compete for responsible public positions. Access to public office was regarded as a measure of esteem, making the proportion of mechanic candidacies an important measure of mechanics' standing in the New York community.

In an excellent quantitative study, Edmund P. Willis has presented a great deal of valuable information concerning mechanics who attained the prestigious offices of assemblyman, alderman, and assistant alderman. His conclusions are pertinent to this study and will be summarized below. Also employing quantitative techniques, this study explores the active participation of mechanics in all local elective offices, including both the prominent positions covered in Willis's research and the lesser posts of assessor, collector, and constable. One aspect of the present work is that it examines both the winners and the losers of political contests each year, thus revealing a more accurate picture of any changes in the kind of candidates offered by the two parties. Second, this analysis touches all offices, including those for which ordinary tradesmen rather than well-to-do mechanics were more likely to run. Finally, this research analyzes the practices of the two parties within the different wards, indicating how many mechanic nominees were presented in a ward as compared with the number of artisans living there.

Prior to examining candidacies, however, it is helpful to give a collective portrait of those mechanics actually elected to office. Willis suggests three general conclusions about artisans holding the high public positions he studied. First, that the craftsmen who reached high office were among the most prominent of New York society; second, that this group was an upwardly mobile body of men; and third, that the Republicans had a distinct advantage in recruiting officeholders from the ranks of the most talented, wealthy, and ambitious mechanics.

The high status of the officeholding mechanics emerges from Willis's data on the wealth and background of these men. While their personal holdings averaged below those of their merchant and attorney colleagues, the assets of these noteworthy artisans were closer to the merchants' wealth than to the ordinary New York tradesmen's. Based on a Fourth Ward sample that could not take into consideration the large number of subsistence artisans living in the outer wards, in 1789 the median personal worth of a mechanic officeholder ranged from $1,250 to $2,000, while the median wealth of the craftsmen community ranged from $250 to $500. In 1815 the figures were, respectively, $10,000 to $20,000 for mechanic officeholders and $2,000 to $5,000 for all tradesmen. Moreover, more than half of the mechanics elected to high office were landlords, and about 40 percent held either a bank or insurance company directorship or a bank account. Unquestionably, this represented one of the most enterprising and successful segments of the artisan population.[1]

Further evidence of the eminent stature of mechanics sitting on the Common Council or in the state assembly is the data on the nationality, background, and generation of these officeholders. These artisans came from either English, Dutch, or German stock (Republicans, 83 percent; Federalists, 75 percent), generally were affiliated with the Episcopalian or Dutch Reformed church (Republicans, 69 percent; Federalists, 65 percent), and came from families who had been in America for two, three, four, or more generations. While the mechanic community as a whole likely contained a considerable number of Baptists, Lutherans, Presbyterians, and Methodists, these faiths combined contained only about one-fourth of the officeholders. Moreover, the emphasis on English, Dutch, and German stock (with Germans a distinct third) and the concentration on later-generation families left little room for immigrants or those of less prominent nationalities.[2]

Another factor illustrating the prominent status of officeholding mechanics is their high percentages of membership in notable societies and public service organizations. These bodies were important both in political training and for achieving general recognition in the community. Half of the artisan officeholders included in Willis's study belonged to the prestigious General Society of Mechanics and Tradesmen. Almost 40 percent of this group were members of a fire company, and one-fourth belonged to the eminent humanitarian and philanthropic societies of Gotham. Finally, over 50 percent of the Republicans holding high positions belonged to the Tammany Society.[3]

Also very clear from Willis's research is the strong upward mobility of New York's most politically accomplished mechanics. Two-thirds of those holding high office came from mechanic homes. While some of these men began their careers at mercantile or professional standing, many others practiced an artisan trade sometime in their lives. Of the 283 men in Willis's study, 60 were originally merchants, and 117 of the sample reached that category before they retired. Many of these latter 57 men were originally craftsmen. As Willis concluded, "only the most energetic and prosperous mechanics were recruited as officeholders."[4]

While artisan officeholders of both parties were generally well off, the major division between the two organizations was the trend of the Federalists after 1800 to become "more and more the party of the social elite." That is, they began to restrict their slates primarily to a select circle of merchants and attorneys. In contrast, the Republicans were receptive to ambitious mechanics. Consequently, during this period there was a decided preference for successfully mobile tradesmen to choose Republican allegiance. Moreover, the Republicans had the Tammany Society to attract and initiate mechanics into the political acquaintances and general knowhow necessary for political leadership. The Federalists had no comparable organization until 1808.[5]

Brief biographies of a number of mechanics elected to responsible positions help to illustrate the process through which an artisan reached high office. Jacob Lorillard is an example of a prominent manufacturing mechanic with wealthy family connections whose fortunes improved quickly. Borrowing $3,000 from his brothers in 1800, he began his own leather-producing establishment. He did well in an expanding market and soon bought new equipment. By 1815, Lorillard, forty-one years old, owned three houses and two leather stores along with forty acres of Manhattan real estate. His worth was assessed at $90,700 that year. He went on to become president of the Mechanics Bank—evidently glad to retain his initial identity. A Federalist, he was elected to the state assembly in 1812 and 1813 and also served as an assistant alderman in the Second Ward from 1815 to 1817.[6]

A similar case among the Republicans involved the political ascent of shipwright Noah Brown, who rose from a "barefoot frontier boy" to a noted shipbuilder. Brown was elected assistant alderman for the Tenth Ward in 1815 and 1816. He was a Republican, and an important part of his party preference may well have been influenced by his rise from poverty. Lorillard, on the other hand, started well and was given every opportunity by his family. The Republican party, the quantitative data show, offered greater hope to the lowly but ambitious "expectant capitalist."[7]

While a large fortune in business was probably the most likely passport for a mechanic wishing to achieve high political office, there were other means. He might attain his goal by a slow and steady effort to make himself known. Membership in various organizations was the method employed by tanner J. P. Anthony. While expanding his father's business and amassing a moderate estate, he was busy making himself a recognized figure. In 1798 he accepted an appointment from the Common Council as a fireman. After declining a military commission, Anthony joined the General Society of Mechanics and Tradesmen in 1801 and served as a vice-president in 1805 and 1806. In 1806 he also became a member of the Republican-oriented Tammany Society. Thus, while doing reasonably well in his business, this tanner had immersed himself in activities involving him with both his fellow mechanics and with the Republican leadership, thereby becoming a possible candidate for an otherwise elite nomination. In his first political contest, for assistant alderman in the Fourth Ward, he was defeated. However, with the help of his fellow tanners, Anthony was subsequently elected to the assembly in 1808 and 1809. Lacking a college degree or the near-merchant status that his more wealthy counterparts had achieved, a mechanic needed the connections offered by fraternal and voluntary organizations for top political consideration.[8]

A final method of entry into politics was for an ambitious mechanic to work his way up through service in lesser elective and appointive offices. An example of one such man was Benjamin Haight, a moderately wealthy ($5,300 in 1808) Federalist saddler from Westchester. A resident of the Third Ward, Haight became well known there serving as an election inspector from 1790 to 1808. In the meantime he was elected assessor in 1804 and 1805 and served as sergeant at arms in the assembly in 1804. Because of Republican political dominance, Haight was unable to win election to the assembly, but he was elected assistant alderman of his ward for three years beginning in 1806.[9]

Before he could run for the Common Council or assembly, Haight had to serve at lesser offices, building up connections with the Federalist political leaders of his ward. (It would have been fruitless for Haight to have attempted to build up Republican connections, since that ward went Republican only three times from 1790 to 1815.) This included service on local ward committees aside from his other offices and duties. A tradesman like this saddler who could not command respect through his wealth or background had to serve a long political apprenticeship. The road to high office was an arduous one for most artisans. The very few who made it could well consider themselves members of a very select circle.

Analysis of the candidacies of mechanics in assembly and municipal elections gives added emphasis and greater dimension to the eminent status of most artisan nominees and to the margin of the Republican advantage in attracting craftsmen. Both of these aspects are apparent in Table 4.1, a description by occupation of candidates running for the state assembly. It should be noted that artisans are divided into two categories: manufacturing mechanics and tradesmen mechanics. This split is an attempt to separate the well-to-do master mechanics who ran a major manufacturing outlet such as a sail-loft, boatbuilding operation, or a tannery, air furnace, or construction concern from artisans who either worked for these men or who owned smaller operations. The latter category takes in a number of tradesmen who accumulated sizable estates but had not yet achieved the eminent stature of a boatbuilder such as George Buckmaster or a sailmaker such as George Warner and Stephen Allen. The manufacturing craftsmen, commonly officers of the Mechanics Society and speakers before tradesmen audiences on the Fourth of July, occupied a significantly higher echelon in New York society than both journeymen and other independent craftsmen.

Table 4.1 reveals that in the assembly elections mechanics made up one-fourth of the total number of candidates (29 men running for 70 terms). Of these nominees, manufacturing mechanics outnumbered their tradesmen brethren by more than two to one, despite the fact that in the General Trade Directory the tradesmen composed a ten to one majority. The table also clearly indicates that for ambitious candidates hoping for high state office, the Democratic-Republican party was the party open and receptive to their ambitions. Twenty-three of the twenty-nine mechanics to run for the assembly during these fifteen years ran as Republicans. Contesting for 54 terms, they averaged 2.3 candidacies per term. In nearly every year they outnumbered their Federalist counterparts among both classes of mechanics. Among tradesmen this gap was particularly wide, as the Republicans offered nineteen such candidates to the Federalists' two. Altogether, the Federalists allotted sixteen terms to mechanics, less than one-third of the Republican total. Eight of these nominations came during the closely contested elections from 1811 to 1815, and equaled 50 percent of all their nominees for the fifteen years of this study. However, these eight candidacies still comprised but 14.5 percent of their slates for those five years. In contrast, the Republican figure for mechanic nominees from 1811 to 1815 was 44 percent. When the Federalists increased their efforts to attract mechanics, the Republicans did the same, and maintained their advantage. This procedure, of course, benefited ambitious mechanics, who saw their opportunities for political office under the two-party system increase in times of greater competition.[10]

Table 4.2 describes the distribution of candidates for elective municipal offices. Once again manufacturing mechanics predominated in nominations for the two most prestigious positions: alderman and assistant alderman. These well-to-do artisans were offered from three to four times as many candidacies (89 to 27) as were tradesmen mechanics. They were second only to the merchants in the number of such nominations received, though the gap between the two groups was considerable. An aldermanic position was the likely pinnacle of the political career of an economically successful mechanic.

For the less prestigious but still respectable position of assessor, tradesmen mechanics did receive a somewhat greater proportion of the mechanics' total nominations. Furthermore, the overall percentage for artisans (28) was higher than that of any other class. If grocers are included in the same general social stratum as mechanics, then over half of the candidates for assessor came from the artisan sector of New York society. While for a manufacturing mechanic this office was a possible stepping-stone toward an aldermanic nomination, for tradesmen this position was very likely the highest level that they might hope to achieve—and that only after a great deal of work spent in local ward committees gaining general community recognition.

The percentage of mechanic nominees dropped off in the contests for collector. Candidates for that post were often identifiable in the directories only as "Collector," and it was impossible to determine any other concurrent or former occupation. This office was not considered particularly partisan, and men often ran for it with the support of both parties; nor was it uncommon for an individual to serve at this post for five years or more. In 1815 the office of collector was removed from the ballot and made appointive.

The public constable was the one office in which tradesmen mechanics predominated. Thirty percent of the candidates for this post could be identified as either a working mechanic or else as having practiced a mechanic trade prior to assuming his police

Table 4.1

ASSEMBLY NOMINATIONS BY OCCUPATION 1801-1815

		Occupational Percentage Within City								
a)		(13.2)	(13.1)	(4.1)	(9.2)	(1.8)	(5.3)	(45.2)		
FEDERALISTS										
b)Occupation:		Merch	Grcr	Retl	Prof	Offcl	M.Mech	Mech	Unk	NC
1801-1805	%:	45.5	4.5	0.0	18.2	0.0	13.6	9.1	9.1	55.1
	N:	(10)	(1)	(0)	(4)	(0)	(3)	(2)	(2)	(27)
1806-1810	%:	46.0	6.0	10.0	30.0	0.0	6.0	0.0	2.0	0.0
	N:	(23)	(3)	(5)	(15)	(0)	(3)	(0)	(1)	(0)
1811-1815	%:	25.5	7.3	12.7	30.9	1.8	14.5	0.0	7.3	0.0
	N:	(14)	(4)	(3)	(17)	(1)	(8)	(0)	(4)	(0)
Total	%	36.7	6.2	9.4	28.1	0.8	10.9	1.6	6.3	17.4
	N:	(47)	(8)	(12)	(36)	(1)	(14)	(2)	(8)	(27)
REPUBLICANS										
1801-1805	%:	57.1	0.0	4.1	10.2	0.0	22.5	6.1	0.0	0.0
	N:	(28)	(0)	(2)	(5)	(0)	(11)	(3)	(0)	(0)
1806-1810	%	37.2	2.0	0.0	27.4	0.0	15.7	15.7	2.0	0.0
	N:	(19)	(1)	(0)	(14)	(0)	(8)	(8)	(1)	(0)
1811-1815	%:	29.1	0.0	1.8	23.6	0.0	29.1	14.6	1.8	0.0
	N:	(16)	(0)	(1)	(13)	(0)	(16)	(8)	(1)	(0)
Total	%:	40.7	0.6	1.9	20.6	0.0	22.6	12.3	1.3	0.0
	N:	(63)	(1)	(3)	(32)	(0)	(35)	(19)	(2)	(0)
TOTAL										
1801-1805	%:	53.5	1.4	2.8	12.7	0.0	19.7	7.1	2.8	27.6
	N:	(38)	(1)	(2)	(9)	(0)	(14)	(5)	(2)	(0)
1806-1810	%:	41.6	3.9	5.0	28.7	0.0	10.9	7.9	2.0	0.0
	N:	(42)	(4)	(5)	(29)	(0)	(11)	(8)	(2)	(0)
1811-1815	%:	28.3	3.8	3.8	28.3	0.9	22.6	7.6	4.7	0.0
	N:	(30)	(4)	(4)	(30)	(1)	(24)	(8)	(5)	(0)
Total	%:	39.0	3.2	5.3	24.1	0.4	17.4	7.4	3.2	8.8
	N:	(110)	(9)	(15)	(68)	(1)	(49)	(21)	(9)	(27)

Sources: ASSEMBLY: *New York Evening Post*, April 30, 1802, April 29, 1803,
May 2, 1808, April 29, 1809, April 28, 1810, May 2, 1812, May 1, 1813,
April 30, 1814, April 29, 1815; *American Citizen*, April 30, 1804,
May 6, 1806; *Daily Advertiser*, May 4, 1801; *Morning Post*, May 6,1811.

COMMON COUNCIL: *New York Evening Post*, November 5,8,15,1802; November 7,
8,9,16,22,29,1804; November 14,21,1806; November 17,21,1807; November 19,
1808; November 6,20,1810; November 18,19,1811; December 3,1812; November
10, 1813; November 13, 20, 1814; April 29, 1815; *American Citizen*,
November 19,1801; November 15,16,1802; December 6, 1803; October 28,1804;
November 1,13,1804; November 4,11,1805; November 14,1807; November 19,
1808; *Morning Post*, November 28,1811; *Columbian*, November 18,19,1811;
November 16,1814; *Public Advertiser*, November 29,1809; *National Advocate*,
November 10,1813; *Morning Chronicle*, November 11,1803, *Longworth's New
York Directory*, 1801-1815.

Notes to Table 4.1:

a) The numbers in parentheses refer to the overall percentage distribution
of occupations as determined from the 1805-1806 *Longworth's New York Directory*.
(See Table 3.1.) Laborers constituted 8.2% of the working population. There were
no candidates from this class for any office.

b) Occupations are categorized as follows:

Merch: (merchant); merchant, broker, auctioneer.

Grcr: (grocer); grocer, boardinghouse, tavern.

Retl: (retailer); dry good store, hardware store, bookseller, merchant
         tailor, druggist, lumber merchant, flour store.

Prof: (professional); teacher, physician, attorney, accountant, shipmaster.

Offcl: (public official); constable, marshal, police justice, collector,
         measurer. NOTE: If a constable or collector is listed under
         another profession either for his year in office or in any previous
         year, he is classified under his previous occupation.

M. Mech: (manufacturing mechanic); tanner and currier, hatter, soap and candle maker,
         coachmaker, sailmaker, harnessmaker, brewer, starchmaker, whipmaker, iron
         moulder, ropemaker, morocco leather manufacturer, air furnace, builder.

Mech   (tradesman mechanic); shoemaker, cooper, silversmith, butcher,
         goldsmith, sawyer, upholsterer, baker, livery stabler, printer,
         coppersmith, mason, carpenter, carver, smith, chairmaker.

Unk: unknown

NC: No candidate put up by the party.

c) The percentages of NCs is calculated from the total of the NCs and the
rest of the candidates; the percentages for candidates is calculated from
the total number of candidates exclusive of the NCs.

duties. Many others who could be found in the directories listed only as "constable" or "marshal" probably also came from mechanic backgrounds—certainly enough to raise the number of tradesmen running for this position to over half of all candidates. More men of the tradesmen-mechanic class were nominated for constable than for all other municipal offices combined.

Not surprisingly, the job of enforcing the laws was not as prestigious as the other elective offices. Historian James F. Richardson has stated that it was often difficult to find people willing to run for this office and that some individuals were actually fined for not accepting a nomination.[11] Washington Irving, on the other hand, noted that even contests for constable provoked great emotional outpourings.[12] In any case, there is no question that the reputation of the law enforcement officials was

Table 4.2[*]

CHARTER NOMINATIONS BY OCCUPATION: TOTAL GROUP

1801–1815

1801–1815		Occupational Percentage Within City[a)]							
		(13.2)	(13.1)	(4.1)	(9.2)	(1.8)	(5.3)	(45.2)	
TOTAL GROUP									
[b)] Occupation:		Merch	Grcr	Retl	Prof	Offcl	M.Mech	Mech	Unk	[c)] NC
Office:										
Alderman	%:	46.0	3.8	12.8	8.9	2.6	17.0	4.7	4.2	15.8
	N:	(108)	(9)	(30)	(21)	(6)	(40)	(11)	(10)	(44)
Assistant	%:	23.4	8.9	10.6	17.9	2.6	20.9	6.8	8.9	18.7
	N:	(55)	(21)	(25)	(42)	(6)	(49)	(16)	(21)	(44)
Assessor	%:	21.8	18.8	10.1	2.3	1.4	10.1	17.9	17.6	21.3
	N:	(95)	(82)	(44)	(10)	(6)	(44)	(78)	(77)	(119)
Collector	%:	6.3	22.7	7.3	4.8	37.2	7.2	10.6	3.9	20.7
	N:	(13)	(47)	(15)	(10)	(77)	(15)	(22)	(8)	(54)
Constable	%:	3.2	11.0	2.1	1.2	48.5	0.7	30.1	3.2	23.1
	N:	(14)	(47)	(9)	(5)	(208)	(3)	(129)	(14)	(129)
Total	%	18.5	13.4	8.0	5.7	19.7	9.8	16.5	8.4	25.6
	N:	(285)	(206)	(123)	(88)	(303)	(151)	(255)	(130)	(390)

[*] For sources and notes to Table 4.2 see Table 4.1

not high, as they were subject to complaints for trying to earn high fees by illegal means, and especially for taking advantage of the poor.[13] This was not a position that would lead to further advancement in the way that the offices of assessor and collector might.

Table 4.3 describes the charter nominations by occupation and party. Here again the Republicans' greater receptivity to placing mechanics on the ballot is evident. For the posts of alderman, assistant alderman, and assessor, the Republicans had sharply higher percentages of tradesmen-mechanic nominees—though these figures were still very low in comparison with the proportion of tradesmen in the city population. The Republicans also held significant advantages in the number of eminent mechanics nominated for the positions of alderman and collector. In the slots on the ticket for which Republicans chose artisan candidates, the Federalists would often select merchants, retailers, or attorneys. Thus, the Federalists had 13 percent less total mechanic nominees than did the Republicans.

An important exception to Federalist bias occurred in nominations proffered mechanics for the post of constable. For this, the meanest of the elective offices, both parties ran a high proportion of tradesmen mechanics. The Federalists regarded this position, and none other, as proper for a man who wore the leather garments of the mechanic trades. If constables are excluded from the totals, the percentage of Federalist nominations given to tradesmen mechanics falls to 8 percent, barely half of the respective Republican figure. Even so, the Republican statistics indicate a similar bias, only to a lesser degree. Thus it would not be unfounded to assume that New York society dictated that all but a few of the ordinary mechanics—and that included nine-tenths of the artisan population—were to be restricted in the level of political office open to them. Unless they were to rise to a higher status, social if not economic discrimination limited the vast majority of tradesmen to posts no higher than that of public constable.

Table 4.4 portrays the character and number of mechanic nominees for charter offices over the fifteen years of this study. From 1801 to 1805, a period of Republican ascendancy, that party had considerably more mechanics competing for aldermanic offices than the Federalists. This was particularly so for tradesmen mechanics. During these first five years the Republicans had almost

Table 4.3 [*]

CHARTER NOMINATIONS BY OCCUPATION: FEDERALISTS

AND REPUBLICANS, 1801-1815

1801-1815		Occupational Percentage Within City [a]								
FEDERALISTS		(13.2)	(13.1)	(4.1)	(9.2)	(1.8)	(5.3)	(45.2)		
[b] Occupation:		Merch	Grcr	Retl	Prof	Offcl	M.Mech	Mech	Unk	[c] NC
Office:										
Alderman:	%:	50.0	1.7	19.8	12.1	0.9	11.2	0.9	3.4	16.0
	N:	(58)	(2)	(23)	(14)	(1)	(13)	(1)	(4)	(23)
Assistant:	%:	24.8	6.0	12.0	25.6	1.7	20.5	1.7	7.7	15.8
	N:	(29)	(7)	(14)	(30)	(2)	(24)	(2)	(9)	(22)
Assessor:	%:	23.3	16.1	10.3	2.7	0.9	11.2	13.5	22.0	19.8
	N:	(52)	(36)	(23)	(6)	(2)	(25)	(30)	(45)	(55)
Collector	%:	7.6	23.6	12.3	2.8	36.8	2.8	9.4	4.7	17.8
	N:	(8)	(25)	(13)	(3)	(39)	(3)	(10)	(5)	(23)
Constable	%:	1.8	10.3	3.6	1.8	48.0	0.4	30.5	3.6	19.8
	N:	(4)	(23)	(8)	(4)	(107)	(1)	(68)	(8)	(55)
Total	%:	19.3	11.9	10.4	7.3	19.3	8.5	14.2	9.1	18.5
	N:	(151)	(93)	(81)	(57)	(151)	(66)	(111)	(71)	(178)
REPUBLICANS										
Office:										
Alderman:	%:	42.0	5.9	5.9	5.9	4.2	22.7	8.4	5.0	15.0
	N:	(50)	(7)	(7)	(7)	(5)	(27)	(10)	(6)	(21)
Assistant	%:	22.0	11.9	9.3	10.2	3.4	21.2	11.9	10.2	15.7
	N:	(26)	(14)	(11)	(12)	(4)	(25)	(14)	(12)	(22)
Assessor	%:	19.8	21.2	9.7	1.8	1.8	8.8	22.1	14.8	22.8
	N:	(43)	(46)	(21)	(4)	(4)	(19)	(48)	(32)	(64)
Collector	%:	4.9	21.8	2.0	6.9	37.6	11.9	11.9	3.0	23.5
	N:	(5)	(22)	(2)	(7)	(38)	(12)	(12)	(3)	(31)
Constable	%:	4.9	11.6	0.5	0.5	49.0	1.0	29.6	2.9	26.4
	N:	(10)	(24)	(1)	(1)	(101)	(2)	(61)	(6)	(74)
Total	%:	17.6	14.8	5.5	4.1	20.0	11.2	19.1	7.7	21.8
	N:	(134)	(113)	(42)	(31)	(152)	(85)	(145)	(59)	(212)

[*] For sources and notes to Table 4.3 see Table 4.1

Table 4.4

PERCENTAGE CHANGES IN MECHANIC NOMINATIONS

1801-1815

	Manu. Mechanics		Tradesmen Mechanics		All Mechanics	
	Fed.	Rep.	Fed.	Rep.	Fed.	Rep.
ALDERMAN						
1801-1805:	7.1	16.1	0.0	6.5	7.1	22.6
1806-1810:	7.0	15.9	0.0	9.1	7.0	25.0
1811-1815:	17.8	31.8	2.2	9.1	20.0	40.9
Total:	11.2	22.7	0.9	8.4	12.1	31.1
ASSISTANT						
1801-1805:	20.7	38.7	0.0	9.7	20.7	48.4
1806-1810:	23.3	16.3	0.0	18.6	23.3	34.9
1811-1815:	17.8	13.6	4.4	6.8	22.2	20.4
Total:	20.5	21.2	1.7	11.9	22.2	33.1
ASSESSOR						
1801-1805:	14.8	7.3	3.7	23.6	18.5	30.9
1806-1810:	12.0	9.1	13.3	20.5	25.3	29.6
1811-1815:	8.1	9.5	19.8	23.0	27.9	32.5
Total:	11.2	8.8	13.5	22.1	24.7	30.9
COLLECTOR:						
1801-1805:	3.4	3.4	10.3	10.3	13.7	13.7
1806-1810:	4.8	14.3	14.3	9.5	19.1	23.8
1811-1815:	0.0	16.7	2.9	16.7	2.9	33.4
Total:	2.8	11.9	9.4	11.9	12.2	23.8
CONSTABLE						
[a]1801-1805:	0.0	0.0	11.8	15.4	11.8	15.4
1806-1810:	0.0	0.0	34.9	27.1	34.9	27.1
1811-1815:	1.1	2.8	37.1	41.5	38.2	44.3
Total:	0.4	1.0	30.5	29.6	30.9	30.6
ALL OFFICES						
1801-1805:	8.4	11.1	4.7	14.6	13.1	25.7
1806-1810:	8.5	9.5	15.6	19.0	24.1	28.5
1811-1815:	8.0	13.3	19.7	22.8	27.7	36.1
Total:	8.4	11.2	14.1	19.1	22.5	30.3

[a] From 1801 to 1805 there were a disproportionate number of constables identifiable only as constables. For sources and other notes see Table 4.1

13 percent more mechanic candidates than the Federalists. With constables dropped from the totals, the differences were 10 percent for tradesmen and 3 percent for elite mechanics. As the Federalists attempted to catch up to the Republicans from 1806 to 1810, the gap in mechanic nominees between the two parties dropped to 4.5 percent. With constables excluded, the difference remained large for tradesmen, 8 percent, though it 'fell to only 1 percent for elite mechanics. The Federalists were bringing in more artisan leaders to replace local retail and dry goods store owners on the ballots.[14]

During the intensely fought campaigns from 1811 to 1815, the overall percentage of mechanic nominees, excluding constables, increased to 27 percent, up 4 percent from the previous ten years. Also without constables, the Federalists raised their percentage of mechanic candidacies to 22 percent, up 11 percent and 7 percent from 1801 to 1805 and 1806 to 1810, respectively. Republican figures for the proportion of mechanic nominees (excluding constables) rose to 32 percent of their total candidates, an increase of 2 percent from 1806 to 1810 and 3 percent from 1801 to 1805. The greater number of mechanic candidacies was no boon for average workingmen, however. The increases in both parties' percentages reflected a larger number of manufacturing mechanics taking aldermanic nominations at the expense of the merchant classes. Only in the sense that a prosperous boatbuilder or sailmaker represented the mechanic community was intense competition helpful to the artisans' representation on municipal slates. In charter elections growing party rivalry caused both parties to raise their antes to the mechanics, mainly in the form of more slots offered the leaders of the artisan community.

Tables 4.5-4.7 depict the charter mechanic nominees by ward. Together they provide comparative information on party preferences for both manufacturing and tradesmen mechanics in the first three "merchant" wards, the transitional Fourth Ward, and the mechanic-dominated fifth through seventh wards. These tables also reveal the average number of terms of office for which a candidate was likely to compete. In analyzing these charts, it should be noted that all nonmechanics (merchants, grocers, dry goods store owners, professionals, and public officials) are put in one category, "All Others," and one percentage calculated for the number of nominations and terms which they received.

The merchant wards (Table 4.5) invariably voted Federalist. The ward leaders of that party did select a number of manufacturing mechanics to compete for the position of assistant alderman, but with only a few exceptions they did not permit tradesmen to contest for any office other than that of constable. Nor did it seem to matter that, according to the Second Ward Jury List for 1816, mechanics made up a larger portion of the area's population (39 percent) than did the merchants (27 percent). Republicans, on the other hand, nominated a considerably higher percentage of mechanics, both manufacturing and tradesmen. However, because the Republicans often failed to produce slates for what were hopeless contests and because they had little to lose in offering high positions to mechanics for offices they were very unlikely to gain, their figures must be interpreted cautiously. Nevertheless, they did put forward more artisans as candidates, though for fewer terms than the Federalists. They preferred to rotate their nominees, whereas the Federalists allowed incumbents to run for reelection. Finally, it is of interest to note that in the Third Ward, a district in which the Republican slate was successful in three of the fifteen years of this study (it was never successful in the first and second wards), more manufacturing mechanics were nominated for office than in the first or second ward. As was found true for assembly elections and in general for the municipal contests, hard-fought contests in which each side had a chance for victory encouraged both parties to bring in broader slates of candidates.

The Fourth Ward was a swing district. Containing a mixture of all professions (mechanics made up just under half of the population), it went Federalist eleven out of the fifteen years of this study, but did so by a margin of less than 3 percent of the total vote in four of these years. Table 4.6 reveals that manufacturing mechanics received a high proportion of the aldermanic nominations in this ward; tradesmen mechanics received none. In an area like this in which mechanics were numerous but not dominant, little effort was made to bring any but the very top of the artisan class into competition for offices that were also desired by merchants and attorneys. At every level aside from alderman the Republicans offered elite members of the mechanic community more candidacies and terms than did the Federalists. Although this may have helped the Republicans attract craftsmen's support, that

Table 4.5

CHARTER NOMINATIONS BY OCCUPATION AND WARD

WARDS 1–3, THE MERCHANT WARDS a)

FEDERALISTS

Office:	(5.3) Manu.Mech					(45.2) Mech.				(49.5) All Others				Total		
	b)NC	C	T	AV	%	C	T	AV	%	C	T	AV	%	C	T	AV
Alderman:	1	0	0	0.0	0.0	0	0	0.0	0.0	18	44	2.4	100.	18	44	2.4
Assistant:	1	4	15	3.8	34.1	0	0	0.0	0.0	13	29	2.2	65.9	17	44	2.6
Assessor:	4	7	13	1.9	15.1	4	7	1.8	8.1	49	66	1.3	76.7	60	86	1.4
Collector:	1	0	0	0.0	0.0	1	1	1.0	2.4	18	40	2.2	97.6	19	41	2.2
Constable:	3	0	0	0.0	0.0	6	21	3.5	24.1	34	66	1.9	75.9	40	87	2.2
Total:	10	11	28	2.5	9.3	11	29	2.6	9.6	132	245	1.9	81.1	154	302	2.0

REPUBLICANS

Office:	(5.3) Manu.Mech					(45.2) Mech.				(49.5) All Others				Total		
	b)NC	C	T	AV	%	C	T	AV	%	C	T	AV	%	C	T	AV
Alderman:	18	1	2	2.0	7.4	2	2	1.0	7.4	18	23	1.3	85.2	21	27	1.3
Assistant:	19	2	4	2.0	15.4	6	6	1.0	23.1	13	16	1.2	61.5	21	26	1.2
Assessor:	53	3	9	3.0	24.3	3	3	1.0	8.1	20	25	1.3	67.6	26	37	1.4
Collector:	25	1	1	1.0	5.9	1	2	2.0	11.8	8	14	1.6	82.4	10	17	1.7
Constable:	57	0	0	0.0	0.0	4	8	2.0	23.5	14	26	1.9	76.5	18	34	1.9
Total:	172	7	16	2.3	11.3	16	21	1.3	14.9	73	104	1.4	73.8	96	141	1.5

TOTAL GROUP

Office:	(5.3) Manu.Mech					(45.2) Mech.				(49.5) All Others				Total		
	b)NC	C	T	AV	%	C	T	AV	%	C	T	AV	%	C	T	AV
Alderman:	19	1	2	2.0	2.8	2	2	1.0	2.8	36	67	1.9	94.4	39	71	1.8
Assistant:	20	6	19	3.2	27.1	6	6	1.0	8.6	26	45	1.7	64.3	38	70	1.8
Assessor:	57	10	22	2.2	17.9	7	10	1.4	8.1	69	91	1.3	74.0	86	123	1.4
Collector:	26	1	1	1.0	1.7	2	3	1.5	5.2	26	54	2.1	93.1	29	58	2.0
Constable:	60	0	0	0.0	0.0	10	29	2.9	24.0	48	92	1.9	76.0	58	121	2.1
Total:	182	18	44	2.4	9.9	27	50	1.9	11.3	205	349	1.7	78.8	250	443	1.8

Notes: a) For sources to Table 4.5 see Table 4.1. The 1816 Jury List reveals that the Second Ward contained 39.4 percent mechanics and 27.3 percent merchants out of the total working population of 1,771.
b) C = Candidate; T = Terms; AV = Average terms per candidate. Percentages are calculated on the basis of total terms.

Table 4.6
CHARTER NOMINATIONS BY OCCUPATION AND WARD:
FOURTH WARD (Mixed) [a]

FEDERALISTS

Occupations:	Manu. Mech (5.3)					Mech. (45.2)				All Others (49.5)				Total		
Office:	NC	C	T	%	AV	C	T	%	AV	C	T	%	AV	C	T	AV
Alderman:	1	2	6	42.9	3.0	0	0	0.0	0.0	5	8	57.1	1.6	7	14	2.0
Assistant:	1	0	0	0.0	0.0	0	0	0.0	0.0	5	14	100.	2.8	5	14	2.8
Assessor:	2	1	1	3.6	1.0	1	2	7.1	2.0	17	25	89.3	1.5	19	28	1.5
Collector:	1	1	1	7.7	1.0	1	1	7.7	1.0	5	11	84.6	2.2	7	13	1.9
Constable:	2	1	1	3.6	1.0	0	0	0.0	0.0	14	27	96.4	1.9	15	28	1.9
Total:	7	5	9	5.2	1.8	2	3	3.1	1.5	46	85	87.6	1.8	53	97	1.8

REPUBLICANS

Office:	NC	C	T	%	AV	C	T	%	AV	C	T	%	AV	C	T	AV
Alderman:	1	3	3	21.4	1.0	0	0	0.0	0.0	8	11	78.6	1.4	11	14	1.3
Assistant:	1	2	4	28.6	2.0	0	0	0.0	0.0	10	10	71.4	1.0	12	14	1.2
Assessor:	6	1	1	4.2	1.0	2	5	20.8	2.5	9	18	75.0	2.0	12	24	2.0
Collector:	2	2	7	58.3	3.5	1	1	8.3	1.0	2	4	33.4	2.0	5	12	2.4
Constable:	8	0	0	0.0	0.0	2	3	13.6	1.5	8	19	86.4	2.1	10	22	2.2
Total:	18	8	15	17.4	1.9	5	9	9.3	1.8	37	62	72.1	1.7	50	86	1.7

TOTAL GROUP

Office:	NC	C	T	%	AV	C	T	%	AV	C	T	%	AV	C	T	AV
Alderman:	2	5	9	32.1	1.8	0	0	0.0	0.0	13	19	67.9	1.5	18	28	1.6
Assistant:	2	2	4	14.2	2.0	0	0	0.0	0.0	15	24	85.7	1.6	17	28	1.6
Assessor:	8	2	2	3.8	1.0	3	7	13.5	2.3	26	43	82.7	1.7	31	52	1.7
Collector:	3	3	8	32.0	2.7	2	2	8.0	1.0	7	15	60.0	2.1	12	25	2.1
Constable:	10	1	1	2.0	1.0	2	3	6.0	1.5	22	46	92.0	2.1	25	50	2.0
Total:	25	13	24	13.1	1.8	7	12	6.6	1.7	83	147	80.3	1.8	103	183	1.8

[a] For sources to Table 4.6 see Table 4.1. Willis has found that of those in the Fourth Ward in 1815 whose occupation could be identified, 49.7 percent were mechanics and 13.0 percent were merchants (1,283 identified residents,559 unidentified). Edmund P. Willis, "Social Origins and Political Leadership in New York City from the Revolution to 1815" Ph.D. Diss.(Berkeley, 1967), pp 126,128-130.

advantage may well have been nullified by the familiarity of workingmen with respected incumbent Federalists. Furthermore, knowledge that one party's chances of winning were significantly higher than its rival's may have swayed voters who wanted to be on the side of those who held power.

Other than in the Sixth Ward where the elections were divided, Republicans generally carried the mechanics wards. The 1816 Jury List reveals that for the Fifth Ward, mechanics made up almost 70 percent of the population and merchants composed 8 percent. One might, therefore, expect to see a high percentage of tradesmen competing for local offices. However, while the figures for artisan participation are significantly higher than those for the other wards, they are nowhere near the proportion of mechanics living in these districts. Thus, in the fifth through seventh wards (Table 4.7), mechanics made up 35 percent of all the local candidates, with 88 different artisans contesting for 178 terms of office. (Excluding constables, the mechanics ran for 31 percent of the terms, with 70 artisans seeking 118 terms of office.)

Once again the Republican party offered more nominations to artisans, both manufacturing and tradesmen, than did the Federalist party. The latter organization could not shake its elitist attitude to the point where it was willing to put up a comparable number of workingmen in predominantly mechanic residential areas. The average terms of office indicate that in these wards, where the Federalists generally did not win elections, they tended to rotate their candidates, while the Republicans often allowed incumbents to run for two or three or, in the case of constables, for five terms. Even with rotation, however, the Republicans still offered more artisan personalities to the voters than did the Federalists. The elitism of Hamilton's party continually inhibited its political growth.

While analysis of the mechanic wards does reveal significant gains in mechanic participation as charter candidates, this achievement is considerably lessened by the fact that mechanics composed three-fourths of the population of these wards. Thus, a 30 percent representation on the ballot was still less than half the percentage of mechanics living in this area. Taking into account the thousands of mechanics who lived in these wards at some time during this period, thirty candidates in one ward over a period of fifteen years

TABLE 4.7

CHARTER NOMINATIONS BY OCCUPATION AND WARD:

WARDS 5–7, THE MECHANIC WARDS[a]

Occupations: Office:	NC	Manu. Mech. (5.3)				Mech. (45.2)				All Others (49.5)				Total		
		C	T	%	AV	C	T	%	AV	C	T	%	AV	C	T	AV
FEDERALISTS																
Alderman:	12	6	7	21.1	1.2	0	0	0.0	0.0	11	26	78.8	2.4	17	33	1.9
Assistant:	13	2	2	6.3	1.3	1	1	3.1	1.0	14	29	90.6	2.1	17	32	1.9
Assessor:	32	6	8	13.8	1.3	11	16	27.6	1.5	17	34	58.6	2.0	34	58	1.7
Collector:	15	2	2	7.4	1.0	3	3	11.1	1.0	8	22	81.5	2.8	13	27	2.1
Constable:	35	0	0	0.0	0.0	10	20	31.4	2.0	24	35	63.6	1.5	34	55	1.6
Total:	107	16	19	9.3	1.2	25	40	19.5	1.6	74	146	71.2	2.0	115	205	1.8
REPUBLICANS																
Alderman:	1	7	18	39.1	2.6	3	5	10.9	1.7	9	23	50.0	2.6	19	46	2.4
Assistant:	1	5	13	28.3	2.6	1	1	2.2	1.0	20	32	69.6	1.6	26	46	1.8
Assessor:	6	5	7	8.1	1.4	14	30	34.9	2.1	28	49	57.0	1.8	47	86	3.3
Collector:	1	3	3	7.0	1.0	1	2	4.7	2.0	9	38	88.4	4.2	13	43	3.3
Constable:	8	0	0	0.0	0.0	8	40	47.6	5.0	20	44	52.4	2.2	28	84	3.0
Total:	17	20	41	13.4	2.1	27	78	25.6	2.9	86	186	61.0	2.2	133	305	2.5
TOTAL GROUP																
Alderman:	13	13	25	31.6	1.9	3	5	6.3	1.7	20	49	62.0	1.8	36	79	2.2
Assistant:	14	7	15	19.2	2.1	2	2	2.6	1.0	34	61	78.2	1.8	43	78	1.8
Assessor:	38	11	15	10.4	1.4	25	46	31.9	1.8	45	83	57.6	1.8	81	144	1.8
Collector:	16	5	5	7.1	1.0	4	5	7.1	1.3	17	60	85.7	3.5	26	70	2.7
Constable:	43	0	0	0.0	0.0	18	60	43.2	3.3	44	79	56.8	1.8	62	139	2.2
Total:	124	36	60	11.8	1.7	52	118	23.1	2.3	160	332	65.1	2.1	248	510	2.1

a) For sources to Table 4.7 see Table 4.1. The 1816 Jury List shows that the Fifth Ward contained 68.8 percent mechanics and 8.0 percent merchants out of the total working population of 2,961.

is not a large aggregate. In all, it is quite evident that a working-man, if he lived in one of the outer wards, would probably have an opportunity to vote for one of the most successful members of his social class, but would be unlikely to have an opportunity to run for office himself.

The overall profile given by the tables on mechanic candidacies reveals that in a time when political office was not the special province of attorneys, mechanics, and especially ordinary crafts-men, still had a disproportionate share of higher offices. However, it also reveals that the Democratic-Republicans, in contrast to their Federalist opponents, were considerably more amenable to welcoming prominent artisans into their leadership ranks. This was likely an important factor in their ability to maintain their strength within the entire artisan constituency. For many lesser tradesmen too aspired to become the elite proprietors of sizable artisan enterprises, with expensive equipment, real estate, and bank shares. They admired those who had achieved such success, took pride in their selection as nominees for high office, and to a great extent were willing to follow their lead. This is not to say that less eminent mechanics were unaware of the common sentiment that they were unsuitable for responsible public office; nor does it deny the serious tensions between prominent masters, including some who were politically active, and a large segment of the journeymen community. But in an age of national political parties, the Jeffersonian choice was the most satisfactory solution. It offered even poorer tradesmen some sense of esteem as well as the important opportunity to personally reject the hated Federalist outlook.[15]

NOTES

1. Edmund P. Willis, "Social Origins and Political Leadership in New York City from the Revolution to 1815," Ph.D. diss. (Berkeley, 1967), pp. 164, 169-170. A caution must be noted: Willis includes in his 1815 ranking under the mechanic category those men who began their careers as mechanics but who in 1815 would have been known in the community as merchants. Furthermore, his figures do not include a large number of unlisted journeymen.

2. These figures are derived from Willis, "Social Origins," Appendix. In

a small survey taken by the Society for the Propogation of the Gospel in the Fifth Ward in 1807 that included nineteen identifiable mechanics out of seventy-three individuals polled, only 31.6 percent (6) were Episcopalian or Dutch Reformed. Presbyterianism, with 31.6 percent (6), was the most popular denomination. There were also three Methodists, two Baptists, one Catholic, and one Quaker. SPG Record Book, New York Historical Society.

3. Willis, "Social Origins," p. 261.

4. Ibid., pp. 156, 169-170.

5. Ibid., pp. 156-174, 243. Especially in the later years of this study, 1811-1815, more Republican officeholders came from mechanic homes than Federalist officeholders.

6. Ibid., pp. 151-152.

7. Ibid., p. 153.

8. Ibid., p. 273.

9. Ibid., p. 303.

10. In terms of mechanics actually elected to office, in comparison with the 24.4 percent of mechanics nominated for assemblymen, they actually held 32.2 percent of the seats (52 of 155 positions). This was the result of greater Republican success at the polls coupled with higher numbers of Republican candidacies. Forty percent of the Republican slots (42 of 105) were held by artisans, as compared with 34.9 percent of the nominations. The corresponding figures for the Federalists were 18.2 percent of the seats (10 of 55) compared with 12.5 percent of the candidacies. It would appear that both parties ran more mechanics in times of electoral success, though if the unidentified candidates are disproportionately mechanics, as is likely, the figures would probably be nearly the same for both candidacies and actual seats held. Compiled from Willis, "Social Origins," Appendix.

11. James F. Richardson, *The New York Police: Colonial Times to 1901* (New York, 1970), p. 19.

12. Washington Irving, *Salmagundi* (New York, 1904), pp. 216-217, has a fictitious traveler to New York from the East declare that "there never happens an election for alderman, or a collector or even a constable, but we are in imminent danger of losing our liberties, and becoming a province of France, or a tributary of the British islands."

13. Richardson, *New York Police*, p. 19.

14. As for mechanics elected to the posts of alderman and assistant alderman, the figures are not that different from those for the nominees. In comparison with the 24.7 percent of mechanic candidacies for these positions, mechanics were elected to 27.3 percent of the top council positions (76 of 278 seats). Federalist artisans took 22.7 percent (29 of 148)

of that party's slots as compared with 17.7 percent of the candidacies, while Republican mechanics represented 36.2 percent (47 of 130) of that party's aldermen as compared with 32.1 percent of the nominations. Again, while it appears that more mechanics ran in times of party victory than defeat, if the unknown candidates are disproportionately mechanic, the differences, never great, might well be minimal. Compiled from Willis, "Social Origins," Appendix.

15. For journeymen-master labor conflict see chapter 10.

Chapter 5

THE AXIS OF SOCIETY

Partisan politics was the principle forum for mechanics' quest of self-esteem and community recognition. Particularly through their liaison with the Democratic-Republicans, artisans did emerge as a critical factor in New York City politics. There were, however, also serious inadequacies in alliances with major parties. One problem, as we have seen, was a lingering elitism among even the Jeffersonians that prevented craftsmen from receiving their full share of places on the ballot. Of equal or even greater consequence was the willingness of the Republicans to manipulate the interests of the artisan community in order to fulfill personal ambitions. This serious issue, which moved many tradesmen either to withdraw from the electoral process or else to seek redress within their own community, is best understood through an analysis of factional Republican politics.

The plague of factionalism haunted New York's Republicans throughout the early nineteenth century. In the city its rise was largely a function of the weakness of the Federalists after 1804. By then that party had lost control of both the city's assembly delegation and the Common Council and showed no signs of ever regaining strength. In the power vacuum that followed, ambitious

Republicans began attacking their fellow party members. The original coalition of Clinton, Livingston, and Burr soon broke up. The first to fall was Aaron Burr. The Clintonians, under the leadership of editor Cheetham, purged him and his followers as betrayers of Jefferson. Then they turned on their other partner. This confrontation, played out over the question of bribery charges in the granting of a bank charter, saw the Clintonian gubernatorial candidate, Daniel Tompkins, defeating the Livingstonian incumbent, Morgan Lewis.[1]

After the embargo, Republican infighting took place chiefly between the Clintonians headed by De Witt Clinton and the Madisonians (a coalition of former Burrites and Livingstonians) whose local headquarters and leaders were situated within the Tammany Society. The War of 1812 found Clinton a presidential candidate in opposition to Madison. Despite the split, however, the mayor did not renounce his party and stayed within the fold after his defeat. Throughout this and the other internal Republican quarrels, the Federalists remained active, occasionally uniting with a minority faction. After 1807, of course, they were again a formidable organization.[2]

Since mechanics were at the heart of Republican electoral strength, much energy was spent by dissenting Democrats wooing their votes. In the Burrite-Clintonian dispute artisans were courted with issues centering around their personal and economic status. Attacks on Burr, both vicious and plentiful, denounced this former Republican hero as a wealthy attorney who had deceived the family of a poor immigrant tailor out of its entire inheritance.[3] The Vice President, also scorned as a supporter of the unpopular and elitist Merchants Bank, was depicted as a "factious" and "ambitious" office seeker.[4]

Mounting a counterattack, the Burrites appealed to tradesmen through the well known issue of suffrage reform. At a number of local meetings they demanded the popular election of the mayor and the transfer of the city's top magistrate's licensing powers to the Common Council. They told licensed mechanics that after the institution of such reforms no single man would have the authority "to tyrannize over the whole body of cartmen in particular, as well as the other numerous classes of citizens." Nor would the "first magistrate" any longer be able to bask in luxury and wealth at their expense."[5] The Clintonians needed to keep the mayor's office appointive to insure that De Witt Clinton remained at that powerful post. Thus, they could say little in response other than repeat Federalist warnings about the dangers of precipitate change.

In other factional disputes all the familiar mechanic appeals used by Republicans to attack Federalists were now employed against other Republicans. These included a charge that one candidate was attempting to monopolize the blacksmith work to be done in the construction of the new City Hall,[6] the question of a mechanic's suitability for office,[7] an alleged disparaging remark about mechanics reputed to Governor Lewis,[8] a claim that the Clintonians belittled butchers attending a political meeting,[9] accusations of "royal blood and patrician descent," [10] the condemnation of a Madisonian baker as a former soldier in the British army during the Revolution,[11] and the formation of a coercive committee to investigate renegade Republicans.[12]

What is significant about these mechanic-oriented issues is that they were used by Republicans against Republicans. This does not mean that any one faction was more exploitative of artisans than another. The Burrites advocacy of mayoralty reform had little to do with the welfare of licensed mechanics, who were not badly treated by De Witt Clinton. What is apparent is the craft of politicans. These men were willing to further their ambitions or those of their faction by manipulating the interests of the mechanic constituency. In such situations perceptive tradesmen must well have wondered just who their real supporters were.

Even in open contests with Federalists not complicated by factionalism, mechanics had reason to question whether or not the Republicans were wholly intent on bolstering their sense of dignity. The problem was that in seeking to secure a continuing allegiance of the artisan constituency, Republicans continually dwelt upon the condescension and haughtiness of the Federalists. This unending concern with the fragility of mechanics' social standing could produce little self-assurance. Not that the arrogant demeanor of the Federalists was not a serious threat, but rather that the constant use of this tactic was unsupportive of a lasting sense of confidence. The following election appeal aptly illustrates this problem:

They [the mechanics] know their leaders, nor will they acknowledge any master. Mechanics and cartmen have as much independence and political honesty as some other folks who are nightly caucusing to misrepresent and mislead; nor will the vile epithets heaped on this class of citizens, such as "silver heels, leather heads, solemn asses, dough heads, etc." ever drive them from their duty, or make them the tools of any man or set of men.[13]

This repetition of disparaging remarks may have aroused trades-men, but it was unlikely to instill confidence or a sense of political independence.

Given this frustrating behavior, it is not surprising that there were signs of political disillusionment within the mechanic com-munity. One manifestation was the withdrawal or abstention of a significant number of tradesmen from party politics. A prominent advocate of this measure was the *Independent Mechanic,* an avowedly apolitical newspaper. In his opening statement printer-editor Joseph Harmer declared that those seeking news of party struggles would have "to look elsewhere for gratification." This paper would offer the weary mechanic a chance to peruse the important news without being forced to read the "filthy sloughs of party declama-tion, those seas of error which have neither bottom nor shore." In the same issue, "Artist" commended Harmer on his decision to shun party politics: "We are tired of the ceaseless cant of party declaimers—we are sick of clamor, invective, slander, and personal animosity." Indeed, politics was like the fatal Upas tree, whose touch "deranges Heaven's noblest plan, perverts life's genial fluids to corroding venom, and changes the healthful, God-like form, to a loathsome mass of corrupted mortality." [14]

In a later issue, "Timoleon," using his experience as an example, also advised mechanics to avoid involvement in politics. Pre-viously, he related, he commonly abandoned his wife and young children in the evening to attend political meetings at a local tavern. True, when "engaged ardently" for other men's ambition, he received many "flattering compliments" from those he was aiding. Yet this was all he gained, and only prior to elections. Afterward, the politicos disdainfully saw him and other tradesmen only as "abject slaves" of a party or faction, and not as indepen-dent citizens of a republic. Consequently, "Timoleon" began to wonder why he was "struggling for the benefit of others" since he achieved only a loss of "individual happiness" and the "destruction of his family." "When," he asked, "has it ever benefited a mechanic to lose a week in electioneering purposes, spending his money in riotous and debauched company, and joining the dregs and filth of society?" The best solution was to retire peacefully from the unfortunate and meaningless squabbles of party politics.[15]

A number of artisans did take "Timoleon's" advice. Figures derived from Edmund P. Willis's tabulation of city and ward populations and from voter eligibility rates for assembly elections indicate that in 1808, a year of high voter turnout, in the mechanic wards (5-7) out of the 6,215 eligible voters, 4,068, or 65.5 percent, cast ballots. In contrast, in the wealthier lower wards (1-4), 3,994, or 85.6 percent of those eligible, voted. While the figures for eligible voters may be slightly skewed because of higher rates of ineligibility in the outer wards, the estimate of knowledgeable politician Matthew Davis indicates that our estimate of the percentage of voting tradesmen may actually have been high. If Davis's statement that there were 4,000 voting mechanics in 1810 is accurate, then assuming that 55 percent of the population were composed of mechanics, and that 80 percent of the ineligibles were also mechanics, only 53.9 percent of the eligible artisan constituency went to the polls. While Davis's figure may well be an underestimate, it is likely that at least one-third of eligible tradesmen did not vote.[16] A number of these mechanics were probably not interested in politics. But clearly there was a sizable bloc of politically alienated craftsmen.

Aside from abstention from the polls there was another alternative for artisans: to take matters into their own hands, as they had done during the revolutionary era, and to form their own organization which would elect mechanics to defend the interests of mechanics. There were a few calls for such independent political action, including two newspaper articles asking tradesmen to reject avaricious party "placemen" along with "the more opulent part of the community," both of which were intent upon making mechanics "subservient in all matters relating to public and private interest." [17] The most notable appeals, however, were those made by Matthew Davis when he urged tradesmen to take independent steps against the Republican supporters of the Workshop proposal

(p. 67); and "Poor Mechanic" who, in calling for mechanics to vote Federalist during the hardships of war in 1814, argued that the rich as a whole were united against the interests of ordinary craftsmen (p. 95).

These pleas were significant signs of conscious and articulate disaffection. Equally important, however, was their failure to co-alesce into a meaningful political movement. The barriers to such organization were formidable. First, the mechanic constituency, despite its common aims, held considerable division within its ranks. These included differences in ethnic background, attitudes toward Great Britain, and, most notably, the economic strife between journeymen and masters (Chapter 10). Second, the absence of a partisan mechanic newspaper together with lasting political issues isolating tradesmen from the rest of the community made independent electoral activity unlikely. Third, craftsmen who could best have articulated a need for separate mechanic representation, prominent artisans such as Stephen Allen and George Warner, chose instead to remain within the ranks of the Republican party where they could advance most quickly and most readily. Consequently, those favoring autonomous measures were left with either obscure spokesmen or else a "faceless, am-bitious, opportunistic, selfseeking" man such as Matthew Davis. This Burrite, who himself harbored contempt for artisans, used mechanic concern over the workshop as a ploy to further the aims of his faction.[18] Finally, as the preceding chapters have pointed out, the Democratic-Republicans, despite their considerable lack-ings, still offered mechanics considerable recognition and oppor-tunity and, most importantly, a vehicle with which to counter Federalist ideals.

If independent political movement was unlikely and even un-wanted, artisans still possessed an antidote to the manipulations of party politics: the festive gatherings of their own fraternal societies. In the privacy of craft celebrations, while dining, drinking and marching together, tradesmen created a spirit of mutual respect and admiration undampened by the wiles of politicians. Moreover, it was at the assemblies of these associations that mechanics themselves defined the proper ideals for the government of the new nation as well as their particular position within the republic.

Artisans of most major trades established fraternal organizations. There is evidence of societies for the tailors, hatters, shipwrights, coopers, masons, carpenters, printers, butchers, bakers, and cabinetmakers. Some of these associations were open only to journeymen and included economic leverage as a major goal; others took in both masters and journeymen. Regardless of economic function, all societies engaged in benevolent activity, pooling funds for the aid of sick members and the families of deceased brethren. Too, all organizations provided ample opportunities for mechanics to meet in a mood of mutual self-esteem and exaltation. The New York Society of Journeymen Shipwrights and Caulkers provides an example. On Independence Day, its members marched in procession along with the coopers, hatters, carpenters, masons, the constituents of other artisan associations. Following the parade and a special holiday oration, they retired to their meeting place for a festive dinner and round after round of patriotic toasts. At regular monthly business meetings, formal proceedings, usually concerned with delinquent dues and society expenditures, quickly gave way to drinking and camaraderie.[19]

The inventory of the Shipwrights Society, drawn up by the secretary prior to dissolution in 1818, is revealing of the group's spirit. Among the items listed were a "Grand Standard and Belt," a "Staff of Steward," a treasurer's "Key and Sash," banners and staffs of naval characters, along with numerous badges, seals, wafers, and membership certificates. Also among the journeymen's possessions was a gallant model of a one-hundred-gun frigate that they had paraded on the Fourth of July and then, with permission of the Common Council, had publicly displayed in the almshouse. With their pomp, ceremonies, and fraternity—often keyed to patriotic themes—the craftsmen reinforced their mutual sense of respect and importance.[20]

Together with the different local benevolent and trade societies, the General Society of Mechanics and Tradesmen acted as a spokesman for the mechanic community of New York. Founded in 1785 by representatives of thirty-one different trades, it won incorporation by the state legislature in 1792.[21] The society, nonpolitical,[22] was organized democratically (as were all the different associations) under a president, vice-president, secretary, and treasurer. Officers were elected by secret ballot at the regular January

meeting. Dues were charged each member and were used to
provide social security and a school for members and their children, as well as to cover expenses for dinners, entertainment,
badges, certificates, rent, and other needs. Failure to pay dues for
six months resulted in expulsion.[23]

The society's membership consisted mainly of the city's more
prominent and well-to-do master craftsmen such as sailmaker
George Warner and cabinetmaker Duncan Phyfe. Other less well
known masters and even a few journeymen were, however, occasionally granted membership. Most important, through the society
these, the city's most respected mechanics, represented the entire
artisan community's aspiration for stature, economic opportunity, and dignity. The society, at its height between 1801 and
1810 with a membership of between six hundred and seven hundred tradesmen, lobbied effectively for goals that all craftsmen,
Republican and Federalist, journeyman and master, shared. These
included the quest of increased tariff protection, the defeat of

Membership certificate of the General Society of Mechanics and Tradesmen.
Courtesy, Henry Francis du Pont Winterthur Museum.

Mayor Livingston's workshop proposal, and, as a culmination of many years' effort, the incorporation of the city's highest-capitalized bank. Because of serious problems in the management of this institution, however, the society lost the respect of the city's mechanics and remained moribund from 1811 until 1820 when it founded a new Apprentices Library, a source of great pride to the tradesmen community. During its years of strength the society served as a prestigious advocate of general artisan causes.[24]

Since the Mechanics Society represented the ideals of many of Gotham's craftsmen, it is instructive to examine its values. The association's handsomely engraved membership certificate is particularly revealing. At the top center stands the symbol of the mechanic: a muscular arm and hand firmly gripping a hammer. Written across this emblem is the society's motto, affirming the fundamental importance of the mechanic crafts: "By Hammer and Hand All Arts Do Stand." America, the land of opportunity, is depicted in the upper-left drawing where an Indian and two women stand, one holding a honeycomb, and also in the lower-left corner, where the brave American husbandman is shown plowing the land and building a mill. The fraternal aid given to fellow mechanics by their brothers is illustrated at the upper right of the engraving where a bereaved widow, her husband buried in front of her house, waits with her arm outstretched as an aid-bearing emissary of the society arrives. Finally, the mechanics' pride in their skills and accomplishments is pictured at the right and left center where able craftsmen deftly work at their various trades.

Like the other mechanic societies, the General Society used ritual and emblems toward a spirit of fraternity and commonality. This is particularly evident in the initiation ceremonies for new members. After brothers were nominated, seconded, and favorably voted upon, they were brought to the next monthly meeting and told to stand outside the meeting room. The Master of Ceremonies then gave notice of the presence of the initiates with three raps upon the door. The president responded with two raps of his gavel. The members-to-be entered the room, and all others rose. The president addressed the newcomers:

> You have been regularly admitted members of this society.
> The mark of favor with which our invitation has honored

you, is the happy result of those flattering recommendations
we have received of your character. Let sobriety, industry,
integrity and uprightness constitute the ornaments of your
name.

We now hail you brothers! Delightful union when the bond
of Friendship is benevolence! To dry the tear from misery's
eye, to succor the afflicted, and to save the sinking is our
present aim, and constituted an original and principal object
of our institution.

... May the interests, harmony and reputation of this
General Association be ever dear to you—on its private transactions be silent as the grave.[25]

The Masonic-like secrecy and mystery, fostering a sense of ex-
clusivity, enhanced the prestige and esteem of the honored mechanic membership.

Other fraternal organizations with large mechanic memberships
were the local volunteer fire companies. Tradesmen composed a
majority of the various companies. Hook and Ladder Company
No. 2, for example, counted five carpenters, one cartman, a watchmaker, a jeweler, two silversmiths, a brewer, and an engraver in its
ranks, along with two grocers, two merchants, and an accountant.[26] Scattered among the wards with their buckets and engines,
the firemen were always on the alert, ready to rush to a fire once
the alarm trumpet was sounded.

The minutes of the local companies reveal that much of these
associations' activities were fraternal rather than professional; indeed, a fire company was very similar to the other mechanic
societies. Organized democratically, electing its foreman each year,
the company had strict bylaws, with fines levied for missed meetings, absence at a fire (except for illness), and profanity against a
fellow member. (One brother paid a penalty in 1810 for yelling at
one of his comrades, "You be damned, you damned Dutch hog.")
Dissension was strictly forbidden. Two members of Fire Company
No. 11 were given "leave to resign" in a dispute over the care of the
engine, while another was ordered expelled for "disorderly
behavior." [27]

Like the mechanic societies, the fire companies evinced a love of
ritual. Each group had its own "watchword" and badges. Each

Membership certificates of the Society of Master Sailmakers (1797), Firemen of the City of New York (1819). Note the themes of benevolent help, civic importance and self-esteem. Courtesy, New York Historical Society, New York City.

Firemen at work and at play in the outer wards, 1809-1810. The caption on the lower picture reads: "The Firemans Washing Day the Meeting of Two Company, then Sport." Museum of the City of New York.

member proudly adorned his own initialed cap, and the foreman donned a special hat. Fire Company No. 11, moreover, had its own "frock committee" to establish dress procedures. Mechanic civic pride also pervaded the activities of these companies. Enjoying the important municipal function they performed, different companies competed to be the first to the scene of a fire. Mutual conviviality, too, was part of a company's life; refreshments and brandy were served after each meeting, and the year was highlighted with a gala dinner accompanied by the usual round of toasts. Finally, seeking to give its members financial security in times of distress, the fire companies invested their dues and initiation fees in bank shares and stocks.[28]

Without question, the most important day of the year for the different mechanic societies was the Fourth of July. As noted, on this occasion the various artisan associations marched proudly in formation down the city's streets. Often accompanied by political and ethnic groups such as the Republican Tammany Society and the Irish Hibernian Society, the paraders trooped to one of the metropolis's finest churches, where they listened to a holiday oration delivered by a prominent member of one of the societies or by an invited guest. In either case, these speeches were addressed to the common revolutionary ideals most vital to the attending mechanics, from the poor journeyman tailor to the eminent master shipbuilder.

A primary theme of the holiday speeches concerned the recollection of the horrors of British rule and of the brave American response to this repression. Sailmaker George Warner called upon tradesmen to remember the Declaration of Independence as "the voice of an oppressed people" rising against a "Government, which while it was arrogating everything to itself, contemplated to leave us nothing." The Declaration, the "language of a bold resistance to tyranny", bequeathed a lesson of importance to the children of mechanics: "to love their country, to contend for liberty and to despise monarchy." The following year, 1798, attorney George Clinton, Jr., elaborating on the theme of British selfishness, explained that the reason George III had plotted "to enslave us" was to keep America's manufactures "in a state of infancy." Thus, "independence was a sublime moment" in which "colonial vassalage" gave way to "the nativity of a mighty republic." [29]

Peter Wendover, like Warner a successful sailmaker, together with counselor John T. Irving, reminded fellow mechanics of the difficult plight of the "contented colonists," forced to arms against men of "tyranny" and "ambition" who wished to make the Americans "submit to terms of the greatest degradation." Though the colonists knew that "death is a terror," they were even more keenly aware that "slavery is death." For but striving to maintain their "privileges," a yeoman's house would be left "a smoking ruin" as the "wife of his bosom and the tender lambs he cherished" were "inhumanly butchered." [30] Yet the courageous tradesmen endured, for as every mechanic listener understood, the "vassalage" that the patriots had fought against was not only British political rule but also the "aristocratic" way of life that cast them as an inferior order.

The endurance of civil liberties, the only real protection mechanics had against a return to "slavery" and an inferior social standing, was a corollary theme to the fight against oppression. "The animating voice of liberty," proclaimed lawyer Thomas King, "was that invaluable blessing in which is concentrated everything that can make life desirable." Echoing the Declaration of Independence, various speakers detailed different rights. Castigating those who stigmatized the "support of religious liberation" with the "imputation of atheism," Republican attorney George Eacker extolled the freedom of worship. Sailmaker Wendover praised the political liberty of American citizens who, protected by the Constitution, and "unawed by tyrants ... enjoy the elective franchise." Printer George Asbridge, speaking at a holiday gathering of the New York Typographical Society, understandably emphasized freedom of the press. Describing the "clogged" British newspapers, whose circulation and number were limited by the government, Asbridge asserted that the press was one of the "most deadly engines of destruction" against the "encroachments of despotic power." These liberties, including the "protection of property" and guardianship of "personal liberty," could never be taken for granted. For, as baker and Mechanics Society President Thomas Mercein told a group of apprentices assembled to honor the opening of the new Apprentices Library, "you may one day be called on to put on the patriot's armour, and nobly and fearlessly to contend in defense of civil and religious freedom." [31]

2 A second prominent theme of the Fourth of July exhortations pertinent to mechanics concerned America's greatness in a new Age of Reason. The United States was far ahead of decadent Europe where one saw "the arm of labor unstrung for want of employ, the withered hand of hungry indigence, risen in vain to implore assistance from a fellow worm, the famished beggar, groaning and perishing at the gate of pampered opulence." America was a republic, its "infant institutions tested and improved upon the experience of six thousand years." Unlike Greece and Rome, it would endure, for not only had it been aided by "the interposition of overruling Providence" but it had been founded by an "enlightened people" in an era when "a general diffusion of science has exploded the absurdities of religious and political imposture." [32]

What made the advent of the new rational age so momentous to mechanics were the new frontiers and opportunities it presented. First, as President Mercein declared, in the field of "mechanical sciences . . . new combinations and new discoveries are constantly developed in the useful arts; and application, and the fervour of genius, may yet lead to inventions valuable and important in the history of man." Second, according to sailmaker Wendover, was the understanding that in the realm of politics "the end of just governments was the *happiness* of the *governed.*" The new nation was rid of the irrational superstitions and impediments of the past such as a "corrupt nobility" and a "tyrant throne." Rather, spokesman Irving proclaimed, concerned with the well-being of all, it sought its talent from the best of its citizens, regardless of social standing:

Every man looks with independent equality in the face of his neighbor; those are exalted whose superior virtues entitle them to confidence; they are revered as legislators, obeyed as magistrates, but still considered as equals.

Americans, attorney Henry Wheaton advised his audience during the difficult summer of 1814, should "thank our stars" that their lot was cast "in a land of liberty—where each man walks forth in the original majesty of nature—where no distinctions are known but those of talent, and virtue, and education." [33] At last, able mechanics would receive their due recognition and acceptance in the life of the republic.

To insure the continuance of this rational age, education was of special importance to tradesmen. First, it guarded their hard-won freedom and independence. The Apprentices Library, for example, was a "perpetual guarantee" for the "free institutions" of America. "A people will," Mercein exalted, "never submit to the subversion of their rights, nor will usurpers dare to invade them, while the great mass of the community are possessed of intelligence, and think and act for themselves." By establishing the library, the mechanics were planting security around "the fortress of Liberty, erected in the glorious and triumphant struggle of the Revolution."

Second, education cleared a path for the advancement of all able men, including the thousands in the mechanic classes. Speaking to the students and apprentices, the Mechanics Society president recalled the many great men who rose from the ranks of tradesmen:

> Franklin, and Rittenhouse, and Godfrey, and Fulton emerged from the mechanical ranks to a sphere of usefulness, fame, and honor; and to the latest ages of the world will be hailed as the benefactors of the human family. Who can tell how many Franklins may be among you? Who can tell how many Rittenhouses, how many Godfreys, how many Fultons may yet spring from the Institution this day opened! Your opportunities are great and liberal.[34]

Education in a free and enlightened society allowed even the humblest artisan the chance of becoming the next Franklin, either as scientist or patriot.

On the other hand, despite all the possibilities and promise a rational America offered, the influence of wealth posed an immediate and constant threat. Congressman Samuel Mitchell cautioned that independence might fail because of the power of capital: "it is soon discovered that *money* is *power*, that power gives the possessor of it *importance*, and that *importance begets respect.*" George Eacker told of similar peril: "Let not wealth be the road which leads to greatness," he alerted mechanics. Rather, "let virtue be the foundation of distinction." Speaker Irving extolled the "simple blessing of an impoverished but emancipated people" in contrast to the wealth that made for "domestic ease." When monetary assets became the measure of ability and prominence, the republic was in danger.[35]

The messages of the Independence Day orators, detailing mechanics' military sacrifices, the meaning of liberty and the importance of an enlightened and educated government and citizenry, culminated in the assertion that mechanics were not only a vital part of the life of the nation but were, indeed, the very "center of population." Irving told assembled craftsmen that they:

> Compose in a manner, the sinews and muscles of our country. Men who formed ... the very axis of society: whose interest and affectations are reposed at home: whose hearts, I trust, are bound and linked with adamantine bands to the welfare of our country. In your hands must the palladium of our liberty rest. You cannot be inflated by distinction; you do not float like the ephemeral bubbles of pride and fashion, on the surface of society; nor are you of that uninformed class too low to be agitated with the current of events, and who, like dull weeds sleep secure at the bottom of the stream.[36]

The mechanics, and not the "ephemeral" merchants and aristocrats or the "uninformed" day laborers, immigrants, and blacks, were the backbone of American society.

The printers were especially proud of their central contribution. Samuel Woodworth, secretary of New York Typographical Society and a noted poet, in a work entitled "Art of Printing," described the pivotal role of his trade. The first verse told of the fall of "imperial Rome," sadly "denied the art which gives fair knowledge birth, refines the human heart, and scatters bliss on the Earth." It was not until a thousand years later that the "sun of Science" rose, bringing printing to man, and with it the advancement of love and peace:

> Hail! art of arts! all hail!
>   Thy praises mock the lyre;
> To reach the boundless theme,
>   Its tones in vain aspire;
> But grateful hearts which feel the bliss
>   Thy magic powers bestows,
> Respond to every strain like this,
>   How dull so'er it flows:

Chorus:

> Ours is the Heaven-descended art,
>   To give fair knowledge birth,
> To mend the human heart,
>   And civilize the earth.[37]

Another poem, entitled "Printing and Independence," described printing's achievement in removing the world from both "feudal gloom" and "clouded superstition." Its final stanzas celebrated this crucial triumph:

> Hail, Freedom! hail, celestial guest!
>   O never from thy sons depart;
> Thine be the Empire of the West,
>   Thy temple every freeman's heart;
> The Art of Printing gave thee birth,
>   And brightens still thy reign on earth.
>
> Arise, ye favor'd sons of light,
>   Professors of our Heaven-born art,
> And in the chorus all unite,
>   While joy expands each throbbing heart;
> "The Art of Printing shall endure,
> And Independence be secure." [38]

As printer Asbridge pointed out, it was the tradesmen who kept the world in motion, built its bridges, brought in its goods and luxuries. "In short," he declared, "in whatever shape we partake of the comforts and conveniences of life, we are more or less indebted to the labours of the inestimable mechanics." [39]

Similar declarations of esteem were apparent in the toasts given at the Fourth of July dinners of the different societies following the orations. The coopers in 1810 lauded "the mechanics of the United States, renowned for their deeds of philanthropy," wishing that "their united exertions in the support of agriculture, commerce and the independence of their country, be crowned with the sweet consolation of having been weighed and found not wanting." [40] At another dinner an artisan raised his goblet to his fellow craftsmen, asking that they be "encouraged in their arts, and prove to the world that as our country abundantly furnishes the raw materials, we can do without foreign manufactures." [41] The journeymen shoemakers, meanwhile, toasted themselves as, in peace, "a useful and intelligent class in society," while in war they asked that "their zeal and intrepidity be admitted by all and exceeded by none." [42]

The toasts of the General Society in January 1806, at their New Year's celebration, vividly expressed mechanics' patriotic spirit and their ideal of republican America. First in their minds were the "People of the United States," the backbone of republicanism, whom the mechanics hailed as "free and independent." Next in adulation came Jefferson, the "patriot, statesman and friend of the people"; Washington, who "Led our armies to victory and thereby established independence"; and those who had fallen "in defense of our country." Second only to these heroes of the Revolution was the esteem of the mechanics. The society proudly proclaimed: "May every member of this society feel himself happy to be a mechanic, and every mechanic be honored in being a member." Other toasts honored free commerce, agriculture and manufactures, the U.S. military ("Each citizen a soldier and each soldier a citizen"), and the "Rising Generation." Finally, the mayor himself ended the ceremonies by lifting his glass to "The mechanics of this city—may prosperity ever attend them in their private pursuits and in their social institutions." [43]

Clearly, the mechanics identified with the new American nation.

It was, in fact, common for tradesmen to incorporate the terminology of their trade in praising their country, so indicating the interconnectedness of the two. Journeyman bookbinder poet John Bradford composed such a poem:

> INDEPENDENCE, the work each Columbian likes best,
> Is an extra bound *elephant folio, hot pressed,*
> By the patriots of old this great work was begun,
> And *bound* and completed by GEORGE WASHINGTON.[44]

Similarly, the Butchers Benevolent Society toasted their nation: "Let the fields which fatten her numerous herd, become the *shambles* and *graves* of her daring invaders."[45]

The outlook of the mechanic community, as expressed in these toasts and orations, relied heavily on the ideal of republicanism that originated among the radical opposition in eighteenth century England, and which was deeply influential in America in both the revolutionary movement and in political development through the age of Jefferson. That is, artisans living in early nineteenth century New York firmly believed that the success of their government depended directly on the virtue and industriousness of its people. Only if they forsook luxury and refinement in favor of frugality and simplicity would the country prosper. Only if the nation preferred merit to the trappings of birth and wealth would it avoid falling prey to the tyranny of a corrupt aristocracy. And only if a vigilant, intelligent, educated, and rational citizenry was prepared to fully defend individual liberties and to sacrifice their personal gain for the public good would the preservation of the republic be assured.[46]

Mechanics were not in accord with the Federalist strain of republicanism. Although supporters of a constitution that had created a strong and honorable nation, and that had measurably improved the economic well being of the seaport, artisans eschewed a distrustful political persuasion that attempted to distance the bulk of the population from government through such means as the "filtration of talent" and, most grievously, property restrictions on suffrage. Neither did they condone traitorous, manipulating politicians whose self-seeking ambitions could easily ground the ship of state. Rather, in harmony with the egalitarian ideals of the

Jeffersonian movement, they hearkened to the political experience of the 1770s and 1780s when, together with yeomen, they had been chosen in considerable number for high legislative office.[47] Such recognition of the critical importance of the artisan to the body politic was at the heart of mechanics' interpretation of republicanism. Within the nation's great metropolitan centers, tradesmen remained the only reliable body of men capable of keeping American government on its proper course. It was their wisdom, their art, and their reason that prevented corruption at the hands of wealthy, aristocratic or ignorant, indigent elements. Mechanics were, indeed, the "axis of society."

NOTES

1. H.L. McBain, *De Witt Clinton and the Spoils System* (New York, 1907); Alfred F. Young, "The Mechanics and the Jeffersonians: New York, 1789-1801," *Labor History,* 5 (1964), 267; James Cheetham, *A View of the Political Conduct of Aaron Burr* (New York, 1802); William P. Van Ness [Aristides], *An Examination of the Various Charges Against Aaron Burr* (New York, 1803); Jerome Mushkat, *Tammany: The Evolution of a Political Machine, 1789-1865* (Syracuse, 1971), pp. 28-29; Jabez D. Hammond, *The History of Political Parties in the State of New York,* 2 vols. (New York, 1842), vol. 1, pp. 185-196, 198, 208, 220-227. Hammond criticizes De Witt Clinton's decision to renouce the U.S. Senate for New York politics and become "a party in the controversies of the bar-room parties of [New York], and to the petty quarrels in the city and state of New York about the pitiful offices of masters in chancery, sheriffs, clerks, county judges and justices of the peaces" (p. 208). The Livingston-Clinton struggle centered on charges that Governor Lewis had accepted a bribe in return for signing the legislation authorizing the Merchants Bank.

2. Craig Haryan, "De Witt Clinton and Partisanship: The Development of Clintonianism from 1811-1820," *New York Historical Society Quarterly,* 56 (1972), 109-132; Mushkat, *Tammany,* pp. 32-53; Hammond, *History of Political Parties,* p. 285. The Federalists, to their great sorrow, gave tacit support to Aaron Burr's 1804 gubernatorial campaign. They also aligned with the Lewisites (Livingstonians) to win control of the Common Council in 1806 and were sympathetic to De Witt Clinton's decision to challenge Madison in 1812.

3. *American Citizen,* April 14, 27, 1804. An entire folio of 1804 broadsides attacking Burr is available at the New York Public Library.

4. Ibid., April 24, 27, 1804.

5. *Morning Chronicle,* January 11, 12, 13, 1804.

6. *American Citizen,* November 14, 1803.

7. *Morning Chronicle,* November 15, 1803.

8. *American Citizen,* April 28, 1807. Lewis was accused of refusing to submit a contested mechanic's account to mediation because a mechanic was going to be one of the arbitrators, and, he said, "HE WOULD BE A DAMNED FOOL IF HE WOULD TRUST A MECHANIC."

9. *Morning Chronicle,* February 29, 1804.

10. *American Citizen,* March 7, 1807. This phrase was used to contest Governor Tomkins' humble beginnings.

11. Ibid., April 18, 1809, November 1, 1809; *Public Advertiser,* November 14, 21, 1809. Jonas Humbert, a Madisonian baker and aldermanic candidate, was charged with having "worn his Majesty's red coat in this very city." Humbert replied that his service had been forced and that he was being persecuted in the election only because he was a mechanic.

12. Ibid., September 12, 1809; *American Citizen,* April 17, 1809, May 2, 1809, September 21, 1809. Clintonians accused the Madisonians and Tammany of excluding Irishmen from office, unless the Irishmen supported the Madisonian ticket. The Clintonians were also incensed at a committee that Tammany formed to investigate how certain Republicans had voted that year. They claimed that were it not for the law, "the blood of the Republicans would be on the street." The Clintonians, by this time, had their own "Whig Club" to rival Tammany.

13. *Public Advertiser,* March 25, 1809.

14. *Independent Mechanic,* April 6, 1811.

15. Ibid., June 29, 1811.

16. Compiled from Edmund P. Willis, "Social Origins and Political Leadership in New York City from the Revolution to 1815," Ph.D. diss. (Berkeley, 1967), pp. 52, 63, 75. These figures were obtained by multiplying the percentage of eligible voters for the total population (14.9 percent in 1807) by the different ward populations. This figure, the number of eligible voters, was then divided into the number actually voting.

17. *American Citizen,* September 4, 1802, March 22, 1810.

18. Mushkat, *Tammany,* p. 36; Matthew Davis to William P. Van Ness, February 13, 1810, William P. Van Ness mss., Misc. Reel, New York Historical Society. In this letter, Davis, commenting on mechanics' efforts to secure their own bank, wrote: "you would smile to see the zeal displayed on this subject by mechanics of every grade,. . . ." The use of the word "smile," cast mechanics as eager children rather than thoughtful, reasoning citizens. See p. 166.

19. Minutes of the Society of Journeymen Shipwrights and Caulkers, mss., October 12, 1815, January 23, 1816, New York Public Library. All but the bakers, butchers and cabinetmakers were listed as attending a number of the Fourth of July celebrations discussed below.

20. Ibid., February 12, 1818; Petition of Shipwrights Society to the Common Council, City Clerk Filed Papers (hereafter referred to as CC), Box 3181, March 31, 1817, Municipal Archives, New York City.

21. Sidney I. Pomerantz, *New York: An American City, 1783-1803* (New York, 1938), pp. 95-97; Thomas Earle and Charles T. Congdon, eds., *Annals of the General Society of Mechanics and Tradesmen of the City of New York, 1775-1880* (New York, 1882), p. 10.

22. The society was purposely apolitical, not wishing to alienate any of its members because of political differences. The president and vice-president were always of different parties. While occasional attempts were made to bring in partisan politics over public events such as the Louisiana Purchase, or the election of society officers, these never proved successful. *Evening Post*, May 11, 1804, January 13, 1816; Pomerantz, *New York: An American City*, p. 215.

23. Minutes of the General Society of Mechanics and Tradesmen, February 6, 1799, January 7, 1801, June 17, 1801, August 5, 1801, June 2, 1813, November 1, 1820, and passim; a typescript of the minutes is available at the General Society in New York.

24. See pp. 165-168.

25. Minutes of the General Society of Mechanics and Tradesmen, November 3, 1802.

26. Roster of Hook and Ladder Company No. 2, CC Box 3126, 1812. See also Roll Book of First Hook and Ladder Company, CC Box 1740, 1818; Roll Book of Fire Company No. 36 (Eighth Ward), CC Box 3214, n.d.

27. Minutes and By Laws of Fire Company No. 11, December 23, 1807, February 20, 1809, August 9, 1809, New York Historical Society; Minutes of Meeting, First Hook and Ladder Company, CC Box 1740, November 19, 1818, May 28—September 16, 1819; Augustine E. Costello, *Our Firemen: A History of the New York Fire Department* (New York, 1887), pp. 29, 53, 61, 78.

28. Minutes of Fire Company No. 11, February 6, 1818; Costello, *Our Firemen,* pp. 29, 53, 65, 78, 158-160; John DeGraw, *Recollections of Early New York* (New York, 1882), pp. 65-67. Some companies collected a considerable amount of assets. Fire Company No. 11, for example, possessed assets of $8,456.57 in 1809, most of which was stock held in such institutions as the Manhattan and New Jersey Bank, the Eagle Fire

Company, and various bonds and mortgages. Minutes of Fire Company No. 11, December 14, 1809.

29. George J. Warner, *The Means for the Preservation of Public Liberty* (New York, 1797), pp. 8, 16; George Clinton, Jr., *An Oration* (New York, 1798), p. 5; Thomas F. King, *An Oration* (New York, 1821), p. 12.

30. Peter H. Wendover, *An Oration* (New York, 1806), pp. 7-9; John T. Irving, *An Oration* (New York, 1809), p. 8.

31. Thomas King, *An Oration,* p. 12; George Eacker, *An Oration* (New York, 1801), p. 15; Wendover, *An Oration,* p. 14; George Asbridge, *An Oration* (New York, 1811), pp. 11-14; John Rodman, *An Oration* (New York, 1813), p. 6; Thomas Mercein, *An Address Upon the Occasion of the Dedication of the Apprentices' Library* (New York, 1820), p. 13. The last oration was delivered on the anniversary of the evacuation of British forces from New York City (November 5).

32. Irving, *An Oration,* p. 3; Eacker, *An Oration,* pp. 17-18; Dr. Cuming, *An Oration* (New York, 1810), p. 5; Wendover, *An Oration,* p. 13. See also John I. Johnson, *Reflections on Political Society* (New York, 1797), pp. 4, 6, 12-13.

33. Mercein, *An Address,* p. 11; Wendover, *An Oration,* p. 12; Irving, *An Oration,* p. 20; Henry Wheaton, *An Oration* (New York, 1814), pp. 8, 22.

34. Mercein, *An Address,* pp. 7, 12.

35. Samuel Mitchell, *Address to the Citizens of New York* (New York, 1800), p. 21; Eacker, *An Oration,* p. 19; Irving, *An Oration,* p. 4.

36. Irving, *An Oration,* pp. 10-11.

37. Samuel Woodworth as quoted in George A. Stevens, *New York Typographical Union Number Six* (Albany, 1912), pp. 84-85.

38. Ibid., p. 89.

39. Asbridge, *An Oration,* p. 20.

40. *American Citizen,* July 16, 1810.

41. Ibid., January 6, 1808.

42. *National Advocate,* March 8, 1813.

43. *American Citizen,* January 9, 1806; for other examples see *Public Advertiser,* July 27, 1810, July 7, 1809 (Hatters Society); *Columbian,* November 19, 1813 (Typographical Society).

44. John Bradford, *The Poetical Vagaries of a Knight of the Folding Stick of PASTE CASTLE, to which is annexed the History of the Garret, &c., Translated from the Hieroglyphics of the Society by a Member of the Order of the Blue String* (New York, 1813), p. 3.

45. *American Citizen,* January 9, 1806.

46. For an overview of the development of republican thought see Robert E. Shalhope, "Toward a Republican Synthesis: The Emergence of

an Understanding of Republicanism in American Historiography," *William and Mary Quarterly,* 29 (1972), 49-80. Also particularly valuable for ideals close to the mechanic community is Gordon S. Wood, *The Creation of the American Republic: 1776-1789* (Chapel Hill, 1969).

47. Ibid., chap. 12.

Part II
THE
TRADITIONAL
MARKETPLACE

Chapter 6

THE ENTREPRENEURIAL SPIRIT

Early nineteenth-century New York was a city of contrasting marketplaces. On the one hand, buoyed by flourishing national and international trade and the adept skill of the nation's most resourceful merchants, extensive amounts of goods and capital entered the seaport. In the wake of this financial growth, considerable achievement took place in the development of capitalist techniques for production and marketing. These efficiency-oriented methods reached well into a number of populous mechanic trades, particularly carpentry, masonry, shoemaking, tailoring, cabinetmaking and printing, dramatically changing the roles of journeymen and masters, with especially serious effects on the income and mobility of journeymen. On the other hand, many crafts still retained traditional shop practices. Masters in these trades catered to local, often neighborhood, clientele, and generally ran family enterprises with only one or two journeymen and apprentices. Journeymen in these crafts still had good hope of moving on to their own shop after a few years of working for a wage.

This was a transitional economic period and the divisions between the two groups of crafts were far from rigid. Traditionally operated trades were affected by the city's increased wealth in the growing volume, expenses and profits of individual businesses. Too, within the ranks of the artisan trades most affected by the capitalist marketplace there remained many small enterprises functioning in a traditional manner. Furthermore, mechanics in these expanding trades continued with the rest of the artisan community to engage in traditional means of promotion such as advertisement in public prints and the search for greater government assistance. Overall, however, the differences are of sufficient significance to warrant treating the two groups of trades in separate parts. This section will describe both the traditional crafts and the traditional promotional and investment practices common to all trades, while the following section will detail the impact of capitalist procedures on mechanic trades.

Discussion of the traditional mechanic trades must begin with a description of those who controlled the crafts: the masters. That these men worked in a traditional manner in no way means that they lacked drive. For, as Carl Bridenbaugh has noted of colonial craftsmen, their most singular trait was the "desire to get ahead in the world. They were men of ambition. They were constantly on the make ... to raise themselves and their families above their present level." [1] This aspiration, which included the hope, so clearly enunciated in politics, of gaining greater standing and esteem, was the paramount financial goal of Jeffersonian masters as well. Indeed, for craftsmen, the central meaning of the Revolution, together with the fulfillment of republican ideals, was the opportunity for unfettered entrance into the marketplace.[2] Evidence of their determination to take advantage of free enterprise can be seen in the nature of their operations and investments; in the ingenious use of newspaper advertisements to gain customers; in continuing experimentation with credit; and with encounters with local and national governments over health regulation, taxation, and, most important, tariff protection.

The life of Stephen Allen, an artisan who achieved prominent economic and political fame, is representative of the financial possibilities for the most successful masters, even in the still traditional craft of sailmaking. Young Allen, whose father died early in his life, was apprenticed to a sailmaker, and in this station he lived a subsistence life through the War of Independence, ardently favoring the patriot cause, even in occupied New York. As an apprentice he slept in the sail loft, ate from a common stew, and wore but a few coarse pieces of clothing purchased yearly at a local "slop shop." Although he received little schooling, Stephen taught himself to read, devouring any book he could lay his hands on. With equal skill and intelligence, he picked up the art of cutting sail. Throughout these years, as he worked with other apprentices and journeymen, his guiding drive was to be his own boss. Always "uppermost in my thought," he recalled, was "progress towards independence . . . which I determined to achieve if possible; which determination was one of my principal stimulants." [3]

Well before he was twenty-one, Allen went to work in a sail loft as a journeyman. Though he received "numerous threats" from other journeymen because he had only served an apprenticeship of four years, his expertise soon silenced them. By the time he was twenty-one, he had joined in a partnership with another sailmaker. When, however, he began to lose accounts because of his partner's "dissipated behavior," Allen went into business for himself. Working a fourteen-hour day, staying out of debt as much as possible, and "employing the utmost economy in all my concerns," he had in 1796, after seven years, earned $4,000. His income continued to rise as Allen, joining in a new partnership with Joseph Lathrop, amassed $32,000 in the next six years, a sum he claimed was "nothing extraordinary for the time it was made." Following his business success with similar adeptness in politics, the prominent sailmaker won election to the Common Council, the presidency of the Mechanics Society, and finally the office of mayor of the city of New York.[4]

The financial success of Allen was not a fluke. Other craftsmen still operating fairly traditional mechanic enterprises and yet accumulating sizable fortunes included painter and glazier Jacob Sherred, who at one point in his life could not afford even his fifty cents in dues to the Mechanics Society, but who by 1815 was a director of the Mechanics Bank and a holder of assets valued at $120,000; and John P. Anthony, who took over his father's tanning

An 1807 scene in the Fourth Ward. This, the most middling of the wards, contained both a large mechanic and nonmechanic population. Artisans residing here would likely be somewhat better off than their courterparts in the outer wards. These homes, however, do not compare to the townhouses of the lower wards. Notice the open sewer. Museum of the City of New York.

business, building his assets to $4,000 in 1808 and $11,000 in 1815. Edmund P. Willis's study of political leadership lists 143 mechanics who attained aldermanic or assembly positions, many of whom worked in traditional trades and nearly all of whom attained significant economic gain. Even potter Clarkson Crolius increased his worth from $8,300 in 1808 to $22,400 in 1815, while baker Thomas Mercein improved his holdings from $2,600 in 1808 to $11,000 in 1815.[5]

Also confirming that success was not confined to a chosen few is another sample conducted by Willis: an 1815 occupation-wealth analysis of the city's Fourth Ward, the ward he considered most exemplary of the metropolis's overall population. The median wealth of identifiable mechanics residing in that ward (which ranked fifth out of the ten wards in per capita assessment) fell within the range of $2,000 and $5,000, the fourth of eight economic classes Willis establishes. Of the 387 masters in this sample, 255, including the cartmen, boatbuilders, shoemakers, leather workers, tailors, sailmakers, and silversmiths, ranked in this class. Ninety artisans, including shipwrights, printers, masons, carpenters, block-makers, blacksmiths, and hairdressers were in the third range ($1,001 to $2,000); only the coopers and cabinetmakers (41 crafts-men) fell in the second range ($100 to $1,000). Overall these masters, ranking on an average but one economic class below that of the merchant community, possessed sufficient means for a comfortable if not wealthy existence.[6]

Not all masters, of course, achieved such notable success. The 1819 Jury List for the city's Eighth Ward, a poor sector of the city, reveals that many masters there operated small, traditional shops, likely without any help aside from their family and perhaps an apprentice. In a sample composed of the 234 masters working in trades in which journeymen were also working, one hundred (44.4 percent) possessed less than $150 worth of personal assets. Along with the well-to-do masters of the Fourth Ward, there were many small craft enterprises in the outer wards that afforded their proprietors only a very modest living.[7]

Few if any records survive of the businesses of these small shops on the outskirts of the city. There is, however, important evidence of the nature of the work carried on by the more established masters, the men who formed the economic leadership within the traditional framework. Newspaper advertisements and account books describe some of the opportunities available. City notices to cartmen for bids to haul materials to be used in the paving of streets, or for other construction projects, could bring in consider-able income. Butchers, too, were requested to submit major bids to the army for large supplies of beef, and to the state to supply the local state prison.[8] There is particularly detailed evidence on the operations of the city's bakers. These entrepreneurs, though they employed but a few hands and ran a local business, still required considerable expense. An 1801 estimate of an average break-maker's daily expenditures and income, given in a public affidavit by three New York bakers, listed the items given in the table found on this page.[9]

For somewhat larger baking operations, the answers of George Arcularius (50 barrels of flour per week) and Phillip McCardle (24 barrels per week) to an 1805 Common Council questionnaire, reveal that, proportionately, most expenses remained the same with the exception of candles ($1 per day) and journeymen's wages ($20, $18, and $15 per month including board) for Arcularius. McCardle paid his one journeyman only $5 per week, a cost similar to that listed in the 1801 questionnaire. McCardle also paid only $70 per year in rent; Arcularius owned his bakery. The latter noted, however, that rent could run $500 per year. Both bakers also noted that they lost about 3 percent of their bread to bad flour and yeast. Total expenditures, even for a small bread-making operation, could easily run to over $10,000 a year, and a larger enterprise could equal twice that much. Since most bakers were men of moderate means, many needed credit. John Stuart, for example, from 1799 to 1804 negotiated thirty- to sixty-day

SUMMARY OF BAKERS' EXPENSES AND INCOME

Expenses:

2 barrels of flour @ 9.53	$19.06
Wood for oven	.50
Yeast (average)	.50
One workman (including board)	1.00
House rent (based on $212.50 yearly rent)	.58
Salt	.06
Candles	.12
Carting (for 2 barrels of flour)	.09
Wear and tear of wagon, baskets and peals	.12
Personal labor and attendance	1.25
Horse feed	.50
Total	$23.78

Income:

192 loaves (according to November 1 assize)	$22.19
Sale of 2 barrels @ 31¢ (many broken)	.62
Total	$22.81
Daily loss	$ .98

notes worth from $150 to $1,000 in order to purchase flour. He paid these notes with sales revenue.[10]

While most mechanics, such as these bakers, ran individual operations, it was not unusual for tradesmen to form joint enterprises. The most common such venture was the partnership. Stephen Allen engaged in three separate liaisons during his career as a sailmaker. Other examples, taken from numerous newspaper advertisements, include such artisans as watchmakers William Welch and John W. Labhart and cabinetmakers, later auctioneers, Charles Christian and Samuel Paxton. These associations were, of course, only as stable as the personalities involved; many were dissolved on account of death, incompatibility, the desire to go it alone, or one partner taking advantage of the other. A sad illustration of the latter was brought before the public in a notice of dissolution of the partnership of Thomas Studman and Peter Skinner, blacksmiths and whitesmiths. In his message mechanic Skinner regretfully remarked that his friend Studman had "lately attempted to abscond from the City of New York, after receiving considerable monies due to the subscriber and himself." Despite these and other problems, however, partnership was a practical means of pooling resources, capital, and risk.[11]

Occasionally mechanics also formed larger groups to engage in a mutual enterprise. Such was the case of the New York Slate Company, a joint-stock endeavor formed in 1802 by the efforts and funds of tradesmen in the building crafts. Intending to produce slate for use in New York State, the business spent $100,000 in its first four years and employed one hundred tradesmen (quarrymen, dressers, packers, cartmen, boatmen)—but with little profit and heavy expense. The problem, according to the company, was a prejudice in favor of slate from Great Britain and Ireland, despite greater cost and lower quality. In a public appeal, the struggling firm asked for greater support from the city's builders and carpenters. While it involved greater speculation and less personal control, joint-stock operations did allow artisans in greater number than two to pool their resources.[12]

A third means of investment beyond individual enterprise and within the range of moderately well-to-do craftsmen in both capitalist-oriented and traditional trades, was the purchase of real estate. The 1819 Jury List for the Sixth Ward reveals that of the ninety-eight masters listed in traditional crafts, twenty-five, or just over one-fourth (25.5 percent) owned real property. The wills of the more prosperous artisans testify to the popularity of such investment. Butcher Michael Varian put his money into lots throughout the city; and Thomas Musgrove, a morocco leather dresser, purchased six acres of land in Harlem. Cabinetmaker Duncan Phyfe, moreover, besides owning expensive property on Partition Street, acquired a farm and other real estate in Brooklyn. New York lots were difficult to acquire, but mechanics who were able often used their earnings to invest in this, the oldest of American speculations.[13]

To prosper, or even to remain solvent, these mechanic enterprises required a steady flow of business. While seeking, of course, to retain their old customers, craftsmen were constantly in search of new business. Their major and longtime traditional forum for reaching potential clients was the newspaper. New York's ten daily papers, together with weeklies and monthlies, were filled with commercial notices of every kind, including many from mechanic entrepreneurs. One collection of artisan advertisements lists nearly 1,200 such ads between 1800 and 1804.[14]

A number of enterprising mechanics found themselves a corner of the marketplace by supplying other craftsmen with needed equipment. Henry Crocheron, for example, operated a wire manufactory at 24 Moore Street. In one advertisement he offered general screens to bricklayers and plasterers; specially made "falling and standing screens" for cleaning "wheat, snuff and indian meal"; washers and dusters for paper mills; and cages and wires for cellar windows. Another would-be supplier, William Peck, notified carpenters and masons in the *American Citizen* that he had house-pipes and gutters made by patent machines ready for purchase at "reduced prices." [15]

Other creative masters sought to make their fortune through the invention of new mechanical devices. Joseph Squire, Jr., in a notice in the *Evening Post,* described his manufactory of "WELDED and OPEN THIMBLES" for sails and rigging. He also carried iron rivets, all made by Jenning's Patent Machine and Jenning's Patent Smith Bellows. The price and quality of his products were attested to by four distinguished sailmakers. Another artisan entrepreneur, Abraham Howard Quincy of South Street, offered both builders and bakers the use of his "Fire Compressing Stone Cabinets," a device that heated shops and buildings with safety, cleanliness, and economy. Displaying business acumen along with his craftsmanship, Quincy made the cabinets available by lease, at a rate of fifty dollars per year per 1,000 inhabitants. Other artisan inventions submitted to the public included scale balances; presses for packing wares; a laborsaving tool for manufacturing bread; a new stove that broiled, baked, and roasted with the same fire; a fire escape and extinguisher; a cutting screw; and a new kind of printer's type. Some creations, such as a novel thermo light, were so popular that admission was charged to those wishing to examine the product.[16]

Masters were no less ingenious in using commercial wit: finding the ablest method of communicating to the public's interest or prejudice. Cognizant of the general desire for wealth and financial security, William Jackson, a "mockasin maker" published a letter "To the Inhabitants of this Renowned City of Gotham," stating that he had brought in sixty-seven of the best workmen in Europe to assist him in his *"infant* establishment." Wholesalers who desired to "make a rapid fortune" and retailers "who wish to make themselves snug and comfortable" were requested to send their orders in (with cash) as soon as possible in order "to prevent his Mockasins lying on the shelf, and himself being eaten out of house and home by sixty-seven imported *gormandizers."* Jackson also noted that he still sold medicinal "LIFE PRESERVERS" which had effectively prevented more colds, coughs, and asthma than "all the quacks in New York have by their drugs." Tradesman William Carver, a shoesmith and horse farrier, appealed to the bias for English products and training, as he reported that he continued to shoe horses in the "best English manner, with a warranty to travel sound." A third mechanic, shoemaker Ruleff Conover, emphasized quality and experience. Noting that he had previously been foreman for a merchant, he respectfully informed the "ladies of this city and his friends in general" that he had opened a store and shop on Broadway. Headed by a picture of a shoe, Conover's advertisement described his "long and unremitted attention" to his profession and promised that he would hire none but the best workmen nor use any but the best materials.[17]

Without question the most original and adept mechanic advertiser was the noted hairdresser, John Richard Desborus Huggins, located at 92 Boradway. Year after year the local newspapers carried the proclamations, poems, literary evaluations, and political views of the self-styled "Emperor Huggins." The following verse, entitled, "Look Here" and "set to music and sung by all the barbers in the United States," is a good example of his work:

> I'm Emperor of Barbers here,
>   My name is JOHN R. D. HUGGINS,
> I'm Shaver, Curler, and Frisseur,
>   In short I'm all but muggins.
> I dress a *Head*—I trim a *Crop*,
>   At *Shaving well* my knack is!
> I fit a wig—liquet a fop—
>   And else would *shave* the chop
> Of little school boy Jackies.
>
> . . . .
>
> At eve by the fire, like a good jolly cock,
> When my day's work is done and all over;
> I tipple, I smoke, and I wind up the clock,
> With sweet Mrs. Huggins in clover—
>   With my Oh! my—come and try,
>   John Huggins,
>   Hard tuggins
>   Savonette paste;
>   Puff—snuff—
>   Huff-Cuff—
>   Trumpery enough:
>   Jogging,
>   Noggin;
>   Smooth *chin* latery,
>   Sharp *razor* shavery,
>   Stripe painted *pole*-ery,
>   *Caricature* drollery,
>   At the Dressing Academy,
>   Where you'll find a Lad, or me,

> Every day,
> 92 Broadway—
> Signery—
> Finery—
> *Pomade*ish—
> *Odour*ish—
> Going—A going! . . .

The Emperor was far ahead of his time in understanding the relationship between sex and commercial success. Not only did he include a bawdy allusion to his wife—"I wind up the clock,/With Sweet Mrs. Huggins in clover"—in the previous ad, but this adroit hairdresser also composed a message that confronted the issue in a particularly modern manner:

THE FIRST LESSON OF LOVE

> In vain I breath'd the tender sigh
> At fair Eliza's feet;
> My soul, which glisten'd in my eye,
> No kindred ray cou'd meet?

> With cold indifference, she repli'd,
> My heart you do not move;
> And I will never be a bride
> Till I have learn'd to love.

> O then, I cried, my pupil be,
> My breast no longer steel,
> Sure I can teach, sweet girl, to thee,
> The lesson which I feel.

> No William, you have tri'd it long,
> And yet I don't improve;
> I'm dull, or you instruct me wrong
> I have not learn'd to love.

> I left her, hopeless, but at eve
> We met, and she exclaim'd,

Now, William, NOW, my heart receive,
With love, for YOU, inflam'd.

Surpris'd, delighted, soon I guess'd
What thus, her heart, cou'd move;
'Twas HUGGINS that my hair had dress'd,
She saw and learn'd to love.[19]

Other Huggins statements, including an account of the Dey of Algiers' fear of an American army of "ten thousand razors," an attack on a man who criticized the Emperor's political parodies (if caught the scoundrel would receive "such a lathering"), and a defense of Tom Paine, offered considerable amusement to the public. It did more than that, however. By making himself a well-known New York personality, Huggins achieved considerable commercial success. This aspiring mechanic was a pioneer entrepreneur in the field of advertising.[20]

Credit was an integral part of masters' marketplace endeavors. Craftsmen often allowed customers to carry an account, and when payment was not made, or was not made in a reasonable time, their businesses would suffer. Bakers McCardle and Arcularius stated that they lost 2.5 to 5 percent of their income each year to bad debts, an amount that exceeded $700 for McCardle and even more for Arcularius.[21] Articles in the *Independent Mechanic* also described this serious problem. "A Mechanic" sent in a piece from London in the hope, he stated, of curing "a practice too prevalent in this city." The essay depicted the plight of a tradesman who himself owed money to a merchant. Asked for payment, he went out to collect his bills only to be told by one of his debtors that the "clerk of cash was out." The next man stated that he was indisposed and would settle later, the third pleaded poverty, and a fourth lamented that he had tied up all his assets in land speculation. Consequently, this honest tradesman was unable to make good his accounts, even though he had conducted an honest and seemingly profitable operation.[22]

Another communication to the *Mechanic* describes the plight of a "poor but respectable artisan" who calls upon a gentleman eight separate times over a bill for five dollars. At first he is either put off

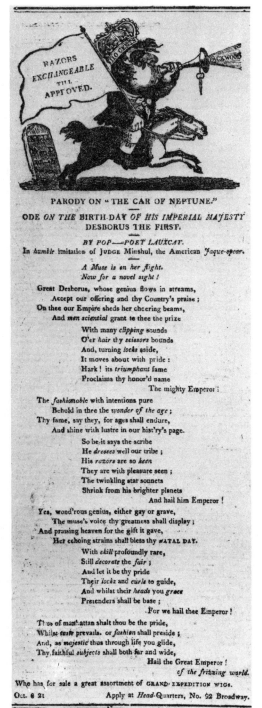

Advertisement of John Richard Desborus Huggins, Hairdresser. Courtesy, New York Historical Society, New York City.

with requests to leave the account or else told that the man is not available. Finally, the customer grudgingly pays the bill while insulting the craftsman: "What insolence! . . . I am determined to procure a less troublesome mechanic." [23] In another insertion, "S" also complained of the weariness of calling on accounts again and again to procure payment. When the craftsman tires of going himself and sends a lad with a note, the boy is insulted:

> You scoundrel! . . . tell Mr. W that I think his message was d——d impertinent; and if he ever sends another such, he shall never have another cent of money from me.[24]

It was sad, indeed, that a mechanic could suffer "an irreparable injury to his business" in order to allow a wealthy customer the "pleasure of counting over his silver."

A barber's shop for gentlemen. Courtesy, New York Historical Society, New York City.

Artisans did take measures to protect themselves from the failure of debtors to pay their bills. Shoemaker Reuben Bunn in 1802 decided to cease extending credit to his retail customers. He notified the public that instead he would charge one shilling less per pair of shoes. An 1811 meeting of similarly concerned tailors, hatters, and shoemakers considered collectively the "subject of giving credit to their respective customers" and resolved to hold general meetings of their professions, though these gatherings apparently took no action. In 1817 and 1819, the city's butchers, worried about losses incurred by accepting bad credit in the form of worthless bank notes, called special meetings to warn each other and the general public "about the extreme injury . . . to the poorer and uninformed who are constantly suffering by the receiving of bank notes without means of information, with respect to current value." The extension of credit was an important part of a master's business, but one that could cause considerable distress and embarrassment, especially in hard times.[25]

On the other side of the ledger, however, in their efforts to expand their operations in line with the growing markets, masters eagerly sought to obtain credit. The most suitable source of capital were the city's commercial banks. Unfortunately, bankers seldom made direct loans to independent artisan manufacturers; they preferred to invest in mercantile-controlled enterprises. Futhermore, merchant bankers, many of whom were Federalists, were disinclined to deal with the predominantly Republican mechanics. Finally, merchants' pervasive bias against treating mechanics as business equals made direct credit transactions rare. The unfortunate consequence was, as the *Evening Post* noted, that all too often "the application of the laborious mechanic is treated with contempt and rejected with disdain." [26]

Despite the seriousness of the obstacles posed by the merchants, the entrepreneurial ambitions of the mechanic community remained undiminished. Rather, from the early nineteenth century on, tradesmen sought opportunities to directly participate in banking. Their first chance came with the formation of the Manhattan Bank in 1799, a Republican-controlled institution that listed twenty-four mechanics among its original subscribers. This firm, however, soon became dominated by the mercantile establishment and did not prove satisfactory to mechanics' desire for a dependable source of capital.[27] If a minority subscription in a merchant-controlled bank was inadequate, a possible solution was the formation of a bank owned and operated by mechanics. Such an institution would be sensitive to the needs of mechanics, open to reasonably small investments in limited mechanic enterprises, and allow tradesmen to continue their traditional means of operation free from mercantile interests. It was not long before such an idea was in the air. Rumors of the possible establishment of such an institution first circulated in 1805 when John Slidell, Jr., a prominent soap-boiler, was said to be circulating a petition.[28] The plan came into fruition five years later when a memorial was, indeed, presented to the legislature, sponsored by the General Society of Mechanics and Tradesmen. A bill was soon drawn up and presented to the lawmakers for approval.

Considerable argument was put forward in favor of the new Mechanics Bank and none against. The lack of opposition was at least in part due to the craftsmen's considerable political clout, particularly in view of the bank's strong support among the city's tradesmen. Matthew Davis, a Burrite politician and former printer, wrote to a friend:

It is impossible for you to imagine how popular the measure is; and you would smile to see the zeal displayed on this subject by mechanics of every grade whether Madisonian, Clintonian Federal or anything else that you can designate them. . . . A disappointment of them in a favorite object, you will readily perceive, would have no inconsiderable effect.[29]

Supporters of the Mechanics Bank described the city's need of and ability to absorb new capital; the importance of an alternative to the "capricious, irregular and arbitrary manner" in which local banks operated; and, finally, the want of an institution that would be oriented to the problems of tradesmen, such as discounting notes of small denomination with which other banks would not bother.[30]

Lacking organized opposition, the act of incorporation passed without difficulty. The law provided the bank with the largest capital of any of the city's banks, $1.5 million. Other provisions required that mechanics be given preference in the purchase of stocks, that seven members of the board of directors be members of the Mechanics Society and that $600,000 be set aside for the state's mechanics and tradesmen.[31] Yet, despite the large capitalization and these safeguard provisions, mechanics who believed that the bank would be a financial bonanza to the city's craftsmen were sorely disappointed. Instead, the institution came much closer to destroying the Mechanics Society than to providing artisans with liberal credit and convenient banking services.

The problem was that as the bank charter was being approved, its sponsor, the Mechanics Society, considerably loosened its membership requirements. Forgoing its practice of admitting only those "brought up to or strictly following a mechanical business" and who were identified "in their interests, their sympathies, and their feelings" with artisans, the society, in poor financial straits, decided not to be "overscrupulous." Consequently, it approved a "large number" of applications of men who were "generally wealthy, were willing promptly to pay their fees," and who were "by no means likely to become pensioners of the Society." [32] These individuals were generally well-to-do merchants whose only connection was that at some time in their lives they had followed an artisan trade or been connected with the business operation of a craftsman. That is, many members of the mercantile community, hopeful of acquiring the capital and profits of the new bank, applied for, and were admitted to, membership in the organization at the same time that the bank was chartered.

A number of these new "mechanics" such as real estate broker Samuel St. John or insurance broker Gabriel Furman, became members of the board of directors. Because they were more familiar with banking operations, as genuine artisans such as Stephen Allen, also a director, were not, they managed to assume the overall management of the institution, including the determination of who would and would not receive stocks and what notes were to be discounted. Shares were sold to those who would "keep the best account with the Bank" rather than to the artisan community as the charter intended. The directors, moreover, resorted to "speculation after speculation," extending the resources of the bank well beyond its means. Forced to stop payments, the bank

soon became insolvent. Seven members of the board of directors
went bankrupt in the third year of the institution's life.[33]

While the Mechanics Bank survived, eventually becoming the
noted Mechanics and Metals National Bank, it was a major
disappointment to many ambitious master craftsmen as well as to
the Mechanics Society. Because of their membership policy and
the bank's errant behavior, the society became embroiled in internal disputes. In December 1810 a resolution was presented before
the association noting that there was at present "great dissatisfac-
tion" among the members, including a "disposition" by many of
them to "withdraw from the Society." The problem, according to
the authors of this motion, were "our Brothers who have been
Directors of the Mechanics Bank" who were guilty of "very unfair
and improper conduct particularly in the distribution of that stock
which was by charter reserved for mechanics." [34] The turmoil was
evident in 1811 when in an election for the bank's board of
directors four separate slates were presented to the shareholders.
Finally, with membership declining rapidly, the society sold 5,000
of its 6,000 shares, divorcing it from any real power over the bank.
This move, however, came too late to restore the trust and leadership previously afforded the society by the city's mechanics. Badly
wounded, the association lay dormant, missing monthly meetings
for lack of a simple quorum. It revived only in 1820 when, under
the leadership of Thomas Mercein, it opened an Apprentices
Library and a noted Mechanics Institute.[35]

Although a number of tradesmen did purchase stock and avail
themselves of the bank's facilities, the Mechanics Bank never
fulfilled its promise nor satisfied the credit needs and financial
services that artisans sought. Consequently, it is not surprising that
within a few years another bank opened, intended for the benefit of
tradesmen. Entitled the Exchange Bank, it was a private, nonin-
corporated institution founded by Joshua Barker, a Republican
merchant and iron molder who put up his assets as capital. The
Exchange Bank was a smaller but more genuine endeavor to
service the mechanic community, and a number of tradesmen soon
patronized the bank for loans, savings, and other transactions. In
1818, however, a bill was proposed in Albany outlawing private
banks and excluding the Exchange Bank from its provisions for
only three years.

Once again the mechanics rallied to their entrepreneurial interests. A large meeting was held at Tammany Hall resulting in a resolution stating that the proposed legislation would oppress the poor and "extend the power of existing aristocracies already too great." Furthermore, the mechanics declared, although they were required to accept merchants' notes, they were not able to "participate in bank favors." Unlike other fiscal institutions that used their capital to accommodate "directors or the friends of directors" (including the Mechanics Bank), the Exchange Bank devoted its funds "almost exclusively" to "laborious and industrious mechanics." No butcher, baker, or shoemaker wished to be deprived of banking privileges any more than the merchant or attorney.[36]

Unfortunately, well before the proposed law could have any effect, the panic of 1819 dealt the Exchange Bank a mortal blow. Owner Barker, despite "commendable foresight and caution," was forced to suspend operations in June 1819. In a public notice he promised to put his entire fortune on the line, including real estate and merchant vessels still at sea, in order to redeem his notes. Once again, however, mechanics were disappointed in their quest for banking services, as the certificates they held from the Exchange Bank became worthless while their debts remained in force.[37]

In sum, the masters' encounters with banks were disappointing. Neither the Mechanics Bank nor the Exchange Bank fulfilled their hope for adequate and readily available credit. A serious problem was undoubtedly tradesmen's inexperience with such complex institutions as commercial banks. Particularly in the case of the Mechanics Bank, they were the victims of men with greater backgrounds in the ways of finance. Their marketplace ambitions remained strong, but in their quest for bank capital, endeavors that began with promise led to considerable frustration and chagrin.

In addition to credit concerns, the entrepreneurial careers of the city's mechanics were vitally affected by actions of the local and the national government. In the continuance of a tradition extending well into the colonial era, craftsmen made both individual and concerted efforts before these bodies in the defense, the protection, and the promotion of their enterprises.

Most of the appearances of artisan proprietors before municipal authorities came in defense of their businesses. Many complaints were lodged against the more noisome of these operations, and mechanics had to prove to the court that their enterprises did not constitute a "nuisance"; failure to so persuade could mean the disbandment of their work. The *City Hall Recorder* relates the trial of two "colored men," carpenters William Hamilton and James Cathaw, who operated a shop in an old wooden building on Stone Street. The danger of fire from their shop and materials threatened fashionable nearby homes, and the two men were prosecuted for a "nuisance." No counsel was employed by the tradesmen, nor did the prosecution press for conviction. The court, emphasizing the importance of this kind of decision to the "generality of mechanics," asked the jury to decide whether or not the defendants posed a greater threat in their present location than in another part of the city. The verdict was "not guilty." [38]

Another trial of interest involved distiller Benjamin Prescott, also indicted as a public nuisance. His cisterns and furnaces were accused of emitting large quantities of smoke, releasing soot to "a considerable distance," posing a danger of fire, and releasing a vapor with a "sickish smell" into the gutters. After the testimony of doctors, who stated both that "a great city is made up, in a measure, of a collection of nuisances," and that Prescott's operation was less noxious than a blacksmith shop, an acquittal was granted.[39]

Not all artisans were successful, however. Stephen Shepherd began in November 1805 to manufacture tripe and wheels at the corner of Jay and Hudson streets. A complaint was lodged with the board of health, and he was ordered to desist. In a petition to the board of health, Shepherd declared that he had invested his entire assets in getting a boiler, a horse and cart, and other items as well as contracted with butchers for the bellies of their oxen. Consequently he requested aid in moving or else, he lamented, his debts would "overawe" him.[40] John Dietz, too, saw his glue manufactory declared a nuisance because of the "stagnation of foul and complacating" materials on the nearby lots. Impelled by a "deep sense of distress and by the apprehension of impending doom," he appealed to the Common Council for permission to continue his enterprise.[41]

The problem for the city was perplexing. On the one hand, the resident complainants, many of whom were mechanics, had real grievances over the "disgusting effluvia" of a sugar refinery, the stench created by the "offals and filth" of a local slaughterhouse, or the "very combustible" quality of a turpentine distillery. But, on the other hand, ambitious master craftsmen needed a place in the city to operate. The threat of a suit, fine, or eviction was a serious concern for artisan entrepreneurs working within a densely inhabited and vulnerable metropolis.[42]

Far outshadowing the consequences of local directives, and of constant and critical concern to entire mechanic branches, were the actions of the federal government in the field of protective tariffs and taxation. These laws and levies touched at once the livelihoods of hundreds of New York City tradesmen. The major efforts in this area were given to lobbying for import duties. Like the quest for banking credit, this campaign began well before the Jeffersonian era. Indeed, during the Confederation period, artisans, through petitions from both individual trades and the Mechanics Society, successfully lobbied for protection. Over the objections of merchants, the New York State legislature assessed significant duties on hats, boots, saddles, chairs, and coaches as well as a lesser general duty of 5 percent on all imports.[43]

With the founding of the stronger national union under the Constitution, tariffs became the responsibility of Congress. On July 4, 1789, it implemented a general import duty with a definite "protective intent." Under its provisions, certain needed raw materials such as furs, wool, hides, and copper were admitted free. Furthermore, a general *ad valorem* duty of 5 percent was assessed as well as a 15 percent tax on imported coaches and carriages; 10 percent on glass, china, and earthenware; and 7.5 percent on clothing, canes, hats, saddles, cabinetwork, and paper. Finally, a 10 percent discount was given to goods shipped in American vessels, and, according to a subsequent tonnage act, a special duty of 50 cents per ton was levied on all foreign-built and foreign-owned ships; this was reduced to 30 cents per ton for ships American-built but foreign-owned, and to 6 cents for those both built and owned by American citizens.[44]

While these duties were significant and were intended to provide some protection for American manufacturers, their effect was minimal. Rather, the act served as the main source of revenue for the new nation. And, in fact, the dominant attitude of Congress from the Federalist period to the War of 1812 was that the intent of the duties should be to produce income. Political parties, particularly the Democratic-Republicans, were, however, at times amenable to requests for adjustments. Consequently, there were many appeals from mechanics for greater governmental assistance. These petitions, which included joint appeals as well as memorials from specific trades, were written chiefly prior to 1808, since after that date the embargo and the war made the cost of shipping prohibitive; furthermore, Congress doubled all duties in 1812 to help pay military costs.[45]

A major source of joint petitions by a number of trades was the General Society of Mechanics and Tradesmen, an advocate since 1785 of increased protective tariffs. In 1799 it wrote its sister society in Providence lamenting the failure of mechanic enterprises: "The attempt of many individuals who have embarked their property in the establishment of particular branches, have successively and with loss relinquished their honorable undertakings." These failures were solely attributable to "foreign importations," which recently had spread a "baneful influence among us—an influence highly unfavorable to mechanical improvement, nourishing a spirit of dependence, depleting in a degree the purpose of our Revolution and tarnishing the luster of our National Character."[46]

Another petition, delivered in 1801 from the "Mechanics and Manufacturers of New York," took a more theoretical position. These tradesmen argued that given the natural resources of the United States which included an available labor supply, suitable equipment, and an "American genius" that was "particularly adapted to mechanics," more attention ought to be given to the promotion of the artisan trades. As long as the United States remained only "a nation of farmers and merchants," paying a tax for its imported goods "which is multiplied in every hand through which it passes," true independence could not be attained. Protective duties would eliminate this unnecessary expense and dependence by encouraging local manufactures. Nor would merchants necessarily be hurt, for their capital would surely find "new employment" in the needs of the growing nation. The point was that at this stage of "infancy," the country's growing crafts must be "nursed by guardian care" until they reached the full "vigor of manhood." [47]

Specific requests of individual trades for favorable legislation were far more common than joint pleas, and far more likely to bring results. A revealing example of such lobbying took place in 1802 when the printers, both masters and journeymen, petitioned Washington against a House Committee report proposing to increase the duty on imported type from 12.5 to 20 percent. This recommendation originated with the request of the owners of a Pennsylvania type foundry and of William Duane, editor of the Philadelphia *Aurora,* who helped establish the foundry. Protests came to Congress from printers in each major American city, arguing against this added expense. In New York the master printers, meeting with the city's booksellers, declared that the increase in duties would "do extensive injury to all persons concerned in printing" as well as indirectly tax American readers—all for the "emolument" of a few adventurers in the type-founding business. Since one foundry could not even supply one-twentieth of the needed type, there was no point and only harm in raising the import duty. Such a move would, indeed, act as a "public evil" in that it would "materially and injuriously affect the whole business of Printing and Bookselling throughout the United States." [48]

The journeymen printers, through their Franklin Typographical Society, sent in a separate letter of protest. These wage-earning tradesmen claimed that the new tariff would force the importation of books in place of local production, thus depriving "two thirds of the Journeymen Printers of the United States of their means of subsistence." Moreover, they argued that by increasing the expense of printing, even fewer journeymen would have the opportunity of operating their own enterprise—an occurrence that was already rare. Finally, they reasoned that the tax would injure the very fiber of the nation by depriving all but the very wealthy of the chance of reaping the benefits of a craft "as conducive to the promotion of learning liberty and happiness" as any other profession. Surely such an act could not become law.[49]

The printers' appeals, although unusual in their stand against a protective tarriff, were typical in their purpose of seeking federal aid for their crafts. The following year, 1803, other trades presented their cases to congress, generally seeking either to retain existing duties, or to procure raw materials from abroad free of imports. Mechanics engaged in shipbuilding delivered a memorial against a proposed law that would admit foreign vessels into American ports on the same terms as native ships. Because foreigners could "build their vessels cheaper, equip them cheaper, and navigate them cheaper than we can do," Americans would lose much of their carrying trade, shipbuilding would stagnate, and "that numerous class of mechanics . . . must cease to find that employment in their own country which they have hitherto done." A separate memorial of the chamber of commerce supported the mechanics, noting that if the legislation passed, then the labor of sailmakers, ropemakers, and other tradesmen "will neither be wanted nor paid for." [50]

Also in 1803, the Franklin Society, in this instance likely concerned with the competition of English-made books and with the price of imported rags needed for making paper, joined with gunsmiths, starchmakers, hatters, papermakers, and other craftsmen in appealing to the House of Representatives for specific changes in the tariff laws. The following year the New York Slate Company asked for increases of levies assessed on foreign slate in order to encourage the purchase of domestic slate. In December of 1807, the city's journeymen hatters sent Washington a memorial for greater protection against imported hats. In a message that gives insight into the problems that Federalist merchants had in attracting artisan support, the journeymen claimed that "mercantile men, particularly in this city," were bringing in so many cheap hats that many hatters "who have served a long time as apprentices and journeymen are obliged to abandon their trade and resort to other means for supporting themselves and their families." Inasmuch as American hats were equal in quality to others and that the petitioners were, at this time of upheaval, "attached to the liberties of this country and willing to hazard everything for the maintenance of its rights and independence," the tradesmen asked for congressional relief.[51]

In 1812 the city's malt brewers also petitioned Congress asking that it promote the use of their product. Describing the consumption of "ardent spirits" as common, "particularly among the laboring part of society," they reasoned that a switch to domestic malt beer would be both "connected with the individual and general good" and "congenial with the spirit of the nation." [52]

The different petitions were duly received and considered by the Committee on Commerce and Manufacturing of the House of Representatives. The last Congress to serve under a Federalist administration was not responsive to the 1801 general petition of the city's "Mechanics and Manufacturers," declaring that it would be "inexpedient at the present time, to further increase the duties on imported articles." The next Congress, meeting under Jefferson's leadership, seemed friendlier at first. In 1802, declaring that manufacturing should be promoted because it could afford the United States an adequate supply of goods, it approved the memorials of the city's tradesmen asking for increases in duties on hats, gunpowder, brushes, and a number of other items. In 1803 it also reacted favorably to the petitions which were submitted by the printers, shoemakers, gunsmiths, papermakers, and hatters. The congressmen noted that the current levies were not sufficient to provide protection, acting only as a tax on consumers. However, it deferred action until the next session. [53]

When it next convened, the Committee on Commerce did recommend a number of small adjustments in the import duties; this included the deletion of the 7.5 percent increase in the tariff on type, a clear victory for the printers' lobby. However, it did not follow through on many of the recommendations it had made in 1803. The report issued in 1804 stated that artisans were already well assisted by drawbacks, bounties, and selected duties. Moreover, it claimed that craftsmen were generally doing well, receiving reasonable incomes while still "not doomed to the strict discipline" of English factories. The committee also declared that the major American occupation remained agriculture and pondered that an increase in tariffs might mean that "we should have no market abroad for our produce, and industry would lose one of its chief incentives at home." Accordingly, the congressmen recommended only a few small adjustments in the duties instead of the major alterations that the craftsmen were requesting. [54]

Congress also reasoned that it should not interfere with the right of citizens, if they so desired, to purchase imported wares. In response to the petitions of the slate companies, the Commerce Committee remarked that it would be "impolitic to increase the impost to a prohibitive amount." American producers of slate should not have a monopoly on the market, preventing a builder "from buying foreign slate, if he prefers it to that of his own country." Moreover, the representatives also declared that it would be unfair for them to grant particular favors to individual trades-men. That would lead more crafts to make such requests and "this cannot be allowed." [55]

This statement by a Republican-controlled committee does not mean that the Democratic-Republicans had deserted their mechanic constituents. They were, first of all, a broadly based party, and while their urban representatives may have favored more protection, the party as a whole was more partisan to agrarian and free trade sentiment. Not, of course, that it did not attempt to satisfy individual needs, as witnessed by the various alterations in general tariff laws. But despite the continuing efforts of the various mechanic crafts requesting higher duties, prior to the war with Great Britain there was no overall change in government policy from a tariff oriented to revenue to one intended to provide protection.

With the coming of the War of 1812, the focus of mechanics' attention in Washington shifted from tariffs to taxation. In order to finance the war, Congress passed legislation imposing highly bur-densome duties on mechanic production, including levies on candles, leather and iron products, paper, hats, and carriages. Spurred on by the opposition Federalists, craftsmen vigorously protested these assessments. Large meetings were called at which speakers condemned as gross violations of constitutional rights laws that required licenses and bonds from all tradesmen commencing business, that allowed tax collectors to search craftsmen's shops without a warrant, and that permitted the imposition of heavy fines on any artisan who did not cooperate with federal officers. Together with these protest assemblies, nearly every mechanic branch met separately to draft petitions to Congress against the "exorbitant" taxes that would surely ruin "thousands of mechanics." [56]

With the cessation of hostilities, attention returned to protective duties. And, in the spirit of national pride following the war, advocates of protection received a much friendlier hearing. This was signaled in 1816 with the passage—over the protests of merchants' petitions—of legislation considerably raising duties and constituting the first "protective" tariff in American history.[57] In this spirit, many articles appeared in the local newspapers praising local manufactures and arguing for their encouragement. Too, the Society for the Promotion of Domestic Industry and the American Society for the Encouragement of Domestic Manufacture, organizations that included mechanics as well as mercantile promoters, lobbied with some effect for policies of greater promotion of manufactures. After the war with Britain, arguments that real independence would be attained only when the United States was no longer dependent on imports and that "national industry is the source of national wealth" carried much more weight.[58]

It appeared that mechanics' viewpoint on protection had triumphed at last. Yet, in this case, as in the ill-fated Mechanics Bank, the initial victory was misleading. In entering unchartered territory by encouraging a "spirit of manufacturing," tradesmen also fostered an atmosphere conducive to large-scale mercantile enterprises in this area. And no institution caused more dread within the artisan community than the factory.

As ambitious entrepreneurs, New York's master craftsmen used many different means to achieve marketplace success. This included individual efforts in invention and advertisement and collective efforts, varying from partnerships, to the Mechanics Bank, to the movement for increased tariff protection. Their goal in these enterprises was twofold. First, these artisans were intent on augmenting their incomes. Although few masters amassed estates of more than a few thousand dollars, there were enough men like Stephen Allen to whet the appetites of the rest of the community. Second, masters were bidding to assert their economic independence. This is particularly evident in their discussion of the need for banking services and import protection. They were attempting both to avoid dependency on scornful bankers for credit, and to prevent their government from deferring mechanic interests to those of international commerce. The ultimate goal of these tradesmen was to establish a marketplace position not demanding subservience to the merchant community.

If the efforts aimed at economic independence and increased fortune sometimes ended in disappointment, this was due not to any lack of ambition but to a limited economic horizon and potency. Mechanics could not, of course, prevent the coming of a war, embargo, and panic. Nor did their experience afford them the knowledge necessary to operate a complex banking operation or to foresee all the consequences of strong governmental protection for manufacturing. Consequently, masters helped to create situations difficult, if not impossible, to control.

NOTES

1. Carl Bridenbaugh, *The Colonial Craftsmen* (New York, 1950), p. 165.

2. Joyce Appleby, "The Social Origins of American Revolutionary Ideology," *Journal of American History,* 64 (1978), 935-958.

3. James C. Travis, ed., "The Memoirs of Stephen Allen, 1767-1852; Sometimes Mayor of New York City, Chairman of the Croton Water Commission, etc." (New York, 1927), pp. 1-49 (Typescript at New York Historical Society).

4. Ibid., pp. 50-80.

5. Edmund P. Willis, "Social Origins and Political Leadership in New York City from the Revolution to 1815," Ph.D. diss. (Berkeley, 1967), Appendix.

6. Ibid., pp. 123, 130. They may be assumed to be masters as journeymen were seldom listed in *Longworth's New York Directory* by 1815.

7. New York City Jury Lists, 1819, Eighth Ward. Historical Documents Collection, Queens College, City University of New York.

8. *American Citizen,* June 7, 1804; *Public Advertiser,* June 7, 1804. See also Cash Book, James Ruthven, carver, 1792-1804, New York Historical Society; Record Book, Solomon Townsend Anchor Shop, 1795-1806, New York Historical Society; Account Book, James Akerly, Blacksmith, 1791-1801, New York Historical Society.

9. *Mercantile Advertiser,* November 19, 1801. Shillings were converted into dollars at the rate of one shilling—eight and one-half cents. The daily loss indicated in these figures was not an accurate indication of bakers' enterprises' profitability, as the holdings of breadmakers generally fell in a comfortable middle range with a few, such as Mercein, having considerable assets. Rather, the figure was intended to prove that bakers deserved better profits. But the scale of business is accurate. Willis, "Social Origins," pp. 129, 130, 346, 349.

10. Report, Committee of the Common Council, City Clerk Filed Papers (hereafter referred to as CC), Box 3080, August 15, 1805, New York City Municipal Archives; Account Book of James Stuart, June 24, 1790-October 29, 1808, Henry Du Pont Winterthur Museum Library, Wilmington, Delaware.

11. Rita Suswein Gottesman, *The Arts and Crafts in New York, 1800-1804,* New York Historical Society Collections, 1949 (New York, 1965), pp. 139-141, 116, 219, passim.

12. *Morning Chronicle,* August 31, 1805; see also *Evening Post,* July 21, 1802; for a copy of a stock certificate see John McComb mss., New York Historical Society.

13. Will Inventory of John Charters, April 29, 1825, C-87; Will Inventory of George Gosman, February 22, 1821, G-84; Will of Thomas Musgrove, November 8, 1827, Liber 61, p. 436; Will of Michael Varian, February 10, 1826, Liber 60, p. 124. Historical Documents Collection, Queens College, City University of New York. See also Nancy McClelland, *Duncan Phyfe and the English Regency, 1795-1830* (New York, 1939), p. 121, and advertisement directed at mechanics for lots in Manhattanville, *National Advocate,* January 9, 1813.

14. Gottesman, *Arts and Crafts in New York.* The newspaper count is for 1807. John Lambert, *Travels Through Canada and the United States, 1806-1808* (London, 1814), p. 78.

15. *American Citizen,* May 14, 1806, September 19, 1806.

16. *Evening Post,* February 16, 1809; *Public Advertiser,* November 14, 1812; Gottesman, *Arts and Crafts in New York,* pp. 211, 212, 310, 417, 415, 424, 432, 434.

17. *Morning Post,* May 31, 1811; *Evening Post,* September 16, 1809. See also advertisements of Garrit Sickles, shoemaker, *Morning Chronicle,* March 19, 1804; "Mrs. Carney's Shoe Manufacture," *Evening Post,* March 27, 1808; William Carver, blacksmith, ibid., November 1, 1808; and Gottesman, *Arts and Crafts in New York,* passim.

18. *Evening Post,* February 9, 1808.

19. *American Citizen,* May 10, 1809.

20. For other Huggins advertisements see *Evening Post,* December 24, 1807, June 4, 13, 18, 1808, February 6, 1809, October 5, 1809, August 31, 1811, March 23, 1812; *Morning Post,* January 16, 1812; *American Citizen,* September 30, 1809, February 21, 1809, April 25, 1809, July 6, 19, 24, 1810.

21. Report, Committee of the Common Council, CC Box 3080, August 15, 1805.

22. *Independent Mechanic,* April 4, 1812.

23. Ibid., September 9, 1817.

24. Ibid., December 28, 1811; see also *Evening Post,* February 1, 1808.

25. *Weekly Museum,* February 6, 1802; *Evening Post,* June 27, 1811, June 17, 25, 1817, June 26, 1819.

26. *Evening Post,* March 3, 1804; a number of mechanics opposed the establishment of a Federalist-dominated Merchants Bank in 1805. Bray Hammond, *Banks and Politics in America from the Revolution to the Civil War* (Princeton, 1957), pp. 149-161; *American Citizen,* January 21, 1801, March 16, 1804, February 8, 1805; *Morning Chronicle,* April 26, 1804.

27. Alfred F. Young, "The Mechanics and the Jeffersonians: New York, 1789-1801," *Labor History,* 5 (1964), 266.

28. *American Citizen,* April 8, 1805.

29. Matthew Davis to William P. Van Ness, February 13, 1810, William P. Van Ness mss., Misc. Reel, New York Historical Society.

30. *American Citizen,* March 2, 6, 8, 1810.

31. The only significant legislative opposition came from seven assemblymen from the western part of the state. *Evening Post,* March 23, 1810; the act of incorporation is printed in full in the *American Citizen,* May 5, 1810; Minutes of the General Society of Mechanics and Tradesmen, January 2, 1811; William Thompson Bonner, *New York, the World's Metropolis* (New York, 1924), p. 406.

32. Minutes of the General Society of Mechanics and Tradesmen, January 19, 1823.

33. Bonner, *New York, The World's Metropolis,* pp. 406-407; Travis, ed., "Memoirs of Stephen Allen," pp. 84-88.

34. Minutes of the General Society of Mechanics and Tradesmen, Deceber 13, 1810.

35. *Mercantile Advertiser,* March 26, 1811; Minutes of the General Society of Mechanics and Tradesmen, January 6, 1813. Prior to the sale of the stock, considerable tension also existed between the board of directors of the bank and the General Society over a loan to the society and the right of the society to vote on its bank shares when they were being held as collateral. Ibid., August 1, 1810.

36. *Evening Post,* April 6, 1818.

37. *National Advocate,* February 16, 1819; *Evening Post,* June 22, 1819, July 1, 1819; Victor S. Clark, *History of Manufactures in the United States,* 2 vols. (New York, 1949), vol. 1, p. 379.

38. *City Hall Recorder,* March 1817.

39. Ibid., November 1817.

40. Petition of Stephen Shepherd, CC Box 3173, November 6, 1805.

41. Petitions of John Dietz, CC Box 3181, December 8, 1817, and CC Box 3176, April 20, 1818.

42. Petition of Residents of Leonard Street, CC Box 3174, May 21, 1810; Petition of inhabitants of Eighth Ward, CC Box 3174, April 12, 1810; Petition of James Phillips of Sixth Ward, CC Box 3176, April 20, 1818. See also fire commissioner's report on cabinet makers' and carpenters' request to store lumber in the city, CC Box 3175, January 27, 1817; and the petitions of the hatters and dyers who wanted permission to discharge colored water into the street (granted), CC Box 3176, December 26, 1819 and CC Box 3176, February 15, 1819.

43. Albert A. Giesecke, *American Commercial Legislation Before 1789* (New York, 1940), p. 138; Curtis Nettels, *The Emergence of a National Economy, 1775-1815* (New York, 1962), pp. 69-70.

44. F. W. Taussig, *A Tariff History of the United States* (New York, 1892), p. 15; Clark, *History of Manufactures,* vol. 1, pp. 270, 288; Nettels, *Emergence of a National Economy,* pp. 109-111.

45. George Rogers Taylor, *The Transportation Revolution: 1815-1860* (New York, 1951), p. 360; Clark, *History of Manufactures,* vol. 1, pp. 271-272, 283; Taussig, *A Tariff History,* p. 17; Nettels, *Emergence of a National Economy,* pp. 319-320.

46. Minutes of the General Society of Mechanics and Tradesmen, January 28, 1799.

47. Walter Lowne and Matthew Clarke, eds., *American State Papers* (Washington, 1832), Finance, vol. 1, p. 694.

48. Rollo Silver, "The Printers' Lobby: Model 1802," in *Virginia Studies in Bibliography,* Frederic Bowens, ed. (1950-1951), vol. 3, pp. 207-210, 213-217.

49. Ibid., pp. 217-219.

50. Lowne and Clarke, eds., *American State Papers,* Commerce and Navigation, vol. 1, p. 509.

51. Ibid., Finance, vol. 2, pp. 80, 107, 257. While the actual petitions submitted in 1803 are not reprinted, these were the concerns mentioned in the report to the House. For printers see also Finance, vol. 3, p. 462.

52. Ibid., Finance, vol. 2, p. 528.

53. Ibid., Finance, vol. 1, pp. 694, 730.

54. Reply of Committee on Commerce and Manufacturing on the Memorial of the Tradesmen of New York and Other Cities, *American Citizen,* February 9, 1804; Joseph Dorfman, *The Economic Mind in American Civilization,* 2 vols. (New York, 1946), vol. 1, p. 323.

55. Lowne and Clarke, eds., *American State Papers,* Finance, vol. 2, pp. 107, 185.

56. The taxes are listed in *Columbian,* March 7, 1815; see also Clark, *History of Manufactures,* vol. 1, p. 274. For protest meetings and petitions see

Evening Post, December 30, 1813, April 20, 1814, April 8, 14, 21, 1815, October 4, 10, 14, 1815; *Columbian,* October 9, 1815, December 12, 1813; *National Advocate,* December 30, 1813. For political debate over this issue see Chapter 3.

57. Sidney Ratner, *The Tariff in American History* (New York, 1972), pp. 12-15; for relevant petitions for and against see Lowne and Clarke, eds., *American State Papers,* Finance, vol. 3, pp. 458, 460, 462, 463, 484, 518-522, 576, 530, 532, 533, 540, 543, 563, 577-578.

58. *Evening Post,* May 25, 1816, November 15, 1817, February 28, 1818, May 19, 1821, *National Advocate,* February 5, 1813.

Chapter 7

THE SPECTER OF
MONOPOLY

Despite the tendency to sometimes let their ambition guide them
into unknown and perilous paths, mechanics working in traditionally oriented professions were not unaware of the dangers that
lay at the ends of such journeys. Indeed, they were most conscious
of the inroads that the factory system had made into a number of
crafts in Great Britain through the creation of large monopolistic
enterprises, and they were determined to fight off any such institutions that might arise in their midst.[1] Like the campaigns for
greater access to credit and for tariff protection, the fight against
monopoly was part of a long-standing struggle by artisans for the
control of their trades free of mercantile interference and domination. And, in a traditional manner, it united both masters and
journeymen in a common marketplace endeavor. The masters,
fearing both bankruptcy and the fall to wage-earner status, led the
struggle; but they were often joined by the city's journeymen, who
believed that monopolies would totally eliminate upward mobility
while driving salaries to beneath a subsistence level. Whenever
such an enterprise began operation in New York, mechanics
quickly came together to oppose it. The problem, however, was
that the system of free enterprise, which many mechanics encour-

aged and profited from, also allowed for the pooling of resources necessary for the inception of factory-type operations.

The most interesting and enlightening example of the interconnection between mechanics' ambition and the entry of monopolistic institutions occurred in 1801 in the wake of a citywide work stoppage initiated by the city's bakers. The events leading to this radical step began in the 1790s with protests against price regulation.

As experienced proprietors of shops that required their extensive expertise as both producers and marketers, bakers were keenly concerned with making what they considered to be a fair profit. American breadmakers had battled city authorities over the assize, a method of profit control, since the seventeenth century. Under this practice, which dated to medieval England, the weight of a loaf costing one shilling was regulated in accord with the prevailing price of flour. When the cost of flour rose, the weight of the shilling loaf fell; and when the wholesale flour price declined, the weight of the loaf increased proportionally. Thus, the profit that a baker could make on a loaf, as determined by the Common Council, remained the same. Flour inspectors were authorized to seize underweight bread, fine offending bakers, and give the confiscated loaves to the almshouse.[2]

During the 1790s, with the bakers' "advance" (the price they could charge above the cost of flour) set at ten and then twelve and a half shillings per barrel of flour, a number of bakers sent petitions to the Common Council asking that either the assize be lowered (less weight to a shilling loaf) or that it not be raised despite public demand for such action. Other breadmakers, however, were not content with only an adjustment of the assize. Influenced by the burgeoning capitalist economy and freer economic attitudes of the early national period, they deemed it grossly unfair for their profession to be singled out for income limitation. Accordingly, they asked the Common Council to give up its regulatory powers over the bakers' profits.[3]

Responding to the breadmakers' demands, the council in 1800 appointed a committee to investigate the suitability of retaining the assize. After meeting with a committee of New York bakers, its members issued a report stating that in their opinion:

... perhaps the only Mode this Board can adopt to afford Relief to the Petitioners and the Citizens at large would be to regulate in future the weight of Bread only and not the Price, leaving that to the Bakers. This would create an emulation among the Bakers and would of course produce good Bread and in the Opinion of this Committee at a reasonable Price.[4]

Willing to experiment with free market "emulation," the council enacted its committee's proposal, fixing the weights of loaves at either one and a half or three pounds, but allowing the bakers to set their own prices. This was a momentous event for New York's bakers. After generations of regulation they were at last free to enter the marketplace unhindered by the bonds of government authority.

Judging by the absence of complaints to the Common Council or to the daily newspapers, the New York community accepted the removal of profit controls. However, in the fall of 1801 after the new system had been in effect for about a year, the price of flour dropped sharply while the cost of bread remained the same. Soon strong protests found their way to the mayor and the council. An editorial in the *American Citizen* claimed that the price of bread in New York surpassed that in England despite the lower wholesale cost of American flour; the reason: lack of regulation. Using the bakers partly as a scapegoat to attack the Federalist-controlled city government, the *Citizen* asserted that the bakers had "frequently been enriched by the negligence of the common council" under Mayor Richard Varick's leadership. In an address directed toward incoming Mayor Edward Livingston, "Parentis Familiarum" wondered if it was not "extraordinary" that "in a country so famed for plenty, ... prices remained as high as those in famine-stricken parts of the world." [5]

The bakers were quick to defend themselves. Because they had laid in their stock of flour well in advance of the drop in wholesale price, they explained, breadmakers were still using expensive flour and could not afford to lower their prices. However, the Society of Bakers had met and determined to reduce charges once the old flour was exhausted. The bakers were not out to exploit the public. There was no just cause for reimposing the assize.[6]

This response, in turn, was immediately answered by "Common

Sense," a self-appointed spokesman for the public interest. Supervision was required because of "necessity, the parent of all law." Since bread constituted the "principle [sic] part of our food," and since most consumers did not have the time to seek out cheaper loaves, open rivalry among breadmakers would not produce a fair market price. If a few men were to monopolize the trade, "the depravity of human nature," following the maxim "get as much as you can," would see them drive prices up—to the ruin of the community. The message was clear: the bakers were using their position as the producer of a vital provision to abuse the citizens of New York.

Bowing to pressure "for a prompt and effectual remedy," the Common Council, whose members were up for election the next month, voted in late October 1801 to reinstitute the assize. The new law allowed the bakers a fourteen shilling advance over the price of a barrel of flour, or a shilling and a half more than the old 1800 rate.[7] Angry at this rebuke to their pride as honorable citizens, to their right to free enterprise, and to their profits, the bakers met secretly and executed a citywide work stoppage on November 3. This action—one of the most decisive steps taken in New York City by a group of tradesmen during the first two decades of the nineteenth century—excited "general alarm" and provoked reactions both immediate and strong.

A frightened New York citizenry, deprived of their main source of nutriment, were outraged at the bakers' action. They were also trapped, however, since they had no other means of procuring bread. Thus, responding to the power of the breadmakers' unity, the Common Council promised the discontented tradesmen quick relief. Thereupon, the Society of Bakers announced that, "intimations" having been given that bread producers would receive "ample satisfaction," the breadmakers would once again "cheerfully supply their customers." [8] True to its word, the council, which had already set up a committee of investigation a day before the strike, in two weeks altered the assize to give the bakers a twenty-eight-shilling advance above the wholesale price of flour—a raise of 100 percent! [9]

The public's indignation found expression in wrathful press criticisms that denounced the bakers' avarice and emphasized the need for regulation. Writing in the *Commercial Advertiser,* "A

Grocer" castigated the breadmakers for not giving the community any notice of their intended strike. "The citizens," he declared, "need not have been put to such extreme difficulty and inconvenience." Consequently, the bakers now deserved "every detriment possible" from those grocers who retailed their bread. One possible response was for the grocers to cease vending the goods of the deceptive tradesmen. Another spokesman proclaimed that the strike was sufficient proof that the "experiment" of nonregulation was a failure. Unless they were under the supervision of society, the bakers would abuse their "privileges"; taken over by "*self-interest* . . . they would accommodate themselves before *they accommodated* the poor." [10]

The bakers defended themselves as persecuted workingmen trying to eke out a decent living. Three prominent New York bakers, Christian Nestell, George Arcularius, and Jacob Beekman, hoping both to "correct" the notion that many New Yorkers had about the bakers' "enormous profits" and to "exculpate" themselves from the charges of "cheating the poor," published an affidavit sworn before no less a notary than Mayor Livingston. Detailing their expenses, they asserted that under the previous assize a baker who processed two barrels of flour a day (192 loaves) ended up losing nearly a dollar a day.[11]

"A Poor Baker," a second champion of the breadmakers, scorned the assertions that bakers were reaping excessive profits and abusing the poor. Such reasoning, he asserted, was but an example of the abuse of hardworking tradesmen at the hands of the educated elite. The leaders of society who attacked the integrity of the bakers knew little of the tradesmen's real nature:

> You may think it a trifle to treat bakers in this way—and so will many a rich noble. The bakers are neither nabobs nor rajahs—but are generally decent and orderly citizens. Virtue is not exclusively the boast of rich men; nor is moral honesty confined to the higher classes.

Like other mechanics, the city's bread producers were honorable men who condemned monopoly and unlawful combinations. (Nor could they speculate even if they so desired, since it was impossible to store bread.) But, if despite all protest regulation was to be

A bakery shop (above) and baker's wagon in delivery of loaves (below). Bakery: Courtesy Century House, Watkins Glen, New York. Delivery Scene: Museum of the City of New York.

forced upon the bakers, then they should at least have a say in its calculation. Rather than allowing merchant and attorney councilmen, who knew little of the flour-processing operation, to make these decisions, bakers should have a role in a process so vital to their livelihoods.[12]

In understanding "Poor Baker's" argument, it is important to note that, though their work stoppage hurt the poor the most, the bakers' offensive was directed against the elite classes. For it was these men who sat on the Common Council and so held the means to thwart the breadmakers' ambitions. What so stung the bakers was that they believed that the affluent wished to inhibit them from becoming anything other than subsistence tradesmen.

The arguments and protests of the bakers reflect their position as entrepreneurs anxious to reap the profits of the free market. Their situation and position shifted very quickly, however, when they realized that the path of unimpeded financial opportunity posed even greater danger than the assize.

On the day of the bakers' strike a number of the city's "wealthy citizens," angered at "an inconvenience so serious, and so unexpected," assembled at the Tontine Coffee House. Philanthropically concerned about "guarding against the inconvenience" of dependency on the local bakers for the city's supply of bread, and more than likely also interested in taking advantage of a profitable situation, they determined to form the New York Bread Company.[13]

Organized as a joint-stock enterprise under the guidance of John B. Church, brother-in-law of Alexander Hamilton, this company was to be so large-scale a producer of bread that the city would be guaranteed an adequate supply regardless of the whims of the bakers. The first six hundred shares of stock, at fifty dollars each, were quickly sold, and another six hundred were put up for sale. A board of directors, composed of nine of the city's most prominent merchants, was elected and a superintendent hired.[14]

Advertisements soon appeared soliciting bakers to work either on contract or else "for labor only" (materials to be supplied by the company). Other ads told prospective customers that in a helpful innovation, the company was issuing colored checks to its patrons which they could exchange for either one, two, or three loaves. Clients would present the checks to carriers and then be billed at a later date. Finally, the directors notified the citizenry that in order "to merit public confidence" particular care was being taken in both the selection of workmen and the construction of bakehouses. The Bread Company went into daily production on February 4, 1802, three months after the work stoppage.[15]

With the appearance of the Bread Company, the bakers' position shifted markedly. Suddenly the bakers rather than the public were in dire fear of monopoly. Ceasing their advocacy of free enterprise, the bakers' spokesmen now forecast, in an anguished if unsophisticated manner, the menacing consequences of monopoly capitalism. Moreover, they proposed that the state legislature intervene in their favor and not grant the company a charter.[16] Proponents of the Bread Company, incorporating the bakers' earlier arguments, argued for the right of this new firm to compete with everyone else in the marketplace. Soon the public prints were filled with debate over the place of factory-type enterprises in America.

A number of articles detailed the deleterious effects that the Bread Company would have on both bakers and consumers. "Investigator" suggested a number of serious concerns. He reasoned that it was possible that a few individuals, in pursuing legitimate and honest personal ends, might bring grief to many decent citizens; such was the case with the New York Bread Company. Although this operation might well become a "lucrative concern," and in so doing supply New Yorkers with cheaper bread, it would also mean the ruin of "a class of men who perhaps were as virtuous as the generality of mankind." Because of the new company, bakers would soon have to either abandon their profession or else "take refuge" in other cities and towns—a fate befitting only those "committing terrible sins." The backers of the Bread Company, despite their benevolent intentions in securing for the city its food supply, would be well advised to redirect their efforts to better causes. A good start would be an inquiry into how "to extract salt from the sea." [17]

Two other spokesmen directed their attention to the plight of consumers. Baker Jonas Humbert asserted that large breadmaking establishments were invariably filthier than small bakeries. "An Observer" argued that speculative concerns posed a grave danger to shoppers. The peril lay, not in manufacturing per se, but in monopolies that were "injurious to the country." The New York Bread Company, unfortunately, was such an establishment. This firm would first undersell all independent bakers, forcing them out of business within a few years. Then, with the market cornered, did the citizens of New York really expect that the company would "continue . . . [to] supply the public with a cheaper rate?" [18]

The threat of monopoly raised by the Bread Company was frightening not only to the bakers but also to many other small-scale mechanic entrepreneurs. These craftsmen were aware that opportunity in the shoemaking, construction, tailoring, printing, and cabinetmaking trades was declining. Aspiring journeymen were being forced into the position of permanent, poorly paid wage earners. Could the same process not engulf the masters as well? Might not the merchant backers of the Bread Company also reduce tanners, butchers, and bookbinders to wage slaves, forced to adhere to an unwanted factory discipline and unable to enjoy the fraternal and social pleasures of economic independence? Would not the pride and dignity of craftsmanship, the noble legacy of the artisan, be extinguished as craftsmen performed laborious, simple, tedious operations? The Bread Company posed a serious threat to the traditional mechanic crafts. [19]

Aware of the danger, a general meeting of mechanics was called for December 8, 1801, in the midst of the Bread Company's recruitment of men and customers. The three hundred tradesmen in attendance passed a number of strongly worded resolutions. The first recommended that the "free and independent mechanics" consider the propriety of "uniting in ONE GREAT ASSOCIATION" which would act to maintain their rights. A second declared that mechanics and tradesmen would not "countenance" the interference of any monopolizers or speculators in the mechanic professions. Because such a course would be "fatal to every description of tradesmen," they would neither employ nor be employed by such men. Lastly, the workers voted to form a committee of three mechanics from each ward to lobby in Albany against monopolistic establishments. [20]

A few days later "Mechanicus" added a suggestion that all tradesmen in the city contribute three cents per day to aid those forced out of work because of their refusal to support "moneyed men of wealth" in their ill-begotten schemes. [21]

Grocers, despite any resentment they still felt toward the bakers because of the work stoppage, were of the same social stratum as mechanics, and were small-scale entrepreneurs themselves. Consequently, they shared the breadmakers' concern over monopolies. Holding a joint meeting, they concluded that they would maintain a baker's dozen at thirteen loaves despite the Bread Company's offer to raise it to fourteen—a figure the local bakers could not match. In a statement of thanks, the Society of Bakers praised the retailers for their decision not to "deprive the bakers a living by a calling they have learned and followed from their infancy." [22]

The climax to the public debate came in two remarkable articles that appeared in the *American Citizen* and the *Gazette and General Advertiser*. The unsigned message in the *Citizen* could easily have been published in a socialist tract during the travails of late-nineteenth-century industrialism. Warning that "monied capitalists" were attempting to invade tradesmen's operations with "combination and monopoly," this radical spokesman cautioned that the time was fast approaching for "mechanics to be united; to be ONE—or a degrading vassalage will reduce the greater part of them to the vile ambition and avarice of *monopolists.*" For the mechanic community to look with "cold indifference" upon the bakers' plight would be a foolish and costly mistake, for the breadmakers represented but "one link of that chain that denominates all MECHANICS." Invoking arguments similar to those used against the bakers' "depravity," he described the profound changes undergone by men gaining large monetary holdings. First, "covetousness" entered their breasts. Then, hoping to amass even greater riches, the opulent proceeded to deceive workingmen with the notion that, because they encouraged trade, monopolistic institutions were in the best interests of the country. This, of course, was a specious form of reasoning, designed to "delude . . . or silence mechanics." For proof of the capitalists' cupidity, artisans needed only to look to Europe where they could see a "picture of wretchedness" created by the monopolistic power of the affluent. The monopolists were attempting to introduce "ignorance and barbarism to America." What could not be achieved in open hostilities against workingmen was now being attempted "through the influence of great capitalists." Indifferent to political allegiance, these men were disdainful of "the common class, as *they* are *pleased* to call them, who are not included among respectable citizens." Were their schemes to succeed, republican government and the *Rights of Man* would soon become the "laughingstock" of European courts. Indeed, America had much more to fear from such a group than from a foreign enemy. Consequently, along with their interest in self-preservation, it was the patriotic duty of mechanics to unite and fight, with every means at their disposal, the entrance of "monied capitalists" in America.[23]

"A Mechanic," the second incisive analyst of the implications that monopolistic institutions held for workingmen, gave more details about the inner operations of a firm such as the Bread Company. He asserted that the elite merchants on its board of directors were not really concerned with the "distress of the poor," but instead intended to "monopolize by degrees all profitable mechanical branches." The wealthy capitalists had all the advantages. First, unlike the small-scale mechanic entrepreneur, who had a family to feed and rent to pay, they were able to make a profit on a return of only 9 or 10 percent of their capital. Second, if necessary to defeat "a few obstinate mechanics" who were "unwilling to become servants," the capitalists could easily forgo a few years' interest and would even absorb a loss. Third, to undersell the local tradesmen, they could afford to purchase large quantities of materials at low cost. Then, having ruined the businesses of these artisans, they would hire hundreds of masons, cartmen, carpenters, and other mechanics at miserly salaries—reserving for themselves the extra profits. And, since it was the "nature of mankind to be always adding to what they have," the monopolists would continue to squeeze craftsmen in every way:

> . . . they will screw down the wages to the last thread; next the independent spirit, so distinguished at present in our mechanics, and so useful in republics, will be entirely annihilated. The workmen will be servants and slaves, and their votes must always be at the command of their masters.

Thus, the pride of tradesmen, which in the early national period was thought to hinge on economic independence, and which had been "so galling" to the stockholders of the Bread Company, would be finally and completely extinguished. Unless, that is, mechanics "of every description" united against the chartering of this evil institution.[24]

Responding to this barrage of criticism, the defenders of the Bread Company upheld the propriety and worth of the firm. Communications to the *Commercial Advertiser* argued that the bakers had forfeited their privileges in the community through "callous disregard" of the public. By ceasing to bake "without giving one day's notice to the Inhabitants," they had left the population without means of securing its most vital staple. This, however, would not happen again. Not only had the local residents now learned how to manage without the bakers, but the Bread Company now functioned to assure them of "a certain supply of good bread ... at a reasonable price." The company had no desire to make itself an object of speculation, but only "to come forward as fair competition with the bakers for custom." If the company was able to sell more loaves at both a higher quality and a lower cost, then the company "deserves and will command a preference." [25]

The most telling and farsighted apology for the Bread Company was put forward by "A Bread Eater" in two cogent essays in the *Mercantile Advertiser*. Dismissing the idea that governmental regulation was an effective measure in securing good low-cost bread, he compared the public demand for supervision to "feeble infants" crying for protection from their "Civil Parent." "No mechanic," he asserted, "should be restricted in his profits by any power—it is fundamentally contrary to every principle of Justice, and it strikes at the root of industry." On the other hand, it was true that the bakers, by uniting in a common deceptive interest, had defrauded the populace. The way to break this unfortunate "chain of union" was through competition, not regulation. With the Bread Company in operation, this was accomplished. The bakers' "narrow policy, in wishing to make money too rapidly," would be defeated by the old economic law that "trade will regulate itself."

"Bread Eater" also explained that society really had little to fear from the New York Bread Company. The workings of the free market would protect the public from any evil practices that the company might try to implement. Should it, for example, attempt to charge inflated prices, its rivals would soon take its business away. If necessary, a 20 percent limit could be placed on the profits of the firm, with the rest going to the community as taxes. But that was hardly the real danger. It was far more important that the Bread Company be encouraged to compete with the organized bakers. This would insure New Yorkers of good bread at the lowest possible prices.[26]

In the end, what had begun as an attempt by the bakers to free themselves from corporate regulation culminated in a full-scale analysis of the operations of monopolies, a test of the validity of laissez-faire in practice, and a challenge by and to the power of aspiring large-scale capitalists. An assault on eighteenth-century mercantilism had turned into a shrill and prophetic debate on the ultimate threat or benefits of free market capitalism. The problem for the bakers was that while they dismissed as negligible the threat to the community posed by their actions, the public did not. In depriving many faithful customers of a staple that they saw as a necessity for survival, the breadmakers had significantly lessened the populace's opposition to a large-scale manufactory of bread.

Had the bakers not asked for unrestricted competition? If so, what laws stated that only small operations were to be permitted, and only single proprietors allowed? Did the local bakers have a right to a monopoly? They did not, of course. But neither in the world of free enterprise did they have the resources to compete with large-scale factory operations. And with the availability of cheap labor, there was little that the mechanics could do to stop such firms. English experience and the anguished appeals of a few spokesmen notwithstanding, the different mechanic trades were not effectively united to prevent the establishment of large joint-stock enterprises.

While the bakers and mechanics were not able to stop the Bread Company, providence found a way. The company's huge main building was destroyed on May 23, 1803, by a spectacular fire that killed two men and injured many others. There was no contemporary suggestion of arson. A witness to that event noted, however, that "the general interest felt in the success of this enterprise caused great excitement when it was known the building was on fire and strenuous efforts were made to save it." The blaze was ultimately attributed to embers left burning in an oven. Evidently unable to recoup its losses, the company was put up for sale a year later, and its stockholders were paid off from the proceeds of the transaction.[27]

With the demise of the New York Bread Company, the bakers resumed their campaign against profit regulation. A breadmaker's entrepreneurial ambition was still a stronger factor in the early nineteenth century than his fear of monopolistic corporations. Although no further incidents of unified defiance are known, individual acts of resistance continued. Outspoken baker Jonas Humbert publicly announced in 1814 that he was no longer going to abide by the assize. He asserted that though it was against his personal creed to defy public authority, he held an even stronger belief that a mechanic, along with other members of society, had a right to judge for himself what a sufficient profit was. It was "arbitrary in the highest degree" for the law to compel a tradesman to sell his goods for less than his customers were willing to pay. "Hopefully," he concluded, "the honorable corporation of New York will not be the means of reducing a laboring mechanic and his wife and children to beggary." His faith was soon shattered when the flour inspector ordered his loaves confiscated for being underweight and then levied a heavy fine when Humbert failed to release the bread to the almshouse. Another defiant baker, Thomas Graham, whose loaves were also seized as underweight, had not even allowed the flour inspector to leave the assize at his bakery. He too refused to give his bread away as charity and was fined accordingly.[28]

In addition to these acts, petitions for repeal of the assize continued on the agenda of the Common Council. The basic argument remained the same: bakers had a right "to be placed on the same ground with other mechanics who make their goods to suit their customers both as to quality and prices." In seeking to make an honest profit, the city's breadmakers were being "trammeled by corporation law . . . exclusively so from any other set of mechanics." [29]

By 1813 the bakers had ceased to be defensive about their responsibilities to the poor. Spokesman Humbert reasoned:

> . . . if a poor man will not purchase inferior bread, and will have the finest, why should the baker be compelled to labor and toil for this man more than the butcher, of whom *he will* purchase the best piece of *beef, paying* the highest price for it.[30]

That beef, unlike bread, was not a poor man's staple was irrelevant to Humbert. His point was that it was a great hardship for the breadmakers—merely for the sake of the less fortunate—to be unable to sell their products "free from corporate law, *as to profit.*" As a number of bakers explained in another petition, the poor were not obligated to purchase bread. They could make their own if they could not afford those loaves offered at public sale. It was unfair to ask the city's bread producers to support the indigent when they themselves were struggling to maintain their own families.[31]

While arguments were also made that the removal of regulations would improve the quality of bread, the brunt of the bakers' statements were against the principle of profit control.[32] The Common Council, while it raised the bakers' allowance during wartime inflation in 1814 to thirty-two shillings per barrel (and lowered it to twenty-four shillings during the panic of 1819), did not discontinue the assize until 1821. In December of that year, a majority of the aldermen, finally won over both by the bakers' arguments and a dawning awareness of a new economic era, voted to remove all price controls while maintaining standard weights for loaves.[33]

The assize, victim of the growing spirit of free enterprise, became a relic of early urban history. Yet the aspiring baker, the greatest foe of profit control, had won but a pyrrhic victory. Because his sense of foreboding over factory-type institutions such as the New York Bread Company was not equal to his aspirations, he contributed to the economic climate that would open the way for similar firms and that would, in large part, put an end to small-scale baking enterprises. It is not that the breadmakers were not concerned, but unless the threat was immediate, their entrepreneurial ambition was the stronger motivation.

A second dramatic encounter that revealed tradesmen's fear of monopolistic factory operations, but which was not tempered by ambition, took place in 1803 over the well-intentioned philanthropic proposal of Mayor Edward Livingston. On New Year's Day of that year, the mayor presented the General Society of Mechanics and Tradesmen with a letter calling on the society to join with the city government in the creation of public workshops that would allow the poor and disadvantaged to learn mechanic trades such as shoemaking and hatmaking. He also suggested that carpenters, masons, and other tradesmen hire poor and unskilled laborers as assistants. In this way work could be given to new immigrants; to those suffering from illness and physical handicaps; and to widows, orphans, and discharged convicts. Livingston intended his plan to reduce mendacity and unemployment, rehabilitate prisoners, and restore dependent individuals to self-reliance. The workshops were to be built by mechanics with a loan from the city. Once in operation, its employees would learn artisan skills while receiving a wage set a certain percentage lower than that earned by fully trained mechanics.[34]

Alarmed, the Mechanics Society responded to the Livingston proposal with great dismay. There was little hope, it explained, of persuading artisans to support a plan that ran "contrary to their interests" by creating a public monopoly that would undersell craftsmen. It was dangerous, indeed, to tamper with the natural workings of the marketplace; the poor would find work when and if the economy allowed. Moreover, such an institution would "check the spirit of industry," for no potential tradesman would wish to serve an apprenticeship if he need only go to jail to be trained in a profession. Finally, the workshop would seriously degrade mechanics' stature by putting them in competition with men "convicted of every violation of the law of the land."[35]

Despite the Mechanic Society's disapproval, the mayor, backed by the inspectors of the state prison,[36] proceeded with his plan, publishing it in the city's major newspapers. "Cornplanter," a writer in the *Mercantile Advertiser*, approved of its merits, declaring that civilized nations, and particularly prosperous countries like the United States, ought to be able to eliminate the evils of poverty and unemployment. By giving work to the unfortunate, the wealth of the nation would increase as these people added to the bounty.[37]

Because of the strong antagonism expressed by a united mechanic constituency, the Common Council tabled the mayor's proposal. Undaunted, Livingston, together with eighty-five prominent citizens, presented the plan to the state legislature, thus continuing the controversy.[38] Artisan spokesman, "Q," asserted that it was not incumbent upon the public to countenance the "idle and dissolute" by giving them special advantages, opportunities that would only encourage wanton behavior. Moreover, those without means of support could always "cultivate the earth." This was a far better solution than associating New York's mechanics, who were "in no country more distinguished than in this city," with the lowest echelons of society.[39]

Most importantly, mechanics argued in Albany over the danger of "monopolising concerns." A project like the workshop threatened the economic welfare of tradesmen as well as their place in the "social compact." Consequently, the philanthropic motives of some of the proposal's backers were suspect. These individuals intended to destroy the "independence in the people" that was the "GLORY of our country" by bringing the laboring part of the community "to the same depressed condition which we find in some states of Europe." [40]

Only a year after they had gathered to protest the formation of the New York Bread Company, mechanics reassembled in even larger numbers to listen to impassioned speeches on the evils of the factory system and the true meaning of the workshop proposal.[41] Soon, as we have seen, the issue became a political football between the Republicans and the Federalists, each party accusing the other of responsibility for the plan.[42] In the absence of any real political power or organization on the part of the poor, handicapped, and alien, particularly in contrast to the potent mechanic constituency, the proposal's defeat in Albany was inevitable.[43] A government-initiated enterprise was more vulnerable to public pressure than a private institution such as the Bread Company.

A third instance of mechanic concern over monopolistic manufactories took place during the embargo in 1809. The New York Phoenix Insurance Company, a chartered institution with $500,-000 in capital stock, unable to sell marine insurance because of the cessation of shipping, petitioned the state legislature to allow it to put its resources into the manufacture of cotton and hemp. This move immediately occasioned "no inconsiderable alarm amongst the respectable mechanics" of the city, who yet retained a "lively recollection" of Livingston's workshop and the Bread Company. The *Public Advertiser* reported that craftsmen feared competing with a "monied institution so rich and therefore so powerful as the Phoenix Company" because such a body could "*monopolise* the raw materials" and reduce the prices of "mechanical labor." [44]

One artisan directly affected by the Phoenix Company's petition, "Ropemaker," expressed his concern. Reasoning that the institution would not invest its capital in areas in which it stood little chance of competing with other, more experienced manufacturers, such as cotton production, he declared that the "sole object" of the company was "the monopoly of hemp . . . to the ruin of our ropemakers." Surely, if the legislature saw fit to grant the memorial, "the only ropemaker in this city will in a short time be the New York Phoenix Company." Once again a monopoly threatened the ruin of an entire mechanic branch.[45]

In defense, "Mechanic" replied that the company had been founded in part by mechanics, who still constituted a "considerable proportion" of the 360 shareholders. Moreover, rather than impoverishing artisans, the Phoenix Company was interested in the welfare of the country. It had been originally launched in order to compete with the foreign-based London Phoenix Insurance Company. Now, when deprived of the use of its capital because of the "oppressive edicts of European powers," the company intended to put its resources into domestic manufacture "to the general benefit of the country, as well as for the interest of the institution." Through "a proper application of machinery and the employment of a small portion of manual labor," cotton and other materials could be produced to rival England, thus strengthening the economic position of the United States in regard to her rival.[46]

It is interesting to note that in this controversy mechanics were arguing for government intervention against the Phoenix Company. Six years earlier, during the workshop controversy, they demanded that the government stay out of the market, while the year before that they had asked for interference against the Bread Company. Similarly, although the breadmakers argued against profit control, when allowed to set their own rates, masters were not adverse to implementing craftwide prices. The printers did so in 1795 under a binding agreement, as did the bookbinders in the early 1800s. Masons, carpenters, and cabinetmakers also established tradewide charges, which they published for the public. Craftsmen were not, of course, ideologues. Their consistency lay in their intention of protecting their professions. This included common actions to prevent the creation or continuance of monopolistic enterprises, as well as semimonopolistic steps to prevent cutthroat competition.[47]

While no other incidents of large-scale enterprises arousing serious mechanic concern are known, the fear of monopoly continued throughout the Jeffersonian era. It was generally expressed in charges, often by mechanic consumers, that other tradesmen, particularly cartmen and butchers, were hoarding goods and forcing up the prices of food and fuel.[48] This was particularly true during times of hardship such as harsh winters, the embargo, and the War of 1812. Indeed, a vigilant alert for monopolistic practices that threatened artisans' well-being, either as producing craftsmen or as consumers, continued throughout the period.

NOTES

1. For a detailed discussion of this question, see *American Citizen,* August 6, 1808. The greater portion of this chapter appeared in slightly different format as Howard B. Rock, "The Perils of Laissez-Faire: The Aftermath of the New York Bakers' Strike of 1801," *Labor History,* 17 (1976), 372-387.

2. Richard B. Morris, *Government and Labor in Early America* (New York, 1946), 161-166. See also Sidney I. Pomerantz, *New York: An American City, 1783-1803* (New York, 1938), p. 170, and William G. Panschar, *Baking in America,* 2 vols. (Evanston, 1956), vol. 1, p. 22. The price of a loaf was determined by dividing the number of ounces (4,032) in a barrel of flour by the number of shillings that the baker paid for the barrel plus the advance that he was allowed. For example, in 1803 when the advance was 28 shillings, if a barrel had cost 72 shillings, the total of the two, 100 shillings, would be divided into 4,032, resulting in a weight allotment of 40.32 ounces for a shilling loaf. *Laws and Ordinances Ordained and Established by the Mayor, Alderman, and Commonality of the City of New York,* (New York, 1803), p. 17. For the nature of bakers' enterprises, see Chapter 7, pp. 155-157.

3. Petition of Bakers, City Clerk Filed Papers (hereafter referred to as CC), Box 6414, January 20, 1789, November 4, 1792, June 22, 1793, April 7, 1795, New York City Muncipal Archives; *Minutes of the Common Council of the City of New York, 1784-1831,* 21 vols. (New York, 1917-1930), vol. 2, p. 141 (April 20, 1795).

4. Report of Committee on the Petition of the Bakers, *Minutes of the Common Council,* vol. 1, pp. 643, 645 (July 14, 28, 1800).

5. *American Citizen,* October 23, 24, 1801.

6. Ibid., October 27, 1801.

7. *Mercantile Advertiser,* October 23, 1801; *Minutes of the Common Council,* vol. 3, p. 49 (October 26, 1801).

8. *Mercantile Advertiser,* November 4, 1801.

9. *Minutes of the Common Council,* vol. 3, pp. 181-184 (November 18, 1801); the council divided eight to five in favor of the raise.

10. *Commercial Advertiser,* November 3, 1801, November 12, 1801.

11. *Mercantile Advertiser,* November 19, 1801. For details, see breakdown above, p. 156.

12. *American Citizen,* November 9, 1801; see also November 24, 1801.

13. *Gazette and General Advertiser,* November 4, 1801; *Mercantile Advertiser,* November 4, 1801.

14. *American Citizen,* December 4, 1801; *Mercantile Advertiser,* November 9, 1801; Pomerantz, *New York: An American City,* p. 172. The directors included Henry Rutgers, Jonathan H. Lawrence, David Dickson (auctioneer), William Bayard, John B. Church, David Grim, Gordon S. Mumford (former congressional candidate), and Walter Bowne.

15. *Gazette and General Advertiser,* January 19, 1802, February 2, 1802. The liberal extension of credit was made possible by the company's capital resources. Local bakers without such assets could not afford to extend credit so freely.

16. No charter was in fact ever presented to the state legislature.

17. *American Citizen,* January 19, 1802.

18. Ibid., November 27, 1801; *Evening Post,* January 12, 1802.

19. See Chapter 9.

20. *American Citizen,* December 14, 1801.

21. Ibid., December 10, 1801.

22. Ibid., November 28, 1801.

23. Ibid., December 14, 1801.

24. *Gazette and General Advertiser,* November 24, 1801.

25. *Commercial Advertiser,* November 12, 13, 1801.

26. *Mercantile Advertiser,* November 17, 18, 1801.

27. Augustine E. Costello, *Our Firemen: A History of the New York Fire Departments* (New York, 1887), pp. 206-207; *Evening Post,* May 23, 1803, May 2, 1804, May 31, 1805; *American Citizen,* April 5, 1804, December 3, 1804. Previous to the fire, the company had regularly paid quarterly dividends to its stockholders.

28. *Columbian,* April 7, 1814; Report of Flour Inspector William Summers, CC Box 3181, January 9, 1815, September 15, 1815; Petition of Thomas Graham, CC Box 3175, October 23, 1815.

29. *American Citizen,* April 11, 1806.

30. Petition of Jonas Humbert, CC Box 3181, November 22, 1813.

31. Petition of Bakers of New York City, CC Box 3180, December 23, 1811.

32. It is interesting to compare the bakers' arguments in the seven-

teenth and eighteenth centuries with those offered in the early nineteenth. Mary Roys Baker found eight separate complaints: that the English rates were used and English flour was heavier than American flour; that measuring was conducted inequitably; that delays occurred in adjusting the assize when wholesale prices rose; that the assize was insufficient to afford a reasonable living; that "wheaten bread" could not be produced at the current rates; that "White Bisket" could not be made at the same rate as the "penny loafe" as required by law; that some of the supervisors, and those in charge of setting the assize, were unacquainted with the profession, commonly setting irregular and arbitrary weights, thus making the bakers' livelihood insecure and *"often* threatening them with a bad name"; and that "most other Trades and Callings but the Bakers are not Confined but have full Liberty to ask what they please for their Labour." Mary Roys Baker, "Anglo-Massachusetts Trade Roots, 1130-1790," *Labor History,* 14 (1973), pp. 374-377. The majority of these complaints have to do with distress over the adjustment of the assize. Only two references are given for complaints against the principle of regulation compared with over fifty citations concerning the other protests. In sharp contrast, the nineteenth century was seeing a strong resentment among bakers over restraints on their income.

33. Report of the Committee of Inspectors of Loaf-Bread, CC Box 3080, July 22, 1805; *Laws and Ordinances* (1817), p. 55, and Amendment, October 25, 1819; Report of Council Committee, CC Box 3176, March 28, 1814; *Commercial Advertiser,* December 13, 31, 1821. In 1824 Jonas Humbert, the most outspoken foe of regulation, together with a number of other bakers, petitioned the Common Council to reinstate the assize at 28 shillings (the 1801 level). It may be that at least some of the bakers quickly became disenchanted with open competition and wished for a return to the security of price controls. *Minutes of the Common Council,* vol. 14, pp. 57-58 (September 13, 1824).

34. *American Citizen,* February 12, 1803.

35. Ibid.

36. Raymond A. Mohl, *Poverty in New York, 1785-1825* (New York, 1971), p. 230.

37. *Mercantile Advertiser,* February 25, 1803; Mohl, *Poverty in New York,* p. 230.

38. *Evening Post,* March 10, 1803.

39. Ibid., March 10, 25, 1803.

40. *American Citizen,* March 25, 1803; *Morning Chronicle,* March 21, 1803.

41. See pp. 66-68.

42. See pp. 65-68.

43. An assembly committee of the state legislature, while reporting

favorably on the plan, put off consideration until the next session because of the proposal's "novel nature." Needless to say, it was never reconsidered. Mohl, *Poverty in New York*, p. 231.

44. *American Citizen*, February 1, 1809.

45. Ibid., February 4, 1809.

46. *Public Advertiser*, February 4, 1809.

47. Charlotte Morgan, "The Origin and History of the New York Employing Printers Organizations," in *Columbia University Studies in History, Economics and Public Law* (1930), p. 28; and see pp. 248-250, 271.

48. See Chapter 8.

Chapter 8

THE DILEMMAS OF THE LICENSED TRADESMEN

While most mechanics working in New York in the early nineteenth century were free to enter the marketplace on their own, two traditional mechanic branches, butchers and cartmen, constituting over one-eighth of the mechanic population,[1] were required (along with porters and hackney coachmen) to obtain licenses before commencing business. The goals of these tradesmen were similar to those of the other masters: to establish economic independence, to gain financial security or more for their family, and to raise or at least secure their social stature. Because of their complex relationships to their licensors, the mayor and the Common Council, the paths of these craftsmen toward the fulfillment of these ambitions were replete with encounters with authority.

Butchers operated out of stalls in one of the city's public markets. In the lower part of the city these included in 1801 the large Fly Market in the First Ward on the East River at the foot of Maiden Lane. Nearby was the smaller Exchange Market on Broad Street. In the Third Ward on the Hudson River between Vesey and Partition streets stood the Bear Market. Also in the Third Ward, but not located near a dock, was the Oswego Market, convenient for farmers bringing in their goods overland. Further

FLY MARKET,
from the cor. Front St. and Maiden Lane, N. Y. 1816
Drawn by J. Evers.

The Fly Market, the city's largest market, located in the Second Ward near the East River docks (1816). Notice female hucksters selling fruit and vegetables outside the market. Museum of the City of New York.

out, the Catherine Market, on the East River in the Seventh Ward and the Spring Street Market in the Eighth Ward, served residents in the remoter areas of the metropolis.[2]

Butchers' enterprises within these markets could entail considerable capital. Aside from any cost in securing his location, a meat handler had to pay his journeyman, maintain his apprentice, settle market fees, and secure enough cash to purchase his hogs, sheep, and cattle at wholesale prices from the country drovers. If, however, he was fortunate enough to obtain a prime market stall, his earnings could put him among the wealthier mechanics. Indeed, while most butchers working in less advantageous positions earned only moderate incomes, a successful man such as John Pell, worth $19,500 in 1815, is an example of the financial possibilities. Such success was contingent upon being in a position to both get the best livestock and have convenient access to customers.[3]

In contrast, cartmen were among the poorer of the city's tradesmen and had very limited economic horizons. They were required by law to own their own horse and cart and often had to save or borrow the few hundred dollars necessary to go into business. Fortunately, the only major expenses were the care and maintenance of animals and equipment. Their hours were their own, and if there was enough work, a driver could earn a modest income, and perhaps save a few thousand dollars over a lifetime. Illness to a horse or driver, however, could cause a serious financial setback.[4]

Butchers' operations were supervised by the Common Council's Market Committee. Following an investigation of the petitioners' credentials, it issued licenses allowing meat handlers to occupy a stall in one of the city's public markets. Once given a certificate, a butcher could sell his wares six days a week at the hours provided by the council. Only licensed butchers with stands could cut and sell pork, beef, veal, and mutton, and the sale could take place only within a stall. Butchers who violated this law could lose their licenses, while men selling meat without a permit were subject to fines of up to $17.50.[5]

Once granted a stall, a butcher generally held it for life, paying, prior to 1821, no rent other than the normal market fees. While there appears to have been no fixed policy within the city government on the sale of stands before 1821, the *Evening Post* reported in 1806 that of the two hundred stalls then active in the city, only twenty had been sold—the rest were given away.[6] For those butchers without a stall, permission was sometimes given to sell meat by the quarter, though the profits from this kind of enterprise were less than those of a licensed butcher.[7] All those selling meat were under the supervision of the Clerk of the Market, who ascertained that the quality of meat offered the public met set standards, and that the various scales were in order. His salary was taken from the market fees which all butchers paid. As a final check, all licensed butchers had to submit to the city comptroller lists detailing the kinds and quality of the meat they sold.[8]

The city's cartmen were under the authority of both the mayor and the Common Council. The mayor issued licenses to drivers and imposed disciplinary measures he found necessary; the council fixed the prices the cartmen could charge for hauling their loads of hay, wood, merchants' wares, and garbage around the city. City ordinances stated strictly that cartmen were forbidden from working for other men or from selling shares in their operations.

They were also prohibited from selling wood to the public, and could cart it only after a purchaser had paid for his cord at the dock. Before he could take his wagon on the public thoroughfares, a driver had to secure his permit from the mayor and affix a prominent tag displaying his number on his cart. In 1797 the city's one thousand cartmen were organized into twenty companies of forty-nine drivers and one foreman. (By 1820 their number had grown to two thousand.) The foreman was to oversee his group, insuring that all members obeyed regulations and reporting any vacancies. (Any driver idle for over two months was liable to suspension.) Until 1800 no minors were allowed to drive carts; after that year the Common Council allowed youths involved in family hardship cases to receive permits—provided security bonds were posted for them.[9]

In all, the city took wide-ranging measures to see that the vital supply of food (including bread, as we have seen) and transportation were available to its residents at reasonable cost and in good condition. These actions included price fixing and the constant surveillance against either faulty quality or fraudulent conduct.[10] Moreover, the executive and legislative branches of municipal government devoted considerable time and effort to securing the enforcement of all standards and procedures.

Licensing procedures placed the city directly in the role of granting employment. This occurred in offers of inspectorships and measuring positions and in the mayor and corporation's power to determine who could and who could not practice his trade. This latter authority was particularly crucial for New York's butchers, because in the early part of the nineteenth century there were more applicants for stalls than there were places available. This put the Market Committee in a difficult position in determining which to approve of the many memorials sent them by worthy, young would-be meat handlers.

The great majority of the Market Committee's documents, which now lie scattered throughout the city's archives, are petitions from journeymen butchers asking for their own stalls; only a few requested permission to sell meat by the quarter.[11] A typical example is the memorial of John Hutton requesting a stand in the

Lower Fly Market. Hutton claimed that he had served out a regular apprenticeship and then had worked as a journeyman for the past eight years. Asserting that a journeyman's wages were insufficient for the support of his wife, four children, and mother, he fervently prayed for a chance to run his own business. Attached to the petition were the testimonials of a number of other respected butchers and citizens affirming the applicant's good character.[12]

The themes in Hutton's petition—long service as an apprentice and journeyman coupled with the inability to make ends meet without an independent operation—were common to almost all memorials. To an aspiring butcher with a family, the plight of working long industrious years only to be confronted with the serious possibility of never receiving his own stand was most difficult to bear. The anguished letter that Robert Coyle sent Mayor De Witt Clinton in May 1803 gives vent to some of these feelings:

I humbly pray that your honour will be pleased to grant me a permit to sell meat outside of the flymarket as I have no stall and I have a parsal of creatures bought in the Contry this some time past and the people says that they sew me if I do not take them according to contract and what to do I know not unless that your honor will be pleased to grant me permition to sell them as there is five or six of my Neibors her in Brooklyn that goes and sells Everyday and they tell me that they have a permit and I have been idel ever since Christmas as I would not come without leave from the authority which I hope will be granted for gods sake as that is my trad and support of me and my family and if I am Debared of that my family must perish as I have no other way to maintain them. I have served my time in the butchery business and has followed it all my life and nothing else, I have sent in a petition a few weeks back for a stand in Catherine Market there is one there is vacant as the man that occupied it is dead. ... But I am afraid I stand no chance being there is so many aplycations for it. If I have said anything improper here I pray that your Honor will be pleased to pardon me for I am so distressed in mind at present

to think I should serve so long a time to Lern a trade and then
not be allowed to get my living by it.[13]

The council was strict in the enforcement of its rule against the sale
of meat outside the public stalls, and it is thus unlikely that this
petition was granted. The paternalism of the council implied in
this letter is significant in that it was a logical result of the absolute
power resting in that body's licensing authority. The language of
other memorials was not as extreme, but the deferential tone was
the same.

The Common Council's jurisdiction extended to decisions concerning the location that a butcher might secure to carry on his
trade. Butchers already holding stands sent the Market Committee
numerous memorials asking permission to remove to another market. As population shifts occurred, some meat handlers found it
difficult to make a living in their original location, or else saw an
opportunity for greater profit in a different part of the city. For
example, in 1812 butcher John Ludlum petitioned the Common
Council for a new "situation." He declared that he had been one of
the first butchers to work in the Duane Street Market, and,
furthermore, that he had stuck it out there until all but one of the
stands had been abandoned. Similarly, Nicholas Boyce asked for
permission to transfer his operation to the Fly or Hudson Market
from the declining Exchange Market.[14]

The Market Committee took its duties as the butchers' super-
visor very seriously. It considered a prospective licensee's "conduct
and merits" and references, as well as his apprenticeship. It was
also concerned about the surplus of applications. At one meeting in
December 1804, it discussed the problem of upward of forty
applicants competing for only four vacant stalls. Noting that many
of the petitioners were deserving young men who had served out
their apprenticeships, the committee proposed the addition of
fourteen new stands at the city markets.[15] On the other hand, its
reaction to the various petitions for removal was less sympathetic.
In 1803 the committee remarked that its members viewed "with
concern" the many requests for the transfer or sale of stalls. The
aldermen decided that "if the practice of trafficking in stalls and
stands" were to become common, "injurious consequences" would

result. Therefore it was decided that before such a petition would be granted, a butcher would have to produce "conclusive evidence" that his memorial met the standards of "propriety and justice." [16]

Because there was no absolute limit on the number of cartmen—other than a general awareness of how many drivers could be absorbed within the city's economy—applicants had an easier time in securing their permits. Furthermore, a petitioner for a license did not need to scout out an empty stall and then apply for it, but needed only his own horse and wagon. Finally, a cartman did not need to serve a long apprenticeship or any time as a journeyman. Petitions sent to the mayor indicate that this occupation was one of the few in New York's preindustrial economy for which semi-skilled or displaced tradesmen were eligible. One such applicant explained that he had been brought up on Long Island without a trade; a second pleaded that his parent's poverty was responsible for his lack of proficiency in a skill, but that a cartman's license would give him a "decent and comfortable support." [17] A third man lamented that he could find no work at his usual occupation, pump- and block-making. Others, meanwhile, claimed disability and sickness in support of their applications, or those of their children and dependents. [18]

Although it was easier for a man to get a cartman's license than a butcher's stand, neither was a foregone conclusion. In both professions city officials had enormous powers over who would be allowed to carry on their chosen trade and, in the case of butchers, who would receive the more lucrative locations. While the mayor and aldermen generally exercised power with integrity and fairness, independent of party affiliation, political maneuvering and coercion were always potential threats. The blackmail of cartmen prior to 1800, a continuing election theme, had turned the drivers solidly into the Republican camp. Too, a major political scandal erupted in 1806 over Federalist charges of political favoritism in the granting of butchers' stalls. These were exceptional incidents, but they served to heighten licensed mechanics' awareness of how much their financial security depended on the honesty of the men holding high municipal office. Every time a permit was up for renewal, a man's job lay at the mercy of the city authorities.

Consequently, the paternalistic aura that surrounded workingmen seeking licenses continued to affect these tradesmen after they began to practice their professions.[19]

While the city's licensing authority placed the municipality in the role of granting a man employment, the Common Council also acted as a direct employer of mechanics who had worked in one of the regulated trades. It performed this function by hiring tradesmen as inspectors, weighers, measurers, and for other supervisory duties. Bakers were generally picked as flour inspectors, and cartmen were given such posts as wood or hay inspectors and charcoal and lime measurers. As in licensing decisions, many applications were received for each opening, and the council had a difficult time choosing among the petitioners.[20]

Mechanics accompanied their memorials with a number of justifications. Sickness and disability were very common reasons. Men claimed such maladies as a "nervous fever" and "rheumatick pains," or the loss of a hand or a foot in an accident as factors which had caused them to leave their trade and look to the city for less demanding jobs.[21] For others the disastrous effects of unemployment even without a disability were reason enough to claim the city's aid. As a further vindication of their right to a municipal position, many of these tradesmen invoked their military experience. One artisan noted that he had "exerted himself to the utmost of his power in the defense of liberty of his country." [22]

The gist of these petitions was an affirmation by the tradesmen that a man who was "sober, honest, industrious and . . . a friend of this country" was entitled to a decent living from society when illness, accident, old age, or misfortune would otherwise force him into the disgrace of poor relief or the almshouse.[23] The Common Council's potential as an employer was often the last resort for a cartman or other mechanic without alternative resources. It was able to offer him a chance to maintain his respectability in a society strongly attuned to the work ethic.

The major purpose of licensing was the protection of the public good. The city took its supervisory responsibilities very seriously, and, in carrying out its duties, occasionally threatened, curbed, or thwarted the ambitions of its licensees, causing considerable controversy and spirited discussion.

A common citizen-initiated complaint concerned the arrogant and careless manner of mechanics. The *Rambler's Magazine* gives a vivid if somewhat biased account of the rambunctious cartman:

Observe the cartman, driving through the streets like a wild arab, upsetting helpless infants in his course, and dashing their brains against the curb stones. Watch him now asking his meager heart with the utmost fury to overtake the trembling female, who in vain exerts her utmost efforts to avoid him; and see, at length he meets the fate he so richly deserves; his cart upsets, and his head, less obdurate than his heart, lies crushed in the ensanguined pavement.[24]

Like sentiments often appeared in the *Evening Post*. One article told of a driver who, upon striking a boy, answered that *"the citizen may get out of the way,"*[25] while a second complained that the cartmen played a nefarious game of seeing how close they could come to "unescorted women."[26] "A New Citizen" lamented that he had been kept awake until early the next morning by the sounds of three hundred racing cartmen, and still another pedestrian remonstrated that he had looked up the license number of an offending driver only to find that more than one man had the same figure assigned to them. The problem, he said, was that because the two thousand cartmen were "a very powerful body of electors," the police were lax in the enforcement of the rules.[27]

The mayor and the Common Council did take steps to answer complaints. Upon his inauguration as chief magistrate in 1808, Marinus Willet called in all cartmen's licenses for reissue, giving each driver a warning against such abuses as number duplication and racing in the streets. The Common Council regularly passed and reissued laws requiring that the figure on the cart be painted in clear black letters, specifying the proper rules of conduct, and warning that violations would bring heavy penalties.[28] Nor were these idle threats; the City Clerk's Filed Papers are replete with anguished petitions from disciplined cartmen praying for the remission of fines. William Ferdon, for example, asked forgiveness from a twenty-five-dollar penalty for driving without a license on the grounds that he was elderly, poor, and the supporter of a large family. Deeming Ferdon a "fit object of relief," the council remitted the fine.[29] It was not so generous, however, with cartman George Stemple's excuse for driving too fast. It found inadequate both the explanation that he was following an intoxicated cartman and the plea that the punishment would distress him.[30] Nor was the penalty of another driver remitted who, when asked by his foreman to explain the absence of his number, replied that "it was none of his business." This chastened offender explained to the council first that he had removed his tag for but a day and a half while his boom was drying, and second that he did not know who the man was. This plea, too, had little effect on the aldermen.[31]

Public fear and scrutiny also extended to the butchers. Two different sources suggest a popular mistrust of meat handlers. In verse, Thomas Eaton pictured the city's markets as a commons where rich and poor mingled to buy their provisions. He has choice words for the local proprietors:

> But butchers here, like other men,
> Have common sense, and sense of pain;
> These weigh the meat, and you must know,
> The meat side of the scale is low,
> And wants your care to balance it,
> If you would have your proper weight,
> Or else two pounds of meat, you'll see,
> Will just two pounds odd ounces be.
> The rich who buy a stately piece,
> Will scarcely know their meat's decrease.
> But 'tis the poor, who little buy,
> That miss the meat and wonder why.[32]

Eaton does qualify his rhyme by adding that " 'tis thus with some—but not with all," yet the danger to the public remained clear. A correspondent to the *Independent Mechanic*, "NO BONE," also complained of the butchers' treatment of poor customers. He asserted that if a commonly dressed shopper decided not to purchase a certain butcher's meat, he or she would be so harried with insults that for fear of similar treatment the unfortunate soul would refrain from moving on to another stall. Even worse, though, were the nightly revels of butchers as they found enjoy-

A butcher and cartman at work. Butcher: Courtesy, Century House, Watkins Glen, New York. Cartman: New York Public Library.

ment in knocking over indigents and laughing at their "tumbling." [33]

While there was little that the city could do to improve the butchers' manners, it did have the power to maintain market regulations. Much of the Market Committee's effort was spent in enforcing its rules against the illegal sale of meat either by unlicensed vendors or at improper locations. One butcher caught in violation of these regulations was Matthew Byrne. In his memorial to the council, he explained that he had been stuck with cattle on his hands and no place to vend them. Regretfully, he admitted making an illegal sale on Front Street. Alas, at the same time that he was committing this infraction, the Market Committee had decided to give him a stall. Byrne pleaded for permission to keep his newly granted stand in spite of his offense.[34] Another petitioner claimed that he was prosecuted for selling meat at his home only because an "enemy" had informed on him, and begged for remission of his fine on the grounds that, having no stall, he had no other way to support his family but by selling from his own domicile.[35] Judging from the clerk's papers, most of the men prosecuted for market violations were the unfortunate butchers who had no permanent stalls and consequently were forced to scramble for their living. This does not mean that violations did not occur among licensed butchers. Rather, individual customers likely were less inclined to report isolated infractions than the butchers were to prosecute those intruding on their territory.

One unusual case of a licensed butcher who was brought before the Market Committee took place in 1805. The proceedings began when the Common Council received a letter from the city's Jewish congregation, Shearith Israel, protesting the actions of Caleb Vandenbergh. They claimed that this meat handler had offered his wares for sale "as Cosher or fit for that congregation to eat," when in fact the opposite was true. Interviewed by the Market Committee, two of the city's Jewish inhabitants denied Vandenbergh's contention that he had "put the seals on the meat . . . but as a joke," and asserted that his intent had been to sell unfit meat to the congregation. Declaring that they did not see "any good cause why this Board ought not to protect the religious people in their religious rights when not inconsistent with the Public Rights," the

Market Committee duly recommended that Vandenbergh's license be suspended.[36]

The loss of his means of support brought this errant butcher to an immediate state of contrition. A few days after the revocation, he submitted a memorial to the Council describing how he had called upon several members of the Jewish congregation and "begged their forgiveness of the offense, in consideration of which they have been pleased to sign the recommendation accompanying this petition." Pleading that he had a wife and five children "destitute of support," Vandenbergh asked for the return of his license and his stall in the Catherine Market.[37]

A third group of licensed workingmen complained of for errant behavior were the hackney coach drivers. An 1816 petition to the Common Council requested that these black drivers be prohibited from the streets on account of their "insults and base conduct." Coming from "immoral parts of the city" and depending on prostitutes for their living, they were "dissipated" beings not worthy of mingling with honest citizens. The council, however, after due deliberation, decided against their removal; such an action, it explained, would only lead to the erection of more livery stables, enterprises equally offensive to local residents. Rather, the corporation decided to limit the number of drivers that could assemble at any one corner in the city.[38] However, this compromise solution did not satisfy the local householders, who sent in a new letter "remonstrating" against its implementation. The memorialists complained that they would be "incommoded, prejudiced and exposed to extraordinary noise, vulgarity and disturbance." [39] The decision of the council, nevertheless, was not reversed.

The miscreant conduct of the licensed tradesmen, aside from that of the butchers prosecuted for selling meat illegally, likely reflects social antagonisms. These arrogant actions on the part of the butchers and cartmen may indicate a displacement of hostility toward their superiors in city government as well as assertions of status. That is, it was less dangerous to bully and harass individual citizens than to tangle with authorities who could curtail one's livelihood. Moreover, such bullying declared that, on the one hand, no citizen, no matter his standing, was immune to the insults of a tradesman, while on the other hand, it reminded those of a lower station that these mechanics were their superiors. The behavior of the coachmen, however, was unlikely to have been provoked by hostility against supervisors. By granting these blacks the privilege of licensing and regulation, the city was affording them a status they were unlikely to resent. Rather, their callousness was probably an expression of class antagonism against their neighbors, residents just above them on the social ladder. Blacks, who generally voted for upper-class Federalists, preferred to harass struggling artisans rather than the elite aldermen of the Common Council.

The public also turned to the city to obtain the services of licensed tradesmen, sometimes against the mechanics' own wishes. Residents in the outer wards, for example, often lived at a distance from the public markets.[40] Consequently, they sent in petitions asking for new stalls to be erected in their areas. Were this an unregulated profession, a number of enterprising butchers—and there was no shortage of them—would certainly have erected stalls in these areas. However, since the Common Council determined where markets were to be located (as well as who could operate within them), conflicts developed between petitioners for new markets and butchers already at work in established markets. While new locations in outlying parts of the city might mean greater opportunity for some meat handlers, for others it could mean the loss of business or else the inconvenience and cost of moving to a new situation at which they might have a less lucrative stall.

In 1817, upon hearing that the Market Committee intended to recommend the construction of a new market in the outlying northern area of the city, the butchers of the Collect Market who were to be transferred there sent in a communication asking that the market be placed south of Hester Street; the proposed Grand Street site would not provide sufficient business.[41] In a more threatened situation, the licensed occupants of the northern Spring Street Market learned "with concern" in 1812 that the council intended to establish a new Greenwich Street Market. Because the new structure was to be only an eighth of a mile from their location, the meat handlers saw but "little utility" and much grief arising from the new market. Having occupied their Spring Street stalls almost from the mart's inception, and "having exerted themselves to the utmost," the butchers complained that only lately had they become hopeful of realizing a decent profit.[42] Despite the petition, the new market was constructed; it did not, however, cause the demise of the Spring Street butchers; nine years later memorials were received asking that that market be saved from destruction.[43]

As in most disputes involving licensed tradesmen, the Common Council tried to find solutions satisfactory to both of the contending parties. The records of one such dispute include the Market Committee's reasoning. The conflict originated when fifty inhabitants living in the vicinity of the Exchange Market petitioned in 1814 for that market's discontinuance on the grounds that only three or four stalls there were still active, and that "greater and greater space" was being devoted to "Improper uses"—leading to a risk of fire.[44] A few weeks later a counterpetition was submitted by the Exchange Market butchers along with other area residents claiming that because of the distance between markets, the Exchange site was convenient and "in some cases indispensable" to nearby inhabitants. The present location had been built in conjunction with the corporation and a number of licensed butchers, some of whom had occupied their stalls for nearly a quarter century. Moreover, the petitioners claimed that many of the signers of the original memorial had been deceived into thinking that they were agreeing to a request for a new market.[45]

Having heard both sides, the Market Committee decided that, because the original petitioners were from the market area, because the location was in a remote part of the city, and because it contained only a "scanty" supply of food, the Exchange site was of no value. Furthermore, it noted that, much to the annoyance of many local merchants, two-thirds of the market area had been turned into a storage area for "coarse merchandise." Accordingly, it recommended that the market be closed and the displaced butchers transferred to the Upper Fly Market.[46] On the one hand, the council was attempting to alleviate grievances without causing undue hardships. On the other hand, however, it must be wondered whether the councilmen were not more sympathetic to the needs of the mercantile sector than to the inconvenience to be suffered by local residents and butchers.

The third and most vital function of the city's licensing authority was the protection that it afforded against the monopoly of essential goods.[47] A preindustrial urban center was extremely vulnerable to the wiles of profit-seeking speculators who attempted to blackmail residents by cornering the supply of food or fuel. In seeking to preserve a fair price for the latter, the Common Council imposed regulations prohibiting cartmen from purchasing firewood other than for the use of their immediate family. They were to cart lumber only after it had been bought by local residents or businessmen. Wood inspectors were appointed to enforce both these rules and others that restricted the length of wood brought into the city. However, despite these safeguards, abuses took place, and the community lived in constant fear that it might have to pay steeply inflated prices for its heating fuel.

From 1800 to 1820 a considerable number of petitions and letters were dispatched to the Common Council and the daily newspapers complaining of monopolistic cartmen. In 1807, "Citizen" wrote the council that due to an "intrigue between the cartmen and the boatmen who bring wood into the city," the inhabitants of New York had been forced to endure "the most gross and hard imposition." By illegally purchasing whole stocks of firewood, the cartmen were able to command "any price they please." The council was advised to enforce its laws and, in particular, to have each family send for its own wood. This would lower the prices, which, if not controlled, could bring disaster in the winter. It was time that an "evil" that "has been even and longfelt" be brought to an end.[48]

In the fall of 1811 letters to the *Public Advertiser* and the *Morning Post* protested similar abuses and rebuked the corporation for not fulfilling its trust. "Poor Man" claimed that the cartmen had been buying up wood in the summertime for sale in the winter at outrageous prices; other drivers, meanwhile, were condemned for purchasing whole boatloads of fuel and selling them for profits of 20 to 25 percent. What was particularly abhorrent about these operations was that they were perpetrated at a time when—due to the difficulties with Great Britain—many a hardworking man was out of a job. The cartmen were attempting to "make a market of the poor man's miseries, . . . all for a dirty gain." [49]

Not only wronged citizens, but nonspeculating cartmen as well protested the illegal actions of their counterparts; monopolistic practices threatened their ability to procure timber for their customers. In 1810, 144 cartmen submitted a memorial to the Common Council stating that they were working under a "great disadvantage." Arriving at the docks with empty wagons, they were constantly told that all the wood had been sold. These drivers asked the corporation to have the wood inspectors take over complete charge of all boatloads of fuel so that each man could have his turn "at the same prices as monopolizing cartmen." [50] An obstacle to this solution, however, was that even the inspectors were not always honest. A petition from residents and cartmen in the Peck Slip area of the city complained of a local inspector who was attempting to buy up all the available wood for himself.[51]

One local occupant, in a letter to the *Morning Post,* offered a considerably more drastic solution than allowing wood inspectors increased authority. He called on the city not only to take over the sale of wood but to also sell it at prices that would vary in accordance with the monetary status of the purchaser.[52] This was a radical solution running against the increasingly popular laissez-faire economic outlook. Generally the city preferred to let the free market operate in the price of firewood, restricting only operations of the haulers. Because of this a tension always existed between the interests of enterprising cartmen and those of the public, a tension that could not be easily resolved in a partially controlled economy.

A few records are available of cartmen apprehended while carrying on monopolistic practices. Their statements hardly reveal cutthroat racketeers. One offender, John Brown, received a twenty-five-dollar fine for purchasing two loads of wood from a boatman. In his petition to the Common Council, Brown claimed that the owner of the vessel had told him that if he purchased two boatfuls of fuel, he could have the wood for two shillings per load less than the going price. Admitting the transaction, Brown based his defense on the grounds that he had sold the wood at the same price at which he had purchased it, gaining only from cartage fees. Also pleading that he had been a very sick man and that the fine would force him to sell his house, Brown asked for and was granted a remission of his fine.[53] In another explanation, a cartman who had overcharged a customer for wood asserted that he had been forced into such practices because of the effects of the embargo and Nonintercourse Acts on his trade.[54]

The responses of these two men hardly depict malicious drivers attempting to bring the city to its knees. It is, of course, quite possible that these statements do not fully represent the motives of cartmen who were, indeed, speculators. But it is also probable that this was another situation in which the Common Council was caught between two genuine interests. Against the need of the public for fuel at reasonable cost was the dilemma of cartmen operating in the midst of fierce competition (from both licensed and unlicensed drivers) and, after 1807, deteriorating business conditions.

Butchers, too, came under fire for monopolizing their wares and forcing up prices. One memorial in 1801, offered by a number of butchers, accused a number of their colleagues, and particularly Henry Astor, of leaving journeymen in charge of their stalls while they rode into the country, met the drovers before they reached the city, and then bought cattle for stalls "other than their own." By keeping the supply limited and selling them at "an advanced price," they forced up the price of meat through a cornered market.[55] In another incident in 1819, a writer in the *Evening Post* noted that the price of meat and vegetables had not fallen by 25 percent, as had both other necessities and wages. He also reported rumors that the butchers and hucksters had entered into a "combination," and that as a countermeasure a public meeting was being considered at which the populace would be urged to refrain from eating meat for a few days. While the writer implied that such a solution would work because the butchers had to kill their cattle at once, the editor responded that this was not so. The meat handlers could refrain from slaughtering their stock until after the boycott. Moreover, he wondered if the real blame did not lie with the "graziers and gardeners" rather than with the retailers who sold the products.[56]

Having to contend with supervision, restriction, and discipline to which other masters were not subject, as well as the difficulties in securing a certificate, licensed tradesmen expected assistance not available to other artisans in the attainment of their social and entrepreneurial goals. Like other mechanics, of most concern were the burdens of excessive competition and the intrusion of inferior tradesmen in their professions.

The petitions to the mayor and Common Council reveal that the fear of competition was of particular concern. In 1800, for example, meat handlers in the Fly Market suggested to the Market Committee that because the market was already crowded, it not fill the ten current vacancies. Rather, they suggested that the space be used to enlarge stalls currently used by butchers.[57] Considering the shortage of stands in comparison with the number of applicants, this statement reveals a disregard for the plight of the younger butchers in favor of a better opportunity for those already holding advantageous positions.

Butchers also lodged a number of complaints against illegal competition, or "shirk butchers." Their most common grievance was toward these country dwellers or those who posed as country-dwellers and who, contrary to the law, sold meat both on the streets and at the public markets. In 1804, 106 butchers signed a protest in which they declared themselves to be "greatly injured" by the unlicensed intruders who were "hawking and vending Meat in this city" at the same time that they, the authorized meat handlers, were slaughtering their stock "with an expectation of selling the same quantity they formerly did." The sad result could only be "spoiled meat on our hands." [58] Such practices, moreover, were to be deplored because of the danger that they posed to the public health. In 1815, 157 butchers signed another petition against unlicensed vendors of meat who were selling their stock outside the public markets. Aside from the lost revenue in unpaid market fees and the injustice against butchers who had to get their meat cut and dressed according to the law, the welfare of the metropolis was threatened by infection.[59]

Responding to these complaints, the council duly investigated the situation. One Market Committee report declared that the licensed meat handlers were, indeed, being unjustly penalized by agents who bought food from country dwellers and then wandered around the city selling the meat illegally. It recommended the doubling of market fees for all goods sold at the special Country

Market except for those goods coming directly from the farm. Also, the council imposed increasingly stiffer fines on men apprehended selling meat without a license or in unauthorized locations.[60]

The licensed cartmen, too, expected the mayor to protect their economic security and the dignity of their profession. Reinforcing their expectation was the potential strength of a bloc of over one thousand voters. One area in which they managed to see that their status was protected was the threat posed by black cartmen. No member of that race was admitted to the profession in New York during the early years of the republic. A traveler in the city reported that one such man did apply to the mayor complete with the necessary certificates of fitness. The chief magistrate admitted that the papers were in order but declared that he could not grant the black a license because such action "would endanger not only the man's safety but his own." And, were he to approve the application, "the populace would likely pelt him as he walked along the streets, when it became known that he had licensed a black cartman."[61]

While the cartmen managed to keep blacks out of their trade, they were less successful with aliens. Immigrants often came to New York penniless and without skills; there was no way for them to obtain a decent living "but by driving a horse and cart."[62] Generally, licenses were given only to naturalized citizens, since the law stipulated that no alien could receive a permit. However, when a labor shortage developed during the War of 1812, many unnaturalized Irish were given certificates. After the war, the regularly licensed drivers returned home only to find themselves confronted with competition from men whom they considered of inferior ability and social standing. To add insult to injury, the Irish cartmen often found favor with the local merchant employers because of their willingness to charge less than was customary. Seeking redress, the licensed cartmen sent an urgent petition to Mayor Cadwallader Colden requesting that the aliens' permits be revoked. Colden replied that while he would no longer license unnaturalized citizens, it would be unfair to take away the certificates of those currently working.[63]

This reply did not sit well with the drivers. In an emotional address they proclaimed that "the Rights, Liberties and Privalages" on which they had based their complaints were "strictly and justly established" by the actions of their fathers who, in fighting for American independence, had "relinquished individual interest and substance with spilling theire Blood and Laying down theire lives to obtain the rights and privalages of free men and bequeathe the inheritance to us their offspring." This was in stark contrast to aliens who claimed the rights of freemen without "swearing allegiance" to the country they claimed to have adopted.

The cartmen also noted that the situation was becoming more and more serious because of the large number of aliens who had "secured the principal part of the merchants' employ throughout the city." The mayor's plan was of little value because under its provisions it "would take fifty years to correct" the current injustice—and how could the actions of a future mayor by predicted? Furthermore, if it was unjust to remove the licenses of the Irishmen, "How much more unjust is it that we should Bare the Burden and pay our hard earnt pittance to support them in such privalage." Nor were the cartmen completely satisfied with the mayor's decision to enforce the laws, particularly against Irishmen who were illegally driving for third parties. Such a process, unfortunately, might require the industrious mechanics to leave their wagons "day by day to go to court." In truth, the way Colden left it, "it would have been better if we had all been aliens." Incensed, the cartmen concluded their message with a warning that while they did not want to have to violate any of the city's laws, they were depending upon action from His Honor.[64]

Mayor Colden delivered his final response a few days later, and it did little to mollify the cartmen. While again sympathizing with their plight, he steadfastly refused to revoke the Irishmen's licenses because of the distress that such a move would cause. The chief magistrate reaffirmed his intention to crack down on violators, but noted that to do this he needed to be informed of any infractions. Finally, the mayor cautioned the cartmen against taking any action that might involve means outside of the law, for such steps would "lead to consequences in which I should be sorry to see you involved." [65]

Although the cartmen's problems reached their most explosive point in 1818, they had been festering for a number of years. In 1806 a Common Council investigation reported that "the most respectable cartmen" were "considerably dissatisfied" that they had to pay for a license and be subject to military duty "whilst citizens who have been only a few months in this country, who have paid neither taxes nor license and who are exempt from public duty, should be put on similar footing." [66] A few years later, a number of cartmen complained to the city about unlicensed drivers traversing the streets with fictitious number plates.[67]

The problem posed by immigrant cartmen was difficult to resolve. From the aliens' viewpoint, it was necessary and just that poor unskilled laborers have a means to make ends meet in their new home. The cartmen, on the other hand, expected their privileges as licensees to be respected, especially their guarantees as to who might enter their ranks. In 1818 aldermen Stephen Allen and Samuel Stearns proposed a compromise under which the Irishmen would be allowed to "cart dirt and nothing else." This would give them work but still protect the economic situation of the authorized cartmen. However, whether this was a practical solution is questionable, since the licensed drivers resented any intrusion whatsoever into their profession.[68]

A third expression of concern by licensed tradesmen over unwanted competition took place in 1816 when the city's licensed porters sent a memorial to the Common Council. These laborers, many of whom, ironically, were Irish aliens, had fixed assignments at locations throughout the city's streets and docks. This petition charged that unauthorized vagabonds, who wandered from place to place looking for work, were intruding on the porters' territory. When these unsavory men took a job, they deprived honest men of their rightful labor—and often robbed their customers as well! Noting that the "depredation . . . of this unlicensed rabble" was harming the reputation of the metropolis, the porters requested the council to refrain from licensing anyone whose integrity had not been fully established, and to enforce its regulations. In closing, they added a further remonstrance against youths who crowded the steamboat wharves in search of trunks to carry. These boys, who only gambled their money away, deprived "with every shilling they earned, . . . a family of some of your memorialists of a loaf of bread." [69]

Mechanics working in the regulated trades also expected the city, as their advocate, to insure them from interference from other laborers and citizens—licensed or not—who disturbed their job security. Thus, the Duane Street butchers complained about local inhabitants, "numerous families . . . mostly of color," who were living in the local cellars under the market and causing a serious fire hazard with their cooking stoves.[70] The Common Council quickly ordered these residents out, but had more difficulty dealing with a complaint that cartmen working in the Pearl Street and Old Slip area lodged against the hack coaches in their district. In a memorial to the council, the local cartmen asserted first that their financial situation had only lately improved, bringing with it increased traffic. If the city were to allow coaches to enter freely, dangerous congestion would develop; and in a case of limited access, the cartmen clearly had precedent. Second, the wanton character of the coachmen would make for "frequent collisions between them, and that useful body of men, the cartmen whose stands are in the adjacent slips." Third, the entry of the coaches and their drivers would demoralize the entire neighborhood, subverting the peace and order of the community and infringing upon the rights of the local citizenry.[71]

A final and more protracted incident of such conflict involved the collection of manure, a most valuable fertilizer. Manure falling upon the city streets was collected by cartmen working under the supervision of Edward Hitchcock, an independent proprietor, who paid the municipality for the right to retrieve the droppings. A separate group of independent cartmen collected manure from the city's livery stables. In 1813 a serious dispute broke out between the two groups of tradesmen over the right of deposit in the Eighth Ward. The independent drivers, having lost their former storage area, asked permission to use a section of that ward. Hitchcock, whose contract required his approval before any individuals were allowed to store manure within city limits, protested this move, claiming that since he also used the Eighth Ward for deposit, the independent drivers would have an opportunity to steal his manure and an unfair advantage in getting their collections to the docks.[72] He had paid a "large sum" for his rights, and did not intend to have them usurped.

The dispossessed drivers, in turn, claimed that without a place of deposit, "a number of industrious craftsmen" would be deprived of their livelihood; moreover, the city would be unable to secure removal of that manure. The Common Council first solved the problem by assigning the independent drivers a location in the Tenth Ward. Within a year, however, this solution proved inadequate. Residents there began complaining of "offensive and pernicious" drinking water, lowered real estate values, "flies and vermin," and even the impending necessity of leaving their homes. Consequently, in 1816 the city ordered all manure removed from city immediately after collection, and assigned both Hitchcock and the private drivers separate piers. Alas, this decision too brought protest. Other city residents, many of them poor tradesmen, petitioned the Council against this move. They declared that they kept a few animals in their yards and needed the money they received from the sale of their stored manure. This time the ruling stuck, however.[73]

This controversy presented the Common Council with a dilemma similar to those it faced at other times when licensed tradesmen called upon the board to act as their advocate. The grievances of the certified mechanics were well grounded; but so were the petitions of the immigrant Irishmen, the unemployed butchers, the hackney coachmen, and the independent manure carriers. When the council had specific regulations to guide it, the aldermen usually followed the law—to the benefit of those lodging complaints. However, as the problems between licensed cartmen and the Irish drivers clearly showed, a rule could be one thing and enforcement another. In situations in which either the law was unclear or in which reasons had arisen for exceptions, the council and the mayor tried to find a middle ground—and pleased no one.

The predicament of the licensed tradesmen was unique among the mechanics. While they shared similar goals with unlicensed craftsmen, they lacked the autonomy of other artisans. Their welfare was subject not only to changes in market conditions but also to changes in public policy. An excellent example of this occurred in 1821 when the Common Council, in order to raise new municipal revenue, decided to abandon the practice of free allotment and auction off the lucrative stalls at the new Fulton Street Market. Claiming that such a move would "disgrace" meat handlers, make them "the objects of perpetual prosecution," and *"set one butcher against another,"* the butchers met and resolved not to bid for the new stalls. The measure worked at first, as only a few stalls were sold, possibly because one man who disregarded the butchers' resolution was dragged to the dock and thrown in the river where he only narrowly escaped drowning. The meat handlers, who wanted the stalls rented out and assigned by lot, claimed that the new policy would see the wealthy "obtain a dangerous influence over the poorest part" of this mechanic branch. The city did not relent, however, and the eighteen stalls were eventually sold for the sum of $18,865—forcing many butchers to quit and others into insolvency.[74]

Because the achievement of their entrepreneurial goals could hinge on a change in government policy, licensed tradesmen displayed more dependence and arrogance than their unsupervised counterparts. Their insecurity forced them to defer to municipal authority, defeating in part their goal of social and economic independence. This dependence also accounted for their expectations of special assistance and partly for the many instances of arrogant behavior. As seen in the many encounters with the mayor and Common Council, these mechanics faced a very difficult road in the fulfillment of their entrepreneurial ambitions.

NOTES

1. Based on occupational directory in *Longworth's New York Directory* for 1806. The twelve hundred listed cartmen must be scaled down since all cartmen were listed while only about two-fifths of other mechanic trades were. For the full table see pp. 87-89.

2. Sidney I. Pomerantz, *New York: An American City, 1783-1803* (New York, 1938), pp. 174-178.

3. Edmund P. Willis, "Social Origins of Political Leadership in New York City from the Revolution to 1815," Ph.D. diss. (Berkeley, 1967), pp. 129, 348; see also pp. 241, 268.

4. Ibid., p. 130.

5. *Laws and Ordinances Ordained and Established by the Mayor, Aldermen, and Commonality of the City of New York* (New York, 1799). Market fees were set at sixpence per quarter of beef or hog, and four pence for a calf or sheep. The laws of 1803 allowed the constable to take a man attempting to sell meat without a license immediately to the mayor or aldermen. If he was not able to pay his fine at that time, he was to be taken directly to Bridewell, where he could be held for up to thirty days.

6. The Market Committee Report, City Clerk Filed Papers (hereafter

referred to as CC), Box 3155, May 14, 1821, New York City Municipal Archives, detailed the successful new policy that the council adopted in 1821 on renting out all stalls as a means of raising city revenues; *Evening Post*, August 8, 1806.

7. Petitions of Daniel Winship, George Goodhart, George Market, John Pell, Cornelius Schuyler and John Corby to Common Council, CC Box 6414, June 1795.

8. *Minutes of the Common Council of the City of New York, 1784-1831*, 21 vols. (New York, 1917-1930), vol. 2, p. 727 (March 23, 1801); see also Pomerantz, *New York: An American City*, pp. 172-178.

9. The *Laws and Ordinances* (1799), pp. 29-39, designated the allowed sizes of carts according to width and length and where the license tags should be displayed. Drivers had to walk their carts through the streets and, under a fine of $25, could not refuse to transport a person or his goods to any place within the city. Prices were also fixed according to distance hauled and according to the material to be transported. The prices were raised after the War of 1812, but then lowered during the panic of 1819. *Evening Post*, April 24, 1816; Report of Council Committee, CC Box 3165, October 16, 1820. For report on the allowance of minors as cartmen, see Report of Common Council Committee, CC Box 3159, May 4, 1810. On details of the organization of the cartmen into classes see Pomerantz, *New York: An American City*, pp. 211-212.

10. The bakers, too, as we have seen, while not licensed, were subject to many of the similar regulations in regard to quality of product and price limitation. Nearly all their encounters with the city concerned the assize, or profit limitations. There is no record of licensed tradesmen ever complaining over this issue.

11. Petition of John Scott to Market Committee, CC Box 3173, July 7, 1812.

12. Petition of John Hutton to Market Committee, CC Box 3181, April 19, 1813. Also see petitions of John Shane, CC Box 3173, July 17, 1812; Caleb Connally, CC Box 8419, July 27, 1812; and John Basen, CC Box 3173, July 18, 1806. According to Pomerantz, it was not the license but the stall that was difficult to get, as the council was forced to give all qualified men certificates. However, no meat could be cut except in a stall, thus forcing butchers without a stand either to work for another butcher (as a journeyman) or to sell meat secondhand after purchasing it from a butcher with a stall. Neither of these alternatives—judging from the petitions—was very rewarding. Pomerantz, *New York: An American City*, p. 173.

13. CC Box 3158, May 31, 1803; a similar petition was sent in by John White, who stated that he had been selling meat by the quarter for all of

fifteen years, and hoped for a regular stall. CC Box 3173, July 24, 1812.

14. Petition of John Ludlum to Market Committee, CC Box 3173, July 24, 1812; Petition of Nicholas Boyce to Market Committee, CC Box 3163, August 9, 1806.

15. Report of the Market Committee, CC Box 3172, November, 1804; Thomas De Voe, *The Market Book* (New York, 1862), p. 401.

16. Report of Market Committee, CC Box 3155, July 14, 1803.

17. Petition of Nehemia Noss to Mayor, CC Box 3181, April 14, 1817; Petition of Charles Williams to Mayor, CC Box 3181, July 19, 1813. The first petition was granted, but Williams's was not.

18. Petition of John Saunders to Mayor, CC Box 3181, April 21, 1817; this one was "laid on the table."

19. See pp. 53-54.

20. Pomerantz lists, as composing the "army" of municipal officeholders, 64 public measurers, 5 weighmasters, 4 weighers of hay, 22 inspectors of hay, 2 gaugers of liquor, and 13 inspectors of firewood. This does not include the flour inspectors. *New York: An American City,* pp. 170-171.

21. Petition of John Lace to the Common Council for the position of flour inspector, CC Box 3173, May 18, 1818; Petition of John McGill, cartman, to be wood inspector, CC Box 6415, February 22, 1796; Petition of James McKevers, cartman, to be wood inspector, CC Box 3173, May 15, 1806.

22. Petition of Abraham Brevoort, CC Box 3173, April 25, 1806.

23. Petition of Henry Halsted to Mayor Varick, CC Box 6415, February 18, 1796.

24. *Rambler's Magazine and New York Theatrical Register,* vol. 2 (1809), pp. 155-156.

25. *Evening Post,* May 26, 1818.

26. Ibid., October 24, 1807.

27. Ibid., August 29, 1817, July 18, 1806, August 31, 1811, February 12, 1808; *Columbian,* June 21, 1815.

28. Ibid., February 12, 1808; *Minutes of the Common Council,* December 28, 1807. See Chapter 3.

29. Petition of William Ferdon, CC Box 3176, August 23, 1819.

30. Petition of George Stemple, CC Box 3181, August 3, 1812.

31. Petition to Common Council, CC Box 3176, May 31, 1819.

32. Thomas Eaton, *Review of New York or Rambles Through the City; Original Poems; Moral, Religious, Sarcastic and Descriptive* (New York, 1813), p. 25.

33. *Independent Mechanic,* December 14, 1811.

34. Petition of Matthew Byrne, CC Box 3155, March 25, 1803.

35. Petition of Samuel Pierce, CC, Box 3181, January 21, 1813; it was refused. See also De Voe, *Market Book,* pp. 380-381.

36. Report of the Market Committee, CC, Box 3080, September 2, 1805. For a similar verdict in 1796 see De Voe, *Market Book,* p. 202.

37. Memorial of Caleb Vandenbergh, CC Box 3155, September 6, 1805.

38. Petition of Citizens to the Mayor, CC Box 3175, December 23, 1816; Report of the Council Committee on Hackney Coaches, CC Box 3181, December 30, 1816; CC Box 3173, April 27, 1818. All coachmen were black; this fact was derived from the New York City Jury List, 1816, Fifth Ward, Historical Documents Collection, Queens College, City University of New York.

39. Petition of Local Residents, CC Box 3176, May 4, 1818.

40. See Petition of Inhabitants of George's Slip, CC Box 3215, August 24, 1812, and Petition of Residents of the Seventh and Tenth Wards, CC Box 3173, May 26, 1818.

41. Petition of Butchers of the Collect Market, CC Box 3175, July 28, 1817.

42. Petition of Butchers of the Spring Street Market, CC Box 3181, October 5, 1812.

43. Petition of Citizens living in the Vicinity of the Spring Street Market, CC Box 3080, June 25, 1821.

44. Petition of Citizens Living in the Area of the Exchange Market, CC Box 3165, April 4, 1814.

45. Petition of Butchers and Citizens of the Exchange Market, CC Box 3165, April 18, 1814.

46. Report of the Market Committee, CC Box 3165, May 9, 1814. See also De Voe, *Market Book,* pp. 336, 349, 392-393.

47. As one petitioner expressed it, the power of regulation existed to guarantee the community against frauds that "could be practiced by so numerous a class as the cartmen of this city, were they to be unlimited and left without restraint." CC Box 3173, September 21, 1818.

48. Letter of "Citizen" to the Common Council, CC Box 3155, October 19, 1807.

49. *Morning Post,* October 1, 1811, November 22, 1811; *Public Advertiser,* December 28, 1809; wood was not the only fuel subject to monopoly. An applicant for the post of a charcoal measurer in 1818 complained that the four present measurers in the city were all licensed cartmen who refused to measure any coal except for their own subscribers. CC Box 3173, January 22, 1818.

50. Petition of Cartmen, CC Box 3174, September 24, 1810.

51. Petition of Cartmen, Residents and Others Doing Business in the Peck Slip Vicinity, CC Box 3173, n.d.

52. *Morning Post,* September 13, 1811.

53. Petition of John Brown, CC Box 3181, March 9, 1812.

54. *American Citizen,* April 27, 1810.

55. De Voe, *Market Book,* pp. 210-211.

56. *Evening Post,* August 7, 1819.

57. Petition of Butchers of Fly Market, CC Box 3172, May 12, 1800.

58. Petition of Butchers to Mayor and Aldermen of New York City, n.d., Van Zandt papers, New York Public Library; De Voe, *Market Book,* pp. 222, 228-229.

59. Petition of Butchers to Market Committee, CC Box 3175, December 8, 1817.

60. *Laws and Ordinances* (1803), p. 15, allowed offenders to be taken directly to jail; in 1805 the market fee was set at three times normal for anyone caught selling articles that he bought in the market for sale in another part of the market (licensed butchers excluded); in 1812 the attorney of the Common Council was authorized to pay informers half of the fines collected for infractions; in 1817 countrymen were specifically excluded from receiving permits to sell in the market (p. 136). See also Market Committee Report, CC Box 3165, September 7, 1818.

61. Roi Otley and William J. Weatherley, *The Negro in New York* (New York, 1967), p. 65.

62. Petition of Samuel Stearns and Stephen Allen to Common Council, CC Box 3173, June 1, 1818.

63. Petition of Cartmen's Committee to Mayor Colden, CC Box 3173, May 26, 1818.

64. Ibid.

65. Mayor Cadwallader Colden to Cartmen, CC Box 3173, June 1, 1818.

66. Petition of Cartmen to Common Council, CC Box 3174, April 16, 1810.

67. Inspector's Report on Cartmen, CC Box 3173, February 22, 1806.

68. Petition of Samuel Stearns and Stephen Allen to Common Council, CC Box 3173, June 1, 1818. An earlier committee in 1816 had suggested limiting cartmen's licenses to men with families and a long residency in New York. It also suggested that a superintendent be appointed by the council to oversee the drivers and prevent frauds, and that the cartmen each be required to pay one dollar for paying the superintendent and for establishing a welfare fund for poor and infirm cartmen. Report of Committee of Cartmen, CC Box 3173, April 22, 1816.

69. For the ethnic composition of the porters, see New York City Jury List, 1816, Second Ward, Historical Documents Collection, Queens College, City University of New York; Memorial of Appointed Public Porters

to the Common Council, CC Box 3175, June 18, 1816.

70. Petition of Butchers of the Duane Street Market, CC Box 3173, July 27, 1818.

71. Memorial of Cartmen Working in the Pearl Slip Area, CC Box 3165, December 30, 1816.

72. Memorial of Edward Hitchcock to the Common Council, CC Box 3181, May 17, 1813; Petition of Manure Cartmen to the Common Council, CC Box 3181, April 12, 1813; Second Report of the Committee on the Deposit of Manure, CC Box 3215, September 20, 1813. The old storage place near the Episcopal burying ground was not going to be considered suitable for deposit by the city, and the cartmen, anticipating this problem, had sought out a new area.

73. Petition of Private Manure Cartmen to Common Council, CC Box 3181, July 9, 1813, August 2, 1813. (These are dated before the council meeting because the cartmen learned of the proposed finding before it was announced.) Petition of Residents of the Tenth Ward, CC Box 3175, July 25, 1815; Report of the Committee on Manure, CC Box 3181, January 29, 1816; Petition of Inhabitants Regarding Manure, CC Box 3175, n.d.

74. De Voe, *Market Book*, pp. 491-493.

Part III

THE NEW
MARKETPLACE

Chapter 9

A CHANGING ECONOMY

Along with mechanic crafts still working under traditional modes of operation, a number of significant professions were moving beyond preindustrial methods. Often tied in with the expanding mercantile and capitalist frontiers, these trades saw marked and dramatic changes in the conditions of work and in the relations between masters and journeymen. To understand the actions and reactions of artisans in these trades, it is necessary first to examine the nature of this new marketplace, and then the position in which it placed both master craftsmen and journeymen.

New York City in the early national period was at the forefront of a rapidly growing American economy. This was, in the words of Thomas C. Cochran, an era of "business revolution." Enormously expanding foreign and domestic trade, multiplying in the wake of the Napoleonic wars, led to greater consumer demand and expanded merchant operations. Subsequent reinvestment of capital led to improvements in communication and transportation as well as to specialized mercantile functions such as investment banking, stockbrokerage, and auctioneering. New York's many daily newspapers, for example, aided by an improved postal system, circulated widely throughout the metropolitan region and hinterlands, allowing those interested in trade and manufacture to quickly learn of market conditions and shipping schedules as well as other pertinent information. Stable and systematic business procedures, particularly incorporation, also aided commercial growth, as did sophisticated mercantile enterprises such as those conducted by the Girard, Astor, and Brown families. These firms had specific departments for southern and hinterland trade, for foreign imports and for local auctioneering, each directed by knowledgeable men capable of harnessing financial institutions and favorable economic conditions to their advantage. Indicative of the success of these operations and of the growth of the American economy as a whole are recent estimates that per capita income in the United States rose from 55 to 62 percent between 1800 and 1840—all before industrialization.[1]

At the center of the "business revolution" stood the nation's seaports, and especially New York. Together with its excellent deepwater harbors and the finest hinterlands in the nation (including those areas bounded by Newark Bay, Long Island Sound, and 150 navigable miles of the Hudson River), Gotham possessed local officials and farsighted merchants with "more entrepreneurial daring" than those of any other American city. The state, too, encouraged growth, regulating standards of cargo and passing a general incorporation law in 1811 that fostered the appearance of sixty-six acts of incorporation in that year alone. Consequently, the metropolis surged ahead of other seaports to become the country's commercial center, the "hub of inter-urban commodity flow." New York led the nation in both export and domestic trade. Between 1795 and 1810 the city handled one-third of the nation's foreign commerce (one-half in 1825), and by 1810 its share of the coastal trade was 25 percent. The urban center's population grew proportionately, as did its material assets. The number of New Yorkers nearly quadrupled between 1790 and 1820 (33,000 to 123,000), while total capital value increased by 850 percent. This included a 741 percent rise in real property value ($577,000 to $4,275,000) and an increase of 1,208 percent in taxable personal property ($177,520 to $2,322,000).[2]

The expanding economy directly influenced many of the city's mechanic trades. A greater demand for goods caused by the increased population and wealth in the city and the nation gave artisans strong incentive to expand their operations. Furthermore, improvements in communications and transportation as well as the absence of British restrictions made quantity production a viable undertaking. Too, through the "business revolution," mercantile capital and expertise were available to finance the expansion of these crafts and to assist in the procurement of markets and credits. Finally, since the economy was expanding nationally and the growing artisan trades had to compete with similar enterprises in other cities as well as with other local operations, efficient, organized, and cost-effective production was now required within the workshop.[3]

Shoemaking, cabinetmaking, and the clothing trades were three artisan crafts particularly affected by the expanding market system. In the shoemaking trade, ambitious master craftsmen, often with mercantile assistance in procuring credit and in marketing, moved to reach the growing wholesale markets in the city, the hinterlands, and along the Atlantic seaboard. Purchasing the needed leather, they distributed it to their journeymen, who then converted the raw material to shoes and returned it to the masters for marketing. Much of this footwear was low-quality black and brown "slop shoes" intended for slave markets in the South or West Indies, or for the indigent of New York. For these shoes quantity production was essential; costly workmanship, on the other hand, was unprofitable, since the master and his merchant backers had to pay shipping and warehousing costs and to vie in a competitive market. Consequently, journeymen's compensation was set at a considerably lower proportion of the retail cost than that given for high-quality shoes made to customer order. Furthermore, since craftsmanship was of minor concern, masters were inclined to draw on the less expensive labor of paid apprentices, aliens, and a surplus of tradesmen of mediocre skill.[4]

Cabinetmaking and tailoring followed lines similar to those of shoemaking. Besides being sold in increasing number to the growing city populace, furniture was often shipped to the South and the West Indies. One such cargo of five thousand windsor chairs embarked in 1795. A successful master cabinetmaker supervised a large enterprise in which journeymen did very specialized tasks, from veneering to glazing. Duncan Phyfe, for example, at the height of his career employed over one hundred such hands in his workshop. Wholesale merchants, moreover, were ready to buy up whole inventories and ship them to out-of-city markets. While the decline of craftsmanship in cabinetmaking may have been less severe than in the shoemaking trade, the shift toward quantity-oriented, efficiently organized operations was similar.[5]

In the clothes-making profession, however, workmanship did suffer in some instances as merchant tailors, intent on augmenting their profits through increased production at a lower expense, began to cut costs by employing relatively untrained and poorly paid seamstresses. The large number of tailors working in high-rent districts and vying for the custom, for the slop (ready-made clothing), and for the southern markets, forced a highly competitive situation requiring efficient production and reduced labor costs.[6]

The building trades were as strongly altered by the expanding economy as the manufacturing crafts. Financial and population growth saw the city expand into three large new wards between 1800 and 1820, requiring a great deal of new building. Merchants, moreover, particularly inclined to venture in real estate, erected elaborate homes, countinghouses, and stores. The construction business grew accordingly: by 1819 it employed two-fifths (over two thousand) of the city's journeymen and was a crucial factor in the city's economic cycle. Due to the complex nature of the new buildings and to the rising cost of land, a single carpenter assisted by his few journeymen and apprentices could no longer finance or complete an entire structure. Replacing the eighteenth century entrepreneur was the "master builder." Hired by the prospective owner of a dwelling or store, or by real estate speculators, his duties were those of a contractor: responsibility for procuring supplies and for hiring journeymen carpenters and masons. In this highly competitive market, "bosses cut . . . [wages] to the bone in order to gain advantage over their competitors." [7]

Printing outfits were also affected by the growth of capitalist organization. Aggressive publishers, in fact, played a key role in creating the information flow necessary for secure investment. As printing establishments expanded, helped considerably by the increasingly large volume of governmental and business needs, master printers' traditional position of craftsmen working alongside their journeymen and apprentices became less common.

Building a house in the Tenth Ward. Notice the master builder directing his journeymen in this relatively small project. This house was constructed at the very edge of the city. Museum of the City of New York.

Masons at work. New York Public Library.

Rather, it became that of a "fledgling capitalist," the capital consisting of presses and equipment. It was the masters' responsibility to secure hands and oversee shop operations and acquire accounts—all at the least possible expense.[8]

Essential to the expansion of these trades was an available pool of labor of average or less than average skill. (Printing shops, for example, required skilled journeymen for only half of their operations). This labor supply, which was often available at a lower wage than that demanded by highly skilled craftsmen, was acquired from three major sources. The first was the work of apprentices. Beginning in the late eighteenth century, the traditional apprenticeship system, in which a lad was indentured at the age of about fourteen to serve seven years until the age of twenty-one, had begun to break down. A shortage in the work force and the temptations of earning an early wage saw quite a few boys leave their masters early to take on paid positions at salaries less than that of fully trained journeymen. Since apprentices remained a good source of semiskilled, inexpensive labor, this practice continued into the nineteenth century when the labor shortage was less prominent.[9]

The growing immigrant community was a second source of workers. The percentage of the city's population composed of immigrants rose from 6.3 to 9.8 between 1806 and 1819 (5,163 to 11,764). These new residents lived mainly in the outer mechanic wards and worked at either unskilled labor or mechanic trades. In the Sixth Ward, for example, where aliens composed 15.5 percent of the population in 1810 and 24.3 percent in 1819, half of these immigrants worked at day labor with the other half tending to work in journeymen trades, particularly shoemaking, tailoring, and construction. Some of these artisans were highly skilled, but many others were not. In either case, they added to the growing labor pool.[10]

The third major source of moderately skilled tradesmen were the populous hinterlands of New York. A sample of 132 New York City mechanics drawn from various watch lists in the municipal archives reveals birthplaces of city artisans. Nearly two-thirds of the mechanics in this sample came from either New York State or New Jersey, a sharp contrast to the eighteenth century when most craftsmen were born in the city. Tradesmen such as carpenter Jacob Archer of Westchester County in upstate New York or Pierre

Demarest, a shoemaker from New Jersey, found the opportunities of a growing seaport to their liking. These figures suggest that in their decision to come to the metropolis they created not only a labor pool (and market) necessary for the expansion of the mechanic trades, but also a situation that allowed employers to keep wages down.[11]

ORIGINS OF NEW YORK CITY MECHANICS

Place of Birth	Number	Percent
New York City	28	21
New York State (except NYC)	46	35
New Jersey	39	30
New England	9	9
Pennsylvania and Virginia	1	1
Foreign	9	7

The six trades just described—shoemaking, cabinetmaking, tailoring, construction (carpentry and masonry), and printing, which will hereafter be known as "conflict trades" because the bulk of labor unrest took place within these crafts—appear to have been most affected by the "business revolution." A number of professions, most notably shipbuilding and coopering, in which journeymen formed trade unions but did not engage in protracted disputes, were also substantially altered by the changing American economy.[12] The trades of other mechanics, such as bakers, butchers, blacksmiths, goldsmiths, and cartmen, as noted in Chapter 6, generally remained traditional enterprises composed of a shop employing one or two journeymen and apprentices. Yet even these crafts, as we have seen, were at least partially touched by the influx of wealth and the emergence of modern business practices. The considerable expense required in the day-to-day operation of a bakery or a sail loft and the sizable incomes that could come from such shops reflect this. No doubt masters whose account books contained such sums were likely to take on some of the traits of the modern mechanic entrepreneur. Conversely, not all enterprises involved in the conflict trades became part of the growing capitalist matrix, instead remaining family operations. But no artisan could totally escape the consequences of the developing American marketplace.

It is also noteworthy that a large proportion of the city's me-

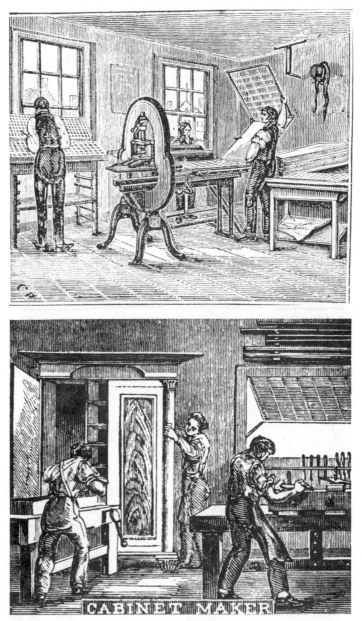

Printers and cabinetmakers at work. These trades had become extensive operations, entailing considerable capital equipment and commercial expertise. Printer: Courtesy, Century House, Watkins Glen, New York. Cabinetmaker: Courtesy, New York Historical Society, New York City.

Shipwrights and coopers at work. New York's large mercantile business allowed these trades to flourish. Shipbuilding was the city's most complex operation, involving large numbers of artisans. Shipwright: Courtesy, Century House, Watkins Glen, New York. Cooper: Courtesy, New York Historical Society, New York City.

chanics worked within the conflict trades, the professions most
geared to the mercantile world. Based on an 1819 sample of
artisans living in the fourth, sixth, and eighth wards, about 40
percent of the entire mechanic community (5,600) and, most
important, 65 percent of all journeymen (3,600) labored in one of
the expanding and conflict-ridden trades. Apprehensively or expec-
tantly, these masters and journeymen, together with perceptive
craftsmen in other mechanic branches, had to be concerned about
their position in the increasingly complex financial network.[13]

For the masters, the changing economy often meant a change in
function. With the restraints of the eighteenth century (a limited
market hemmed in by British imports, British technology, local
rural production, and poor access to credit) considerably lessened,
their role took on a more mercantile character. They now operated
as either small-scale men of commerce seeking wider commercial
outlets, as local contractors seeking mercantile connections, or as
agents of speculative investors, supplying merchants with goods
and services. Involved in highly competitive enterprises, their
relationships with employees tended to be strict and impersonal.
With maximum income and minimum expense paramount, the
easy rapport between a master and his journeymen was less
common.

This change in function, combined with the opportunities of the
growing American economy, often meant earnings and advancement unthinkable but a few decades earlier. One artisan achieving
significant financial success was the well-known cabinetmaker,
Duncan Phyfe. Born in an obscure part of Scotland, he came to
Albany with his mother and sisters at the age of sixteen. After
serving six years as an apprentice, Duncan moved to New York
where he opened a small shop on Broad Street. Lack of work
almost forced him to return to Albany, but at the last minute he
was befriended by the daughter of John Jacob Astor, whose
patronage allowed him to remain in business. Through exquisite
skill and strict Calvinist work habits his enterprise prospered,
reaching national and international markets. Located in a large
workshop and elegant salesroom on Partition Street, Phyfe, by the
time of his death in 1853 had accumulated assets of over $500,-
000.[14] As noted, shipwright Noah Brown, too, reached notable
heights from origins as a "barefoot frontier boy." Beginning in the

shipyards as an unknown journeyman, he became a prominent builder, receiving a naval contract during the War of 1812 that was worth $200,000 and that required the services of over two hundred craftsmen.[15] By 1815 his personal assets totaled $53,000. Others in these crafts taking good advantage of the expanding marketplace include tailor Jonas Mapes, who had amassed $15,900 by 1815; builders Anthony Steenback and Gideon Tucker, whose wealth in 1815 equaled $49,500 and $9,100, respectively; and shoemaker John Wolfe, who had holdings of $18,300 in 1815.[16]

Not all masters in these mercantile-oriented trades, of course, did so well. Edmund P. Willis's summary of the economic stratification of the Fourth Ward in 1815 puts most within the range of $1,000 to $5,000.[17] Often masters were forced to give up their economic independence to work as foremen in mercantile establishments. There they received a good salary, but the profits of the business

Shop and warehouse of Duncan Phyfe, 1815. Phyfe was one of New York's most successful artisans, both artistically and financially. The Metropolitan Museum of Art, Rogers Fund, 1922.

went to the owner. For example, the anchor shop of merchant Solomon Townsend, whose capital was required for the purchase of iron, was run by salaried mechanic foremen who received a weekly wage in the same manner as the five or six men working under them. (This enterprise, it is interesting to note, went out of business in 1806 because of a failure to maintain a cost-effective operation, particularly when orders lagged.) Other masters just failed to expand their businesses, or else, unable to make it in the increasingly competitive market, went bankrupt, their fate attested to by the many insolvency notices in the daily newspapers.[18]

The position of the city's journeymen, in contrast to the mixed but often quite advantageous situations of the master craftsmen, was decidedly unfavorable. The wages, hours, and living conditions of these craftsmen were more a reflection of the need to cut costs in efficient operations than of the influx of new capital into the city.

Unlike masters (other than salaried foremen) whose earnings were their business profits, journeymen worked for set compensation that was paid either by piecework or the daily wage. Printers, shoemakers, tailors, and cabinetmakers as well as goldsmiths, silversmiths, and blacksmiths were paid according to established piece-rate schedules. The cost of work for cabinetmakers, for example, was published in price books that listed either journeymen's rates or retail prices. Typical listings of the pieces produced, their labor, and their retail cost in 1796, are given in the accompanying table.[19]

LABOR AND RETAIL COSTS: CABINETMAKING

Article	Price (labor)	Price (retail)
Mahogany Dining Table	$ 8.80	$ 16.05
Pembroke Table	3.50	14.00
Square Card Table	3.22	14.00
Cradle	2.67	9.33
Splatt Back Chair honeysuckle pattern	1.93	7.67
Heart Back Chair	2.09	7.67
Circular Bureau	9.45	30.00
Clock Case	8.00	30.00

Special detail work was also included in these books as journeymen were paid for each additional item of work they performed, such as adding two small drawers to a bureau (two pence) or extending a bureau an extra ten inches (seven shillings, sixpence).[20]

Similar documents are available for journeymen shoemakers and printers. A sample of prices paid cordwainers for their labor is given in the accompanying table.[21]

JOURNEYMAN SHOEMAKER RATES

Back strap boots, fair tops	$ 4.00
Back strapping the top of above	.75
Ornament straps closed outside above	.25
Back strap bootees	3.25
Suwarrow boots, closed outside	3.00
Suwarrow boots, closed inside, bespoke	2.75
Suwarrow boots, closed inside, bespoke inferior	2.50
Binding boots	.25
Shoes, best work	1.12
Shoes, inferior work	1.00

Printers were paid for piecework operations according to a list that was circulated among all journeymen and masters. It included all types of procedures from setting common type (25 cents per em) and broadsides (30 cents per em) to extra charges for using Greek and Hebrew letters. Time rates were also established for the work necessary in setting columns and taking down presses (15.5 cents per hour).[22]

Journeymen masons and carpenters (and occasionally cabinet-makers) were paid by daily rates. This custom was peculiar to New York and dated from at least the 1790s.[23] Price books did exist in these trades, but when used were usually applied only for retail prices charged by the master builders (a perched stone wall cost one pound, ten shillings for material and labor).[24] The wage rate was set each year in early May (the beginning of the building season) at a meeting of the master carpenters and master masons.

The overall take-home pay for the different journeymen mechanics ranged roughly from eight to fourteen shillings per day (one shilling = 12.5 cents; eight shillings = one dollar). Charles Montgomery states that journeymen cabinetmakers received an average of but eight shillings per day from 1795 to 1810. However, details of public appeals during a strike in 1802 indicate that wages reached as high as fourteen shillings, probably averaging ten or eleven shillings per day.[25] Shoemakers' daily rates are not available for New York, but information is on hand from the transcript of the Philadelphia conspiracy trial, at which one witness stated that prices there were competitive with New York.[26] During the trial a journeyman claimed that he and his brethren could earn no more than $8.50 per week (eleven to twelve shillings daily), and that only by laboring from five in the morning until midnight.[27] On the other hand, the masters replied that journeymen could earn twelve dollars per week (sixteen shillings per day). The truth may have lain with the testimony of master shoemaker Lewis Ryan, who stated that most journeymen received from six to seven dollars per week (eight to ten shillings per day), but that the best men could make twelve dollars per week (sixteen shillings per day).[28] Since those journeymen working for piecework prices at their homes and cellars (shoemakers, cabinetmakers, and tailors) were paid only for what they produced, the discrepancies in the testimony are understandable. The more skillful and quicker journeymen making high-quality shoes received more than their counterparts making footwear of lower standards. Tailors, in 1819, reported that they could earn as much as thirteen to sixteen shillings per day, but because of underemployment they generally could work only six months per year, cutting their salary in half.[29] Carpenters and masons, who were paid strictly by the day, saw their wages fluctuate between ten and fifteen shillings per day from 1800 to 1820.[30]

The hours journeymen worked were also quite different from those of the master craftsmen. While masters often set their own working periods, those who toiled at shops for contractors had specific hours of work. According to a broadside issued by the master builders, carpenters and masons worked a ten-hour day in the spring, summer, and fall, and a nine-hour day during the winter months, November through February. (Masons, who could not work in inclement weather, were paid one shilling more per day than carpenters, while both trades received one shilling less per day during the winter months.) Their workday began at six in the morning during the spring and summer, and at seven during the winter and fall. An hour was allotted for breakfast in the spring and summer, and from one to two hours for lunch during the entire year. Work ended at six-thirty or seven in the evening in the

A bill of Duncan Phyfe (1802) and a business card of one of his competitors (1818). Museum of the City of New York.

fall, summer, and spring, and at five in the winter.[31] Indoors, journeymen had to work for five months (October 10 to March 10) by candlelight until eight or nine in the evening. In all, a journeyman's workday, inside or out, consisted of ten or more hours of labor for six days a week, including, for indoor tradesmen, the strain of working for hours by the glimmering light of candles.[32]

It should be noted that the attempt of the masters in the construction trades to establish through a joint broadside specific work hours for carpenters and masons was a significant change from the more flexible hours and work habits of the preindustrial era. As we shall see (Chapter 11), these traditions were still common among journeymen both in conflict and nonconflict crafts. But the move by these masters to systematize a work schedule is indicative of the changing marketplace of early national New York.

A third area of contrast between the journeymen and the masters was in the scale of earnings. Donald T. Adams, who has computed a cost-of-living index for the early national period, has found that real wages increased by 63 percent during the forty years between 1790 and 1830, a rate of 1.6 percent to 2.0 percent per year. There were two periods of substantial growth during this period: the 1790s and the years from 1815 to 1830. However, during the period of most interest to us, 1801 to 1820, much of the growth in real wages during the prosperous 1790s was dissipated by the rising cost of living. Especially during the war years, prices rose quickly while wages continued their slow gains, shilling by shilling.[33]

Corroborating Adams's work are two budget estimates from journeymen carpenters and masons. The carpenters' statement appeared as part of an appeal to the public for support during a strike in April 1809. It was based on an annual salary of $400 that included three hundred days of work, two hundred from May to November at eleven shillings per day ($275), and one hundred from November to May at ten shillings per day ($125).[34] The masons' figures appeared similarly in a strike appeal in May 1819 and were also based on an annual salary of $400. This was calculated from 213 working days per year at fifteen shillings per day and differed by $187 from the masters' estimate of journeymen's wages because—according to the journeymen—the masters did not account for all the days that the journeymen could not work.[35] Based on these yearly salaries, the journeymen gave sample budgets. Since these calculations were made by the journeymen to convince the public of the severity of their plight, it may be that the estimates are exaggerated to impress the populace. However, the message was intended for people living in the same city who certainly knew the current price of rents, food, and fuel. Indeed, as the following chapter will show in detail, the journeymen were barely making a subsistence living, with less than ten percent owning more than $150 of personal property.[36]

SAMPLE BUDGETS: CARPENTERS AND MASONS

	1809 Carpenters	1819 Masons
House rent	$ 55.00	$ 60.00
Fire wood	30.00	18.00
Food for family[a)	162.50	195.00
Wearing apparel[b)	60.00	100.00
Tools expense[c)	10.00	---
Contingent expenses[c)	20.00	---
Total[d)	$337.50	$373.00
Left for wife's and children's clothing[c), recreation, illness, education of children, and other emergencies	$ 62.50	$ 27.00

Notes to Sample Budgets:

[a) Carpenters stipulate that this meant "victualling for a family of five at 50 cents per day."

[b) Carpenters stipulate personal apparel for themselves only while masons state that this amount covers apparel for a family of five.

[c) Carpenters only.

[d) Amount given in advertisement, $357.50 was incorrect by $20.

The drop in the growth of real wages was not due to a lack of resources or capital. The rising incomes of the successful master craftsmen reveal the ready supply of assets. Rather, it is symbolic of the increasing concentration of wealth in New York during this period. In 1815, in the sample Fourth Ward, the wealthiest 10 percent owned the same proportion of the district's personal property (three-fourths) as the top 30 percent had owned in 1789. That same year the ward's lower 80 percent possessed 13.4 percent of the area's personal property as compared with 33.1 percent twenty-six years earlier. While the proportion of residents owning some real estate rose together with the proportion able to pay a minimal tax, the lower half of the ward's population owned a smaller percent of the area's real estate in 1815 than they had in 1789. Moreover, by 1815 there had been a decrease of 20 to 23 percent in the median assessment of the lowest 30 percent of the ward's taxpayers, a class that included nearly all of the journeymen. This group now owned but 0.9 percent of the total property value, a drop from 4.9 percent in 1789. The lower 50 percent owned only 8 percent of the property, a decrease from 13.5 percent in 1789.[37]

The meaning of these statistics is best seen in the conditions and life of the outer wards where most journeymen resided. By the nineteenth century the colonial practice of journeymen residing with their masters was unusual. Rather, were a traveler to walk through Gotham's streets during this period, he would find several such mechanics and their families sharing a single dwelling. For example, the house at 556 Broadway in the Sixth Ward contained three journeymen households. The building was owned by a shoemaker, Nathaniel Kilmaster, fifty, who rented out parts of his home to fellow cordwainer Peter Gass, twenty-two, and to John Harriet, forty-three, a carpenter. In a similar situation, at 129 Orange Street, two journeymen carpenters and a journeyman jeweler, their families, and an alien painter shared a building. Twenty-two people lived in the house, or slightly more than twice the average of 12.7 inhabitants per dwelling. This was still far less than the 103 who shared a building at 10 Hester Street.[38]

Many of these homes were sparsely furnished, perhaps containing a few windsor chairs, a chest, a table, a bedstead, clothing, and other accessories. Even this was more than could be found in the boardinghouses along the waterfront where many of the younger and a number of older, unmarried journeymen lived. At 6 Rose Street in the Fourth Ward, for example, four workers in the leather trade resided in a roominghouse. Three were journeymen, two in their early twenties and one forty-eight; the fourth was a twenty-six-year-old alien morocco-leather dresser. Also in that ward at 9 Dover Street, nine journeymen and an alien mechanic, ranging in age from twenty-two to thirty-seven, lived in Hannah Christie's boardinghouse.[39] These residences could be uncomfortable, such as the one near the Wallabout shipyards in which twenty-five men slept in two chambers, one of which was only ten to twelve feet square and without a privy.[40] However, they provided the most inexpensive housing, allowing a young craftsman to gain independence both from his family and his employer.

Nearly all journeymen, and the majority of independent craftsmen as well, rented their homes, often from the agents of major landowners such as John Jacob Astor. These magnates bought land in the outer wards before it was settled, renting but seldom selling the dwellings they built on their property. In the Eighth Ward, for example, only 1.5 percent of the journeymen (and 8.1 percent of the masters) owned their own land.[41] The amounts of rent due varied, of course, but landlord affidavits for 1811 and 1819 suggest that a mechanic renting a house in the outer wards paid about $150 per year (from $88 to $250). Many of the house rents were further reduced by partial sublets, lowering the costs to perhaps the $55 to $60 that the carpenters and masons listed in their budgets.[42]

For many of the journeymen, the date that rents were due, either quarterly (the first of each February, May, August, and November) or else annually on May 1, was awaited with dread. In the Eighth Ward in 1819, for example, with 97.6 percent of the 593 journeymen owning less than $150 worth of personal property, the minimum assessment figure for that year, any kind of setback could make it impossible to pay for lodging. Problems such as illness or unemployment or just a lack of sufficient funds led to a large and often illegal migration of poor mechanic tenants each "quarter day." Observing this phenomenon, Moreau de St. Méry was astonished at the "mania" for moving of New Yorkers who "do not own a house." This, he remarked, "must be seen to be believed." But if money was short, as it often was, a change of residence offered the possibility of finding cheaper lodging or else of leaving without paying the rent, though this brought a very real chance of a "distrainment of property."[43]

Besides the procurement of shelter, other serious problems faced the journeymen. Living in drafty wooden homes heated by fire-places, an adequate supply of wood was essential during the cold winter months. Unfortunately, bad weather, embargoes, and wars created shortages and high prices that were further raised by unscrupulous "forestallers" who, cornering the market, drove the cost of fuel beyond the reach of the poor mechanic. In 1807, for example, the price of wood increased 43 percent, from fourteen to twenty shillings per load, because of a "combination" of boatmen and cartmen. The situation commonly grew critical, and few years passed without a substantial distribution of firewood to the poor, including many journeymen. In 1812, the New York Fuel Association handed out 100,000 loads to more than 3,000 needy citizens.[44]

Food, too, was subject to severe shortages because of weather, recession, war, and the intrigues of monopolists. An 1818 letter to the Common Council from "A Citizen" protested that only the rich could afford to purchase food at the markets; the poor were shut out by evil forestallers, miscreants who deserved "branding with a hot iron." When journeymen were not able to afford food, charity, despite the shame accompanied by its receipt, was the only answer. During the bitter wartime winter of 1814-15, for example, soup kitchens fed 3,516 families, or 16,417 inhabitants, at the considerable expense of $25,485.[45]

The problems of food, fuel, and rent hit journeymen hardest in the winters when work was scarce and prices high. A commentator in the *Evening Post* stated that "during our winters, even a moderate one, many of the lower class of artificers, labourers, cartmen and others, have not sufficient employ to enable them to support their families except in a very uncomfortable way, and are, of course, obliged to struggle with difficulty through the inclement season." [46] A further problem at this time was taxes. Personal property levies constituted a heavy burden. As prominent landowner Henry Rutgers, arguing against any increases, warned Mayor De Witt Clinton: "Consider the heavy assessments laid upon the city, especially in the out-wards. I am afraid the Bone will snap." Reports from the tax collectors of these areas give evidence of this distress. In the spring of 1803, collector Anthony Brown of the Sixth Ward petitioned the Common Council for extra time for submitting his funds. Such a postponement, he declared, would not only relieve him of "much embarrassment," but also "enable the poor of the sixth ward who have just emerged from a winter which has consumed their previous earnings, to discharge their taxes with convenience." Similarly, in 1812 collector John O'Neale, also of the Sixth Ward, asked for a delay in the filing of the "insolvent" list in order to enable "a great number of citizens" who were "desirous" of paying their taxes the opportunity to do so. The failure to pay taxes could mean, of course, the seizure of property.[47]

A final threat posed by harsh winters and economic recession was insolvency. While all classes were vulnerable, the journeyman mechanic who had few assets was particularly liable to fall into unredeemable obligations and find himself in debtors' prison. The *Evening Post* reported that "a great proportion of these debtors are of that class of citizens who are easily led to contract debts with small grocers, who like the spider, sits and imperceptibly widens his web around the denoted victim." Debtors' prison meant, of course, dishonor and destitution for one's family as well as a continuing inability to pay. Yet many tradesmen were unable to remain free of its clutches. In 1809, for example, of the 1,152 men incarcerated for debt, only 326 owed more than $15, while 500 were imprisoned for amounts of less than $10 (a week's salary).[48]

It must not be thought from the listing of these conditions that journeymen were constantly starving, freezing, and in jail. Most of the time, they and their families managed to get by. The point is, however, that living in the midst of a city that was in a financial boom, they were forced to manage on tight and sometimes subsistence budgets that left little room for error. These conditions help to explain why so many labor disputes took place during times of prosperity. Journeymen resisted receiving an increasingly smaller piece of the growing economic pie. Moreover, if they were to remain relatively poor, then of that much more importance was the pride and dignity of skilled craftsmen, a holding they would not surrender easily.

NOTES

1. Thomas C. Cochran, "The Business Revolution," *American Historical Review*, 79 (1974), pp. 1449-1466; Alan R. Pred, *Urban Growth and the Circulation of Information: The United States System of Cities, 1800-1840* (Cambridge, 1973); Elizabeth Wood, in David T. Gilchrist, ed., *The Growth of the Seaport Cities, 1790-1815* (Charlottesville, 1967), p. 199; Paul A. David, "The Growth of Real Production in the United States before 1840: New Evidence, Controlled Conjectures," *Journal of Economic History*, 27 (1967), 153-193; Douglass C. North, *Growth and Welfare in the American Past*, 2nd ed. (Englewood Cliffs, N.J., 1974), pp. 68-86.

2. Pred, *Urban Growth*, p. 139; Willis, "Social Origins and Political Leadership in New York City from the Revolution to 1815," Ph.D. diss. (Berkeley, Cal., 1967), pp. 97-98, 113, 119; Robert Albion, *The Rise of New York Port* (New York, 1939); Gilchrist, ed., *Growth of the Seaport Cities*, pp. 41, 56, 68-78, 114; Sidney I. Pomerantz, *New York: An American City, 1783-1803* (New York, 1938), pp. 149-166; J. Leander Bishop, *History of Manufactures from 1608-1860*, 2 vols. (Philadelphia, 1864), vol. 2, p. 173.

3. The problem of urban market relationships and the mechanic trades during the early national era is complex and needs more study. Significant general works include David Saposs, in John R. Commons, et al., *History of Labor in the United States*, 4 vols. (New York, 1926-1935), vol. 1, pp. 88-107; Alan R. Pred, "Manufacturing in the Mercantile City, 1800-1840," *Annals of the Society of American Geographers*, 56 (1966), 307-325; Glenn Porter and Harold Livesay, *Merchants and Manufacturers: Studies in the Changing Structure of Nineteenth Century Marketing* (Baltimore, 1971).

4. Master shoemakers used a number of different methods in selling their wares. Based on conspiracy trial transcripts, John R. Commons declared that masters did their own retailing, including travel to other domestic ports. Saposs, on the other hand, states that merchant capitalists were investing their funds in shoemaking and other mechanic enterprises, lending masters their marketing expertise and sometimes marketing for them, with the masters acting as foremen. In a recent study of Lynn, Massachusetts, Paul Faler has shown how commission merchants worked during this period both as wholesalers and as retailers of masters' foot-wear and as creditors to master craftsmen who preferred to do their own procurement of materials and marketing. All of these methods were likely prevalent in New York at this time. John R. Commons, et al., eds., *A Documentary History of American Industrial Society*, 10 vols. (Cleveland, 1909-1911), vol. 3, pp. 34-39; Saposs, in Commons, et al., *History of Labor in the*

United States, vol. 1, pp. 88-107; Paul Faler, "Workingmen, Mechanics and Social Change: Lynn, Massachusetts, 1800-1860," Ph.D. diss. (University of Wisconsin, 1970), pp. 31-54. See also Blanche Hazard, *The Organization of the Boot and Shoe Industry in Massachusetts before 1875* (Cambridge, 1921), pp. 3-64; Dorothy Brady in Gilchrist, ed., *Growth of the Seaport Cities,* pp. 94-95; and Victor S. Clark, *History of Manufactures in the United States,* 2 vols. (New York, 1949), vol. 1, pp. 354-355, 443.

5. Charles F. Montgomery, *American Furniture: The Federal Period, 1788-1825* (New York, 1966), pp. 13-14; Wendell P. Garrett, "The Matter of Consumers' Taste," in John D. Morse, ed., *Country Cabinetwork and Simple City Furniture* (Charlottesville, Va., 1969), pp. 205-233; Nancy McClelland, *Duncan Phyfe and the English Regency, 1795-1830* (New York, 1939), p. 123; Dorothy Brady, in Gilchrist, ed., *Growth of the Seaport Cities,* p. 95; Thomas Ormsbee, *The Story of American Furniture* (New York, 1938), pp. 33-39.

6. Egal Feldman, "New York Men's Clothing Trade, 1800 to 1861," Ph.D. diss. (New York University, 1959), pp. 5-7, 35-37, 65-75, 148-158, 168. Feldman puts the changes generally after the early national period. This is partially mistaken, I believe, as indicated by the evidence of journeymen strife in this trade. He actually has very little data pre-1825, and it is likely that there was considerable activity during these years. See the discussion between him and Elizabeth Wood in Gilchrist, ed., *Growth of the Seaport Cities,* pp. 197-199. See also *Evening Post,* July 13, 1819.

7. Robert Christie, *Empire in Wood* (Ithaca, 1956), pp. 10-12, and "Empire in Wood, a History of the United Brotherhood of Carpenters and Joiners of America," Ph.D. diss. (Cornell University, 1954), p. 35; Pred, *Urban Growth,* p. 193; *Evening Post,* June 19, 1810. The figure of two-fifths was derived from a sample composed of all journeymen residing in the fourth, sixth, and eighth wards of New York City in 1819 as found in the 1819 Jury Lists. (The exact percentage was 42.7.) Historical Documents Collection, Queens College, City University of New York.

8. Rollo G. Silver, *The American Printer 1787-1825* (Charlottesville, Va., 1967), pp. 1-96, 103; Richard P. Brief, "The Philadelphia Printer: A Study of an Eighteenth Century Businessman," *Business History Review,* 40 (1968), 46.

9. Ian M. G. Quimby, "Apprenticeship in Colonial Philadelphia," M.A. diss. (University of Delaware, 1963), pp. 74-83, 140-147.

10. The number and occupations of immigrants in New York is thoroughly discussed in James Owre, "The Effect of Immigration on New York City, 1800-1819," M.A. diss. (Queens College, 1971), pp. 5-13, and in Carol Groneman Pernicone, "The 'Bloody Ould Sixth': A Social Analysis of a New York City Working-Class Community in the Mid-

Nineteenth Century," Ph.D. diss. (University of Rochester, 1973), pp. 29-35. See also Pomerantz, *New York: An American City,* pp. 201-209, and Table 10.1 below.

11. Return of Watchmen, May to June 1800, City Clerk Filed Papers (hereafter referred to as CC), Box 6464, Box 3155, New York City Municipal Archives; for a discussion of the availability of skilled labor see also H. J. Habakkuk, *American and British Technology in the Nineteenth Century* (Cambridge, England, 1962), pp. 21-25, 128-131, 151-156, and Stuart Bruchey, *The Roots of American Economic Growth, 1607-1861* (New York, 1965), pp. 162-173. Jackson Turner Main, *The Social Structure of Revolutionary America* (Princeton, 1965), pp. 183, 186-187.

12. It is likely that shipbuilding, long an extensive and complex operation, was less susceptible to the convulsions of rapid economic growth. Journeymen shipwrights had come to accept impersonal profit-oriented enterprises and worked out reasonably comfortable relationships with employers. Moreover, shipwrights frequently moved from yard to yard, according to the availability of employment, thus lessening the possibility of protracted conflict. However, the presence of a journeymen shipwrights' society and constitution does indicate that the shipwrights, like other members of expanding trades, were aware of the possibility of being undermined by unqualified workers. (See Chapter 10.) Alan R. Pred, *The Spatial Dynamics of United States Urban Industrial Growth, 1800-1914* (Cambridge, 1966), pp. 197-200. Coopering, on the other hand, remained a local and relatively simple operation: supplying barrels for the city's maritime commerce. Yet the growth in volume stimulated by the expanding economy did pose a threat to journeymen, who moved to protect their position through trade societies. Franklin E. Coyne, *The Development of the Cooperage Industry in the United States* (Chicago, 1940), pp. 14-21.

13. The figures are calculated from the 1819 New York City Jury Lists for the Fourth, Sixth, and Eighth wards. These were the three outer, or "mechanic," wards for which figures are available. Artisans made up about two-thirds of the wards' population.

14. McClelland, *Duncan Phyfe and the English Regency,* pp. 98-125.

15. Willis, "Social Origins," p. 154.

16. Ibid., Appendix.

17. Ibid., pp. 123, 130. These may be assumed to be masters as journeymen were seldom listed in the *Directory* of 1815.

18. See Alan S. Marber, "The New York Iron Merchant and Manufacturer: A Study of Eighteenth Century Entrepreneurship," Ph.D. diss. (New York University, 1974).

19. These are taken from the 1796 *Philadelphia and London Book of Prices* (journeymen's wages) and the 1796 *Philadelphia Cabinet and Chair Makers' Book of Prices* (retail prices) as found in Montgomery, *American Furniture,* p. 23.

20. Ibid., p. 25.

21. *People v. Melvin* (1809), in Commons, et al., *Documentary History of American Industrial Society,* vol. 3, pp. 368-369.

22. Broadside, "To the Master Printers of New York" (1809), New York Historical Society.

23. Colonel Stevens to James McHenry, July 9, 1798; Col. Stevens misc. mss., vol. 1, no. 51, New York Historical Society.

24. *Masons' Price Book* (New York, 1805), in John McComb misc. mss., New York Historical Society.

25. Montgomery, *American Furniture,* pp. 23, 24, 26; *Morning Chronicle,* November 1, 1803; *Evening Post,* April 10, 1805.

26. *Commonwealth v. Pullis* (1806), in Commons et al., *Documentary History of American Industrial Society,* vol. 3, p. 111.

27. Ibid., p. 121.

28. Ibid., p. 106.

29. *Evening Post,* July 13, 1819.

30. *American Citizen,* April 10, 1809, May 10, 1810, June 6, 1810; *Evening Post,* May 14, 1809, May 27, 1819, June 7, 1819; *Columbian,* November 13, 1816. Stonecutters were paid from $1.00 to $1.25 per day (eight to ten shillings) in 1808. Journal of John McComb, John McComb misc. mss., New York Historical Society.

31. Broadside, "To the Journeymen Carpenters and Masons," March 11, 1805, New York Public Library.

32. John Bradford, *The Poetical Vagaries of a Knight of the Folding Stick of PASTE CASTLE, to which is annexed the History of the Garret, &c., Translated from the Hieroglyphics of the Society by a Member of the Order of the Blue String* (New York, 1813), p. 50; Rocellus Guernsey, *New York During the War of 1812* (New York, 1889), p. 35.

33. Donald T. Adams, "Wage Rates in the Early National Period: 1785-1830," *Journal of Economic History,* 28 (1968), 415. Adams notes that despite the hardships under which skilled artisans worked, unskilled labor was paid much less, averaging a ratio of 1.7 to 1.0 for the wages of skilled to unskilled. In times of economic distress, the differences tended to lessen (p. 410). See also Adams, "Some Evidence on English and American Wage Rates, 1780-1830," ibid., 30 (1970), 499-521, and U.S. Department of Labor, Bureau of Labor Statistics, Bulletin No. 499, *History of Wages in the United States from Colonial Times to 1928* (Washington, D.C., 1929).

34. *American Citizen,* April 10, 1809.

35. *Evening Post,* May 31, 1819.

36. See pp. 265-267.

37. Willis, "Social Origins," pp. 108-122.

38. 1819 New York City Jury Lists, Sixth Ward, passim.

39. Nancy Goyne Evans, "Unsophisticated Furniture Made and Used in Philadelphia and Environs, 1750-1800," in Morse, ed., *Country Cabinetwork and Simple City Furniture,* pp. 166-196; 1819 Jury Lists, Fourth Ward.

40. *American Citizen,* July 19, 1804.

41. Kenneth W. Porter, *John Jacob Astor: Businessman,* 2 vols. (New York, 1966), vol. 2, pp. 917-919. Sample from New York City Jury List, Eighth Ward.

42. Landlord Affidavits, Records of New York City Mayor's Court, February 1, 1811, February 1, 1819, August 1, 1819, Historical Documents Collection, Queens College, City University of New York. See also List of Houses rented in Chatham Street, Box 3181, March 12, 1806.

43. *Moreau de St. Méry's American Journey, 1793-1798,* trans. and ed. by Kenneth and Anna Roberts (New York, 1947), p. 165. Landlords could impound and sell property of delinquent tenants after filing an affidavit before the local justice of the peace. *Laws of New York,* 34th sess., chapt. 202, section 19 (1811). One enterprising man took advantage of the moving mania by establishing a house registry service and advertising with the words, "Quarter Day Approaching!!" *The Shamrock or Hibernian Chronicle,* January 26, 1811.

44. Letter of "A Citizen" to Marinus Willet, CC Box 3155, October 19, 1807; *Morning Post,* October 1, 1811, November 22, 1811. See also *Columbian,* October 5, 9, 1813; *Public Advertiser,* December 28, 1809; Thomas N. Stanford, *A Concise Description of the City of New York* (New York, 1818), p. 49; Raymond A. Mohl, *Poverty in New York, 1783-1825* (New York, 1971), pp. 108-110.

45. Letter to the Mayor and Corporation, CC Box 3173, July 14, 1818. On butter monopolies see *Evening Post,* November 12, 1813; *National Advocate,* October 5, 9, 1813; Mohl, *Poverty in New York,* pp. 112-116.

46. *Evening Post,* October 12, 1804.

47. Letter of Henry Rutgers to De Witt Clinton, February 14, 1806, De Witt Clinton Papers, vol. 3, p. 25, Columbia University. Petition of Anthony Brown to Mayor Livingston, CC Box 3155, May 9, 1803; Petition of Collector of the Sixth Ward, CC Box 3181, January 29, 1812. See also petitions of collectors of taxes, second, third, fifth, and ninth wards, CC Box 3080, May 27, 1811; Petition of Collector of the Seventh Ward, CC Box 3080, May 27, 1811; Petition of John McKinnon to the Common Council, CC Box 3175, September 23, 1816.

48. *Evening Post,* February 7, 1818; Smith Hart, *The New Yorkers, The Story of a People and Their City* (New York, 1938), pp. 45-49; Edward R. Ellis, *The Epic of New York* (New York, 1960), p. 210; Mohl, *Poverty in New York,* pp. 121-130.

Chapter 10

MASTERS AND
JOURNEYMEN

The city's large journeyman constituency, constituting two-fifths of the artisan population, played a fundamental role in the life of the mechanic community, particularly on the labor front. During the Jeffersonian era, journeymen in six major trades affected by the expanding marketplace (carpenters, masons, shoemakers, tailors, cabinetmakers, and printers) staged protracted battles against masters and their merchant associates. This labor strife, marking a formative period in American working-class history, generally occurred during periods of prosperity and seriously disrupted the city's economy. In fact, in 1810 the situation became so grave that a number of the city's major "architects and surveyors" took out lengthy public advertisements deploring the "increasing evils and the distressing tendency of the disputes between the Master and Journeymen Mechanics" and the "altercations that so frequently occur among the Mechanics of this city for wages." [1]

To understand the meaning of this labor conflict, it is first necessary to examine the contrasting positions of journeymen in the conflict and nonconflict trades. The differences in the outlooks of the two groups perceptively reveal the effects of capitalist expansion upon the disposition of the journeymen. With this comparison in mind, the ensuing description of the serious labor disruptions of the early nineteenth century can be properly seen as the efforts of journeymen to find a place of strength and dignity within the limits of the new marketplace.

The difficult position of New York's journeyman population, particularly in comparison with the standing of many of the masters, has been noted. This situation was prominently in evidence among the mechanics working in the conflict trades. An analysis of the 1819 Jury Lists for the Fourth, Sixth, and Eighth wards indicates the large gaps between the two groups in monetary possessions (Table 10.1). Only a small proportion (8.4 percent) of journeymen owned $150 worth of personal property, while most employers (72.9 percent) held at least that much; and about one-fourth (25.5 percent) of the masters owned a house or a store, in contrast to a small fraction (2.1 percent) of journeymen.

The disparities in wealth were compounded by the difficulties journeymen had in rising to independent status. The high numerical ratio of journeymen to masters and the small differences between the ages of the two groups (Table 10.2) reveal this condition. Wage earners outnumbered master craftsmen by between three and four to one. Moreover, since some masters still operated small outfits that employed only one or two journeymen, and since many journeymen were not included in the jury lists, the ratio in the larger shops—where most journeymen worked—was considerably higher. A historian of printer-employers in New York states, for example, that the ratio between journeymen and masters in 1818 was eleven to one (55 to 5).[2] With regard to age, journeymen were generally only four to seven years younger than their masters, and many remained wage earners well into their thirties, forties, and fifties. In the Sixth Ward, three-quarters of all artisans under fifty were still journeymen.[3]

For the majority of journeymen laboring in these six trades, the outlook was bleak. The considerable mobility that historians have pictured for the eighteenth century, when "master craftsmen and journeymen had become indistinct from one another," and when master craftsman status was more common than journeyman standing (even if a growing stratification of wealth was pushing mechanics into an insecure lower middle class) was no longer present.[4] For these crafts had become in many instances extensive

Table 10.1

A COMPARISON OF JOURNEYMEN AND NON-JOURNEYMEN IN

MAJOR MECHANIC TRADES OF NEW YORK, 1819: WEALTH STATUS

(Wards 4, 6, 8)[a]

	No.	Personal Property $0 - 149	Personal Property $150+	Freehold $150+	Percent Property or Freehold $150+
SHOEMAKERS					
Journeymen:	154	144	9	1	6.5
Non-Jrnymn:	86	27	36	23	67.0
Aliens:	37	33	4	0	10.8
MASONS					
Journeymen:	151	146	4	1	3.3
Non-Jrnymn:	43	18	11	14	58.1
Aliens:	35	32	3	0	8.6
CARPENTERS					
Journeymen:	407	357	34	16	12.3
Non-Jrnymn:	96	19	46	31	80.2
Aliens:	66	59	7	0	10.6
TAILORS					
Journeymen:	47	44	3	0	6.4
Non-Jrnymn:	57	11	36	10	80.7
Aliens:	66	66	0	0	0.0
Women:	23	21	0	2	8.7
CABINETMAKERS					
Journeymen:	50	49	1	0	2.0
Non-Jrnymn:	42	13	23	6	72.5
Aliens:	19	18	1	0	5.3
PRINTERS					
Journeymen:	38	36	2	0	5.3
Non-Jrnymn:	12	3	7	2	72.5
Aliens:	6	6	0	0	0.0
TOTAL					
Journeymen:	847	776	53	18	8.4
Non-Jrynmn:	336	91	159	86	72.9
Aliens:	229	214	15	0	6.6
Women:	23	21	0	2	8.7

Source: New York City Jury List, fourth, sixth, and eighth wards, 1819.
Historical Documents Collection, Queens College, City University of New York.

[a] Non-Jrnymn refers to both master craftsmen who employed large numbers of journeymen and to those who worked mostly by themselves with only one or two journeymen.

Table 10.2

A COMPARISON OF JOURNEYMEN AND NON-JOURNEYMEN IN

MAJOR MECHANIC TRADES OF NEW YORK, 1819: AGE

(Wards 4, 6, 8)[a]

	No.	Average Age	Age 20-29	Age 30-39	Age 40-49	Age 50+	Age Unknown
SHOEMAKERS							
Journeymen:	154	31.9	65	40	21	6	22
Non-Jrnymn:	86	39.9	13	24	18	15	16
[b]Aliens:	37						
MASONS							
Journeymen:	151	34.2	29	26	17	10	69
Non-Jrnymn:	43	40.2	5	13	6	8	11
[b]Aliens:	35						
CARPENTERS							
Journeymen:	407	34.6	95	101	59	20	132
Non-Jrnymn:	96	41.7	10	29	27	17	13
[b]Aliens:	66						
TAILORS							
Journeymen:	47	32.3	19	16	7	3	2
Non-Jrnymn:	57	36.7	14	20	8	10	5
[b]Aliens:	66						
[b]Women:	23						
CABINETMAKERS							
Journeymen:	50	27.3	28	9	6	0	7
Non-Jrnymn:	42	33.4	11	11	4	1	15
[b]Aliens:	19						
PRINTERS							
Journeymen:	38	31.9	15	17	4	0	2
Non-Jrnymn:	12	32.5	3	6	2	0	1
[b]Aliens:	6						
TOTAL							
Journeymen:	847	33.1	251	209	114	139	234
Non-Jrnymn:	336	38.9	56	103	65	51	61
[b]Aliens:	229	0	0	0	0	0	0
[b]Women:	23	0	0	0	0	0	0

Source: New York City Jury List, fourth, sixth, and eighth wards,1819, Historical
Documents Collection, Queens College, City University of New York.
[a] Non-Jrnymn refers to both master craftsmen who employed large numbers of journeymen and to those who worked mostly by themselves with only one or two journeymen.
[b] Ages not listed.

and complex operations well beyond the means of a young journeyman. As the journeymen printers lamented in 1802, "the business of Printing being very expensive to establish, from the high
price of materials, very few of those, who are obliged to resort to
journey-work when they become free, ever have it in their power to
realize a capital sufficient to commence business on their own
account." [5] While opportunity was still possible for artisans with
exceptional skill, access to capital, or good business sense, no longer
could journeyman status be considered a temporary position. Whatever their hopes at the onset of their careers, for journeymen in the
conflict trades there was no guarantee of advancement, but rather a
good likelihood that they would become permanent wage earners,
making a subsistence salary and struggling with their family under
the constant threat of poverty.

Although they too were affected by declining wages, and were
often as poor as their counterparts in the conflict trades, journeymen working in the nonconflict crafts (or in small enterprises
within the conflict trades) were less likely to organize and take
concerted action against employers. Greater opportunity for advancement, indicated in the Eighth Ward, for example, by a near
equality in the ratio of masters to journeymen in nonconflict trades
(112 to 126), worked against such measures. So, too, did the lack of
concentration of these journeymen, as in the Fourth, Sixth, and
Eighth wards, the 35 percent (456) of the journeymen population
employed in nonconflict trades worked in over sixty separate
professions.[6]

Two revealing examples of the attitudes and life-styles of these
journeymen are available. The first is the account book of Elisha
Blossom, a highly skilled journeyman cabinetmaker who worked
for a small-scale entrepreneur, David Loring. Blossom's account
book covers his work in New York between 1811 and 1815. The
first entries find him just arrived from Argentina and briefly self-
employed constructing parts of tables, benches, and kitchen
shelves.[7] Within a matter of weeks Blossom gave up this existence
and began working for Loring. This relationship continued, on and
off, for the next four years. Working at his employer's shop,
Blossom continued to make shelves, frames and tables for a weekly
wage of $8.25 (eleven shilling per week) out of which he paid Mrs.
Loring $3.31 a week for board and washing. Although this salary

allowed Loring a considerable profit—in one week Elisha finished a sideboard worth thirty dollars—it was not an unusual rate, since a ratio of 3.5 to 1 for labor to sale price was common.[8]

Aside from his efforts for Loring, Blossom did occasional work for other master cabinetmakers. In 1812, for example, he worked for George James, usually for from two to six days at a time. The personal income from his labor was evidently quite sufficient, as in 1813 Blossom purchased a gold watch from Loring for seventy-five dollars.[9] Yet in February 1814, the journeyman cabinetmaker suddenly renounced his profession and took a position as a clerk for bookseller Robert Scott at $375 per year. Within ten days, however, an entry appeared in the margin of his journal stating that he "could not agree as it was too confining and Quit." He thereupon returned to Loring "by mutual consent" where he remained through the end of his account book a year later.[10]

Blossom was a journeyman of extensive individual talent. For one French bureau which he constructed he had to do the gluing, mitering, veneering, fitting, hanging, banding, dividing, and carving.[11] Literate, he appears to have led a rather quiet life. He also seems to have done reasonably well financially, although his apparent lack of children may have had something to do with this. Evidently a solitary worker, Blossom was able to maintain this independence, as well as steady employment and a reasonable income, in part due to his exceptional skill. His isolation also removed him from any participation in concerted action by fellow tradesmen.

Our other example is John Bradford, a journeyman bookbinder who published a book of poetry, much of which concerned his work. The most apparent theme of his verses is his pride in his skills, a sentiment directly expressed in two poems. The first describes his feelings toward his first set of tools, instruments bought "at his own expense" while still an apprentice. In a "PROCLAMATION" he warns all other inhabitants of "Paste Castle," whether "journeyman, 'prentice or in whatever station," to keep their distance from his new possessions. This caution out of the way, Bradford eagerly boasts of his acquisitions:

> The tools I have stiled as my own are but few,
> They are triangle, a knife, stabbing awl and a bodkin.

> A hard hammer, baking and cutting boards too,
> An oil stone, a cutting press, ploy and press pin.
>   Plow knife, candlestick
>   A tarbulum for Dick,
> Needles, sewing keys, compasses and foldingstick;
> Not one of these tools above mentioned are thine,
> For while I work with them I stile them all mine.[12]

In a second poem, the "Knight of the Folding Stick of PASTE CASTLE" celebrates the act of bookbinding:

> First fold it and gather it,
> And if it's complete,
> Then solid and even
> The book must be beat;
> Then press, saw and sew it,
> And line it and glue it,
> And scrape the slips, back it
> And put the boards to it.
> Then lace in the slips,
> In the standing press put it,
> And paste wash the back,
> And when press'd enough cut it;
> This done gild the edges,
> Or colour them, . . .[13]

To Bradford the bindery was not only a place where one put in hours of labor, but also a universe containing all aspects of society. One poem, "All the World's a Bindery," compared artisans to governors:

> Some forward, some finish, and often you'll see,
> To a good workman ten mutton thumpers there'll be.

The rhyme also had choice words for politicians, lawyers, and doctors, the greediest of whom were labeled "*chap books* scarce fit to peruse." [14]

The bindery was a cheerful place, with a spirit of fraternity, competitiveness, and humor. The previous verses illustrate this atmosphere, as do these lines written as an "Elegy on the Death of a Bookbinder":

> He loved both friends and foes,
>   Excepting whom he hated;
> He never was known to be in drink,
>   But when intoxicated.
>
> By him his neighbors were us'd well,
>   When by him kindly treated;
> He ne'er defrauded any man,
>   Of whom he'd never heard.[15]

Toward master craftsmen Bradford displays a sense of assertiveness, particularly in a poem celebrating his release from working nights at the bindery (p. 301). His verses, however, do not reveal serious antagonism. Moreover, there is also an important poem decribing a sense of mutual support and interest. It is aimed at competing masters who, in an attempt to gain accounts, have "injured the business" by working under established prices. Invoking "A MOST SOLEMN CURSE" on these "ungenerous elves," the journeyman's sentiments imply that he sees his master's interest as one with his own:

> Tell me why have you made,
> Bookbinding such a ruin'd trade,
> That now for binding we're scarce paid
>   One fourth of its worth.
> What motives had you in doing it,
> Ye scourings of the eternal pit,
> Curse on your heart ye are scarce fit
>   T'exist on earth.

The "curse" continues:

> May rats and mice devour your parts,
> Your paper and your leather.

> May your hand letters be defaced,
> Your types all mixed together.
> . . . .
> May your apprentices run away,
> Your business be diminished,
> And may booksellers never pay
> You when your work is finished.[16]

Bradford and Blossom appear to live in relative harmony with their employers. In the case of Blossom, the relationship was close to that of respectful equals, while with the younger Bradford it was more paternalistic. Although the evidence based upon these two artisans is far from conclusive, it does suggest that journeymen working in smaller enterprises did not harbor collective class antagonism toward their employers, and in some cases held a moderately hopeful outlook.

The situation, however, for most journeymen laboring in the conflict trades, was markedly different. Whether or not they were aware of the matrices of financial development, these tradesmen could not help but sense the growing instability of wages and the decline in mobility. Unwilling to voluntarily countenance this condition, those most threatened, the more highly skilled members of these trades, banded together into militant trade associations, governed democratically and operating under strict rules of discipline.[17] These organizations, as described earlier, had significant recreational, fraternal, benevolent, and political activities. Their primary function, however, was the maintenance of a fair wage and the exclusion of unqualified cheap labor from the professions. This was to be accomplished by unified action. Some societies employed the practice known today as the "closed shop." The shoemakers, for example, required that all members of their society work only with fellow members at a set wage. Others required that members neither work for less than an established wage, nor with those who did. The bylaws of the New York Typographical Society reveal this practice:

> No member of this society shall work for less than the wages which may be established; neither shall he engage or

continue in any office where there is a journeyman working for less than the established price.

Any member detected "undermining or supplanting a fellow member" or filling the place of a fellow printer who had been discharged because of his refusal to work below established wages would be expelled and his name "reported to the different typographical societies of the United States." [18]

The success of the societies rested on the ability of the journeymen to enforce their bylaws and pressure master craftsmen into giving desired salaries. The journeymen employed four tactics: noncoercive methods, including both collective bargaining and spirited appeals to employers, the public, and errant brothers; the establishment of journeymen-operated enterprises; selective walkouts against offending bosses; and an occasional general strike by the journeymen of one trade.

Journeymen preferred to resolve disputes with master craftsmen at joint meetings. From 1805 though 1810 the cabinetmakers achieved such harmony through the New York Society of Cabinetmakers, an organization of journeymen and masters. Established following a series of conflicts to "maintain good understanding between employer and employed," it mixed fraternal and promotional activity with an arbitration panel ("Standing Committee") to investigate and settle any disputes.[19] Accord was also gained by the printers in 1809 when they settled their wage differences through collective bargaining. In this case the journeymen submitted their demands to the master printers, who responded with a counterproposal. After a number of meetings in which each article was discussed "with an eloquence that would have graced a senate house," the society voted to accept a compromise agreement.[20]

After reaching their general agreement, the printers were forced to use walkouts against a few unyielding employers. When they later forsook such measures, however, these journeymen learned that noncoercive tactics alone tended to deteriorate into unilateral and often desperate appeals for help. In 1810, a year after the agreement, enforcement of society regulations would have required two members to leave their jobs at the *Public Advertiser* because of the presence of journeymen working below established rates. Instead of demanding that these workers leave, however, the society suspended its rule. Unable or unwilling to enforce its bylaws, the journeymen chose to address a passionate entreaty to the master printers concerning the threat posed by large numbers of semi-skilled "halfway" journeymen. Terming the hiring of such help as "illiberal and unjust," they chastised employers for taking on these "miserable botches," foreigners willing to work "for what they can get." [21] Another circular expressed similar anguish over the hiring of apprentices, a devious practice that would not only bring "almost certain ruin to the boys themselves," but would also force half of those working in "the noblest art with which the earth is blest" to seek another trade.[22]

Besides issuing such appeals to employers, journeymen turned to the public, particularly to enforce a boycott. The tailors used this tactic in 1804 when a number of men who had joined the newly formed United Society of Journeymen Tailors were discharged by their employers. The society responded by publishing the names of the offending merchant tailors along with those who were cooperating with the society, and asking the public to patronize only the stores of the latter.[23] Similarly, the journeymen ladies' shoemakers in 1813 asked the populace to boycott poor-quality, mass-produced "slop shoes" and to purchase only the high-quality products of skilled journeymen. This would not only save "hundreds of honest tradesmen" from the "scanty and precarious existence" of making large numbers of cheap shoes but would also protect the health of their families' feet.[24]

Social ostracism was a third noncoercive weapon. The journeymen printers considered it a force strong enough to restrain comrades from working in situations harmful to their fellow mechanics. An entry in the Typographical Society's minutes notes that there is nothing "more powerful in the human mind than shame." Its might was enough to make "the coward bold, the miser generous." The common feelings of the brotherhood would be strong enough to "deter" a journeyman from actions harmful to his fellow workers, even "when innate principle is wanting." [25]

The problem with noncoercive tactics was that they lacked punch in a competitive, changing capitalist world. It was unlikely that master printers concerned with profits were terribly worried about the ethical or the human side of the excessive use of apprentices and unskilled labor. Nor were women shoppers likely to be moved by journeymen's reasoning if they had a large family and a tight budget. Finally, while social ostracism might be effective among members of a fraternity of skilled journeymen, aliens and apprentices were less vulnerable to this threat.

Establishment of journeymen-owned and -operated shops was the first of the militant measures used against uncooperative employers. In 1802 journeymen cabinetmakers, angered and insulted by the master cabinetmakers' unilateral promulgation of a new price list lowering their wages 15 percent, took such action. Eighty strong, they announced to the public that they were setting up their own warehouse at 49 John Street, where shoppers would find on sale at reasonable prices furniture "as elegant as has ever been exhibited for sale in this city." [26] Unfortunately, the enterprise failed for lack of public support; after holding out for six months the journeymen finally settled for an adjustment of a few prices according to increases in the cost of living.[27] They did not, however, lose faith in this tactic. In 1819 a number of the highly skilled craftsmen working in the workshop of Duncan Phyfe set up their own store. Disagreeing with the master's decision to lower wages during the panic, the journeymen notified New Yorkers that they offered "work executed in a style equal to any on the continent." [28]

A selective strike directed against a recalcitrant employer was the second coercive tactic used by discontented journeymen. In 1809 the New York Society of Journeymen Cordwainers invoked this measure following the expulsion of Edward Whitess from their organization because of his failure to pay fines for nonattendance and misconduct ("raising a rumpus" during a meeting). Under the bylaws of the society, Whitess's employer, Charles Aimes, was required to discharge him or else lose the services of all other society members in his employ. When Aimes complied, but then refused to dismiss an apprentice who the society claimed was working in violation of its constitution, the journeymen walked out of his shop, declining to work until he let the boy go.[29]

The selective strike was the favorite weapon of the journeymen. As noted, the journeymen printers walked out in 1809 on the master printers who refused to accept the negotiated wage.[30] Also in 1809 a number of journeymen in the building trades left their jobs and set up their own "hiring house," announcing that they would be available to cooperative master builders.[31] The popularity of this tactic was due to its ability to stifle a particular employer without alarming the community with the threat of widespread action.

The final alternative available to journeymen was a general walkout against all masters of a particular trade. This measure was seldom used, most likely because it touched the public's fear of monopoly—an alarm usually associated with attempts to corner the firewood or foodstuff market—and could lead to court action. However, in times of stress some journeymen did resort to this tactic. There were at least two such incidents in New York. In May 1819, all journeymen masons walked off their jobs when the builders attempted to lower their wages by one shilling per day. Although some masters continued to pay the previous salary of fifteen shillings, the masons' society decided to cease working for all employers. They explained that they left the cooperating builders with "great reluctance," but that to succeed it was necessary to "all stand together." The point was to prevent the isolation of those masons working for employers unwilling to retain the old wage. A complete work stoppage would force good-willed master masons to pressure their more selfish counterparts into giving their workers an honest day's compensation.[32]

The other and more famous general strike involved a turnout by the Cordwainers Society in 1809. This tightly disciplined and militant organization [33] became incensed when it learned that its strike against Aimes had been thwarted by other master shoemakers who were taking in his work. The journeymen met and resolved not to work for any master until their demands were met. This bold action, posing a serious threat to the masters, forced them to turn to the courts for redress.[34]

On the other side of the labor front, merchants and master craftsmen were equally resourceful in their efforts to keep the cost of labor down. Criminal proceedings, their most potent weapon, were seldom used; their availability, however, was clearly announced to all members of the mechanic community by the indictment of twenty-five shoemakers in 1809 for "perniciously and deceitfully forming an unlawful club and combination to govern themselves and ... to extort large sums of money by means thereof." At issue was the closed shop, a tactic the prosecution maintained was "oppressive" and an "evil example" to both employers and "divers other workmen and journeymen." The masters argued that it was unjust and illegal for mechanics to force fellow artisans to join their society in order to obtain employment, or to require employers to hire only association members.[35]

Judicial hostility was clearly evident at the trial. The journeymen were allowed to plead neither that they were receiving only a "bare maintenance" in comparison to the excessive profits of their employers, nor that the masters had similar organizations of their own. Moreover, in his charge Mayor Radcliff directly instructed the jury that the journeymen had used "arbitrary and unlawful means," though he conceded that they were pursuing legitimate ends (higher wages).[36]

The shoemakers were quickly convicted. Although the mayor fined them but one dollar each and upheld their right to "meet and regulate their concerns, and to ask for wages, and to work or refuse," the cordwainers' force in the marketplace was severely impaired. While they and other journeymen were still free to walk out over salary demands, they faced the full force of the law if they organized against an employer who hired nonsociety hands. Since the shoemakers could no longer control the make-up of the labor pool, they now lacked a compelling means to prevent the entry of cheap, semiskilled labor. And, indeed, after this verdict, rendered in 1810, there are few known walkouts for any reason until the extreme financial conditions caused by the panic of 1819. It is little wonder, therefore, that the journeymen, sensing the importance of the trial, wished to appeal. In a letter requesting aid from their brothers in the Typographical Society, they stated their "determination ... to carry it from court to court into the Court of Errors." [37]

Another tactic the masters found useful against the journeymen was the formation of trade associations of their own. While no constitutions for these societies are extant, the newspapers listed notices of meetings of master masons and carpenters as well as statements by the master cabinetmakers concerning joint action that they had taken. The conspiracy trial transcript indicates that the master shoemakers also had their own organization.[38] These groups provided masters the means to give unified responses to their employees. One method was a lockout. During a construction trades strike, "Candour," after admonishing the journeymen to return to work, encouraged the builders to remain steadfast in their resolve by instructing them to say: "if they will not work for the wages I offer them, cover up my walls—I will suspend building for the season." [39]

Masters' combinations were also effective in stifling journeymen's attempts to set up their own operations. In 1802 the master cabinetmakers were accused by their employees of running with "great zeal" from shop to shop, persuading nonmembers not to employ any cantankerous journeymen. Then, with the rival shop open, they were said to have used both threats and cajolery in persuading carvers and upholsterers not to deal with the independent journeymen.[40] Similarly, in the 1790s the master shoemakers were accused of seeking to persuade the city's tanners not to sell leather to balking journeymen.[41]

The tactic that probably was most feared by the journeymen was the importation of unskilled or out-of-city labor to compete with, displace, and demean the skilled craftsmen. Immediately after they negotiated a settlement in 1809, the printers claimed that their employers were trying to bring in other journeymen to "fill the city with hands and thereby be enabled to reduce the prices of work in the city to their former standard." [42] To combat this threat the journeymen formed an elaborate intercity defense, notifying other communities of false advertisements for help, circulating the names of uncooperative journeymen, and keeping lists of offending printers in other cities in case they sought work in New York.[43]

Despite these defense systems, the threat of an oversupply remained grave. For example, in 1810 after a walkout of several weeks by a large number of carpenters and masons who were seeking a salary of twelve shillings a day, the master builders placed an advertisement in various newspapers for "one to three hundred carpenters." These out-of-town laborers were offered the current wage of eleven shillings per day. At the same time an editorial in the *American Citizen* warned the carpenters that unless they "dissolve and go immediately back to work at the old prices," preparations for replacing them would be "immediately carried into effect." [44]

While the outcome of nearly all these disputes is unknown, the master craftsmen enjoyed the advantage. They were at the forefront of economic change, able to exploit the opportunities arising at the end of the preindustrial era. A growing country meant increased markets, production, and profits. With a surplus of labor to draw upon and the power of judicial sanction, they could dispense with rebellious employees or disrupt their associations. When highly skilled craftsmanship was required, the journeymen stood a chance; but the outlook was bleak as quantity production and large-scale construction grew common.

Yet, in their difficult position, the journeymen were reaping benefits from their struggles. They were gaining much needed experience in methods of collective action. In their societies and in job actions they were experimenting with and understanding the need for united ventures. The changing economy and the demands of their employers were forcing the tradesmen to see themselves as a common group with similar goals and fears. Although they had largely to surrender the hope of becoming independent craftsmen, they were gaining a new identity as skilled workers who still had their corner of the marketplace to defend.

Economic stakes were clearly at the center of the journeymen-master disputes. Yet to see these conflicts, as most historians have, only as struggles for economic leverage, or as financial disputes with political parallels, would be to miss an important dimension.[45] To the journeymen more than the wage was in jeopardy; their very standing in society was at risk. For, as the journeymen were forced closer to the position of immobile, subsistence working-men—a place in society occupied by blacks, women, and Irish aliens—they were faced with the loss of their sense of status as worthy and consequential citizens, a priceless footing.

Buoyed by the democratizing spirit of the American Revolution, journeymen, as part of the mechanic community, were striving against deferential expectations and contemptuous treatment. At the Fourth of July ceremonies, as we have noted, the journeymen trade societies marched in formation along with other artisan fraternal associations, listening attentively to orations praising the role of the craftsman in American society. So, too, the journeymen organizations' fraternal activities, including rituals, secret ceremonies, and festive dinners, notably enhanced journeymen's self-esteem and were part of the overall mechanic quest for improved self-image and societal standing.

This goal of increased respect and esteem was, in all likelihood, responsible for the nearly complete absence of violence in labor disputes. The response of the Cordwainers Society to an allegation that during the embargo they had tarred and feathered a Federalist foreman for "vilifying the government of the United States in the presence of the body" is revealing. The shoemakers, while avowing support for the Republican cause, denied they would have committed an act "so anti-republican and contrary to the letter and spirit of the Constitution." Violence was too great a threat to respectability to be useful as a labor tactic.[46]

Yet for the journeymen threatened by the "business revolution," stature was in jeopardy. Were they to become subsistence laborers, they would be vulnerable not only to the Federalists' elitist contempt but also to the scorn of Republican thinkers, including Jefferson, their political hero. The first Democratic-Republican president held an at best ambivalent attitude toward journeymen. While respecting their electoral support of Democratic-Republican ideals, he distrusted their standing as wage earners, a station he considered prone to producing "mindless beings" who, lacking an independent freehold and income, were "fit tools for the designs of ambition." [47] The growing permanency of their position as journeymen had already made these journeymen susceptible to Republican disdain, but to lose respectable salaries, dignified treatment, and the time and funds to engage in leisurely craft traditions would inexorably cast them among the dregs of society.

Accordingly, the central concern of the journeymen's public statements justifying their actions was the preservation of the artisan's self-esteem. The journeymen tailors in 1804, announcing the formation of a trade society, declared their intention to prevent employers from "forcing any imposition upon them," an event that "too frequently occurs on every mechanical branch." [48] The cabinetmakers vented similar apprehensions when, upon the submission of a new book of prices to their employers, they demanded to be "treated as men possessing an ingenious art." A walkout then took place a few years later when the masters refused to honor an oral wage settlement. The journeymen informed the citizenry of

New York that they would return to their employers, but only when these masters were willing to "fill their obligations." [49] The masons, too, invoked the issue of dignity when a number of journeymen bricklayers deserted their master builders. Noting that every other "mechanical branch" had recently received a salary increase, the tradesmen asserted that a refusal by the masters to grant them similar compensation would see "the journeymen of their branch sunk below every other, which inevitably must be the case if we now lie still, and hereafter be considered a poor spiritless set of beings." [50]

The journeymen also protested against masters who injured their employees' standing by compelling them to work alongside of inferior hands. This was at issue in a walkout by journeymen tailors against the use of seamstresses in their profession. Because women possessed inherently inadequate abilities, their labor insulted the trade. "Journeyman Tailor" explained the problem with the following logic:

> A journeyman tailor not above the level of mediocrity cannot make a superfine plaincoat to pass the ordeal of criticism—much less many other garments that might be named; yet this very man can make waistcoats and pantaloons and that, too, with more judgment and solidity than a woman can; *hence* we infer that women are incomplete, and if incomplete, they ought to disclaim all right and title to the avocation of tailor.[51]

Along with his pocketbook, a mechanic's dignity was at stake when he was required to work side by side with female hands.

The pursuit of self-esteem, too, led the journeymen to angry, indignant words against those whose selfish demands stood in their way: the masters. Their harsh resentment was against men who, they maintained, were contemptuously striving to destroy the journeymen by further reducing wages "only barely sufficient to maintain the most industrious mechanic." In 1810 the carpenters asserted that the master builders treated them with "the haughtiness and overbearance [and] conduct better fit[ting] them to give laws to slaves than assuming the prerogative of depriving freemen of their just rights." Rather than give their workers a decent wage and basic respect, they chose to "glide past in their carriages, or build brick houses." The cordwainers similarly described their employers as "evil disposed and selfish" men who enriched themselves by producing cheap shoes without regard for the "humble instruments that fill their cellars." With equal ire, "Journeyman Tailor" compared the merchant tailors to the "merciless tyrant" unable to appreciate the plight of even the most "wretched helot." [52]

These affirmations of dignity and declarations of moral outrage were, of course, deeply felt. They were, however, generally personal attacks directed at individual masters, and not against an economy that was becoming inherently exploitative. That is, journeymen's understanding of their situation was often circumscribed by their relationships with particular masters and merchants. There is, however, evidence of at least a partial consciousness of the underlying causes of their distress. The formation of militant trade societies in itself signals journeymen's awareness of the need of a potent economic force. Moreover, two instances of farsighted thought reveal a dawning cognizance that to securely retain appropriate wages and dignity, journeymen required an economic stance suitable to the modern marketplace.

The first statement, an eloquent strike declaration published by the journeymen carpenters, argued that in revolutionary America, society had an overriding obligation to provide its workingmen with social security:

> Among the inalienable rights of man are life, liberty and the pursuit of happiness. By the social contract every class in society ought to be entitled to benefit in proportion to its qualifications. Among the duties which individuals owe to society are single men to marry and married men to educate their children. Among the duties which society owes individuals is to grant them just compensation not only for current expenses of livelihood, but to the formation of a fund for the support of that time of life when nature requires a cessation of work.[53]

Mechanics living in the new nation proudly asserted the right to a secure and dignified life, even at the expense of private gain.

Subsistence wages were incompatible with the spirit of '76, and masters would have to adjust their operations accordingly.

Second, as argued by the journeymen cordwainers' noted counsel, William Sampson, journeymen had a right to the economic strength sufficient for attaining their goals. Defending the shoemakers' right to a closed shop, Sampson argued that if employers were able to use such methods as "crowding their shops with apprentices" and hiring cheap labor, then, to counter this "rapacity," journeymen were owed a countervailing force of their own. Each party had its goals: the journeymen to secure the highest possible wage and to protect the dignity of their labor, and the masters to obtain the most work at the least cost. Without the right to organize effectively, the journeymen were at an unfair disadvantage: "Should all others except only the industrious mechanic, be allowed to meet and plot?" Did merchants not combine to "settle their prices current," and politicians to win elections? Yet the shoemakers stood "indicted for combining against starvation." Asking only the rights guaranteed by the Constitution, Sampson declared that the cordwainers wanted but an equal chance to fend for themselves in the marketplace.[54]

These statements indicate that journeymen were at least moving toward an outlook that was not a retreat from the burgeoning American economy, but a means of attaining autonomy and self-esteem in a capitalist society; an ideology that would, if realized, enable them to retain their personal and economic dignity even while they remained salaried tradesmen, lacking land or shops of their own. Their contention that the Revolution affirmed their right to create a countervailing market force and to secure adequate compensation meant that wage earners could no longer be seen as "dependent." Rather, their position was one of strength; employers, while still able to seek greater profits, could no longer do so at the expense of the journeymen. Each party had its own inalienable rights.

Given from a much different perspective, the masters' outlook reflected the views of a group of men unwilling to acknowledge that their role in the changing economy meant some loss of economic leadership within the mechanic community. As they were more knowledgeable about the entire operation of the trade,

including production and marketing, the masters considered themselves the guardians of the artisan professions. Accordingly, it was
for them, and for them alone, to determine employees' proper
compensation. Thus, when in 1810 the journeymen carpenters
asked for a raise, the builders' response was that they would not
subscribe to any stated salary, and that was that! [55] In another
dispute in 1819, the master carpenters and masons unilaterally
lowered wages by one shilling per day. Declaring that during the
depression it was neither politic nor right for the journeymen to
insist on their current pay, the masters explained that they had to
consider "the benefit of our employers and ourselves, as well as the
journeymen in our employ." This paternal attitude was a major
cause of the journeymen's complaints that they were treated with
disrespect. Yet to the masters the journeymen had an obligation to
adhere to their employers' decisions. Action to the contrary could
be taken only under "the standard of impropriety." [56]

In response to the journeymen's charges that the masters were
selfish men, bent on holding their employees to subsistence wages
while they fattened themselves on huge profits, the masters again
invoked the claim that they were more aware than their workers of
the general welfare. This rationale was used by the master printers
in 1809. In a "spirit of conciliation and harmony" they explained
that their prices, though two cents per item less than the journeymen desired, represented "a maximum, beyond which it would be
highly injurious, if not ruinous, to the trade to venture." [57] Similarly, the master cabinetmakers in 1802, upon lowering their
wages, claimed that theirs was still an "equitable rate"; their
action was taken for the good of the trade as the old price book had
become so altered as to be unusable. The iron law of profit and loss
was introduced by "Candour" when he explained that the master
builders could not give the journeymen a price hike because such a
raise would eliminate the opportunity of making a reasonable
profit.[58]

Perhaps the most detailed evidence of an employer's attitude
can be found in a letter written by John McComb, the architect in
charge of building New York's new City Hall. In refusing a wage
increase to the stonecutters working for him, McComb denied the
masters' responsibility to maintain salaries at a level concurrent

with inflationary spirals. "It is admitted that the markets and House Rent is high," he stated bluntly, "but we deem it impossible to regulate the wages so as always to be equal to them." To grant an increase to this trade would "be the means of raising the wages of all persons connected with the building line." [59] In a parallel statement, James Cheetham, editor of the *American Citizen,* in 1810 warned that to grant the carpenters their request for a raise would mean that the masons, the painters, the glaziers, and all other mechanics would want a similar increase, an event that would impede the "improvement of the city" and "exorbitantly" raise house rents.[60] Masters reasoned that they had a greater perspective on the needs of the economy. Would not increased wages bring increased prices and then a loss of sales—in which case both master and journeyman would be out of work? If times were hard, that was unfortunate, but there was really not much that they could do without hurting the overall welfare of their professions.

Speaking through the prosecution at the conspiracy trial, the master craftsmen, like the journeymen, considered the place of the laborer in the economic world. Arguing against the closed shop, the masters once more maintained that they were upholding the good of the trade and community against the more selfish interests of their employees. "Public welfare," their attorney argued, was secured by allowing each man freely to pursue his own calling. An organization that impeded this process by forcing a mechanic to join a trade association in order to obtain a job committed "most tyrannical" violations of individual rights. The question was not, as the journeymen had asserted, that of creating a countervailing force in the free market; such a force was not needed in a harmonious society. Rather, it was the shoemakers' obligation to observe the "tacit compact" which they and other classes had entered, "that when they have partitioned and distributed among them the different occupations ... they will pursue those occupations so as to contribute to the general happiness." By uniting to shatter the established order the journeymen were "at war with public policy." Were butchers and bakers to follow their lead and create a similar "monopoly," a "Misfortune worse than a pestilence" would "instantly befall this city." Assurances of the good intentions of the "industrious mechanic" were of little value.

The question was whether "for private interest" the cordwainers would be allowed to "conspire together to inflict the most terrible calamities." [61]

The mistrustful, paternal outlook of the masters can easily be seen as self-serving. Were the journeymen to have accepted such an ideology, they would have become the economic slaves of their employers. On the other hand, there is no reason to doubt the integrity of the masters' claims that their approach aimed for the benefit of all, including the journeymen. First, they unquestionably did assume that they had a better perspective on the trades' needs than their employees. Second, the masters' statements reveal that the employers had not given up the values of an organic society in which each member—apprentice, journeyman, and master— willingly played his part in a harmonious whole. Many of the masters had risen in such a system without the use of walkouts, boycotts, or trade associations. They had been apprentices and journeymen and had deferred to their master craftsmen. Were they not entitled to the same respect? The problem, of course, was that economic conditions had changed markedly. Ease of mobility and the distribution of wealth were considerably altered, and the journeymen were responding to their position as permanent wage earners. The masters, however, despite their active participation in the expanding economy, refused to recognize their employees' need to be treated as an economic class with interests different from those of their employers. Consequently, they brought upon themselves the same charges of elitism and arrogance which during elections they themselves often directed against the Federalists.

Unlike the Federalists, however, the masters emerged triumphant—a result indicated by the short life spans of many of the journeymen societies.[62] The masters' ideals of "individualistic pursuit" and "public welfare" prevailed over the journeymen's conceptions of mechanic dignity and countervailing force. Ideologically as well as tactically, the economic temper of the era favored those at the forefront of financial expansion. First, as Joseph Dorfman has noted, "the dominance of commerce" reigned supreme in American economic thought. The journeymen's experience notwithstanding, it was believed that "opportunity for the capitalist and laborer were richly abundant"; there was little need for trade associations.[63] Second, a lingering spirit of mercantilism, still alive in the early nineteenth century, favored the masters' belief in a "common good"; of men laboring without discord for the betterment of society.[64] Indeed, the insignia of the General Society of Mechanics and Tradesmen, a society of prominent masters, described an economy of only harmony and cooperation between artisans working together to build the republic (p. 130). (This despite the fact that much of the masters' financial success stemmed from their ability to take advantage of a free market economy.) Third, the leadership of the Democratic-Republican Party—which included a number of prominent employers [65]—held a viewpoint similar to that of the masters. Such influential men as James Cheetham, editor of the *American Citizen,* and Thomas Emmet, an assistant prosecutor of the cordwainers, evinced a "generalized passion" against trade societies, institutions they considered incompatible with public comity.[66] Thus, the master craftsmen, enjoying political, judicial, and popular support, found their position to be reasonably comfortable, particularly in comparison to the journeymen's lonely, if courageous, stand.

The antagonism between journeymen and masters was sharp and abrasive. In time of conflict journeymen saw their employers as oppressive paternal tyrants, while the masters saw their employees as misguided and dangerous rebels. Yet in gaining perspective on these disputes, it must be emphasized that they took place within the mechanic community, a community that was not always so bitterly divided. In politics, for instance, as already noted, the egalitarian stance of the Democratic-Republicans generally remained far more attractive than the contemptuous and elitist outlook of the Federalists.[67] So, too, at Fourth of July celebrations the journeymen societies, before retiring to their separate celebrations, did sit together with the masters in the General Society to listen to an oration in praise of the common accomplishments of the mechanic population. Even in economic concerns, journeymen often followed the lead of the masters, as in their quest for tariff protection and for the chartering of the Mechanics Bank. Too, in 1803 when Mayor Livingston proposed the establishment of a public workshop to teach mechanic crafts to the poor, journeymen joined masters in opposition. Masters, while willing to use low cost labor in their own enterprises were fearful of competing against a monopolistic municipal operation, while journeymen were concerned that their position, already endangered, would be further jeopardized by a new supply of poorly trained, inexpensive workers.[68]

These instances of mechanic unity are critical to an understanding of this labor conflict. They emphasize that the craftsmen on both sides clearly understood their common bonds. Most important, they underline the middling position of the mechanic community. The journeymen, as the workshop encounter discloses, did not comprise, in their own view or in the view of the public, the lower class of New York City. Master craftsmen, despite their increased wealth and standing, were making their way in a new and uncertain marketplace, in which they were vulnerable either to the reformist projects or mercantile policies of upper-class merchants and lawyers. Both groups, moreover, bristled from the contempt of elitist Federalists and other condescending gentry. The two bodies of mechanics, masters and journeymen, represented a "lower middle class" and an "upper middle class." The masters were striving toward merchant standing and, in so doing, forcing their employees towards the lower class rank of subsistence wage earner. The journeymen, on the other hand, were attempting to maintain their position as socially respectable skilled craftsmen. In the course of these bitter internal struggles, tactics and ideology were formulated suitable to the growing capitalist economy, many of which would continue to be viable long after the era of the preindustrial mechanic.

NOTES

1. These mediators suggested that the piecework system be substituted for the daily wage, a suggestion that was impractical in that it asked for a return to preindustrial methods in a growing urban economy. *American Citizen*, June 1, 1810.

2. Charlotte Morgan, "The Origin and History of the New York Employing Printers Organization," in *Columbia University Studies in History, Economics and Public Law* (1930), p. 25. In the Sixth Ward, there were 2,390 entries for adult white males, while the ward's male population was 6,832. Allowing just over half of this number for males under 21, as is to be

found in the 1820 census, then 930 adult males were not listed in that ward alone. These were likely to be aliens and journeymen, both of whom were ineligible for jury duty. See David T. Gilchrist, ed., *The Growth of the Seaport Cities, 1790-1825* (Charlottesville, 1967), p. 35, and Carol Groneman Pernicone, "The 'Bloody Ould Sixth': A Social Analysis of a New York City Working-Class Community in the Mid-Nineteenth Century," Ph.D. diss. (University of Rochester, 1973), p. 48, n. 15.

3. Ibid., p. 28.

4. Samuel McKee, Jr., *Labor in Colonial New York, 1664-1776* (New York, 1934), p. 22; Charles S. Olton, *Artisans for Independence: Philadelphia Mechanics and the American Revolution* (Syracuse, 1975), pp. 7-25; Jackson Turner Main, *The Social Structure of Revolutionary America* (Princeton, 1965), pp. 185-186, 194; Carl Bridenbaugh, *The Colonial Craftsman* (New York, 1950), p. 134; Eric Foner, *Tom Paine and Revolutionary America* (New York, 1976), p. 32. For descriptions of a deteriorating position of the middling artisan classes see Alan Kulikoff, "The Progress of Inequality in Revolutionary Boston," ibid., 28 (1971), 375-412: James A. Henretta, "Economic Development and Social Structure in Colonial Boston," ibid., 22 (1965), 75-92; Gary B. Nash, "Urban Wealth and Poverty in Pre-Revolutionary America," *Journal of Interdisciplinary History,* 6 (1976), pp. 545-584. For a contrasting view see G. B. Warden, "Inequality and Instability in Eighteenth Century Boston: A Reappraisal," ibid., pp. 585-620.

5. Rollo Silver, "The Printers' Lobby: Model 1802," in *Virginia Studies in Bibliography*, Frederic Bowens, ed., (1950-1951), vol. 2, pp. 217-218.

6. 1819 New York City Jury Lists, fourth, sixth, and eighth wards, Historical Documents Collection, Queens College, City University of New York. Since jury lists for all wards do not exist, to give a reasonably accurate sample, one was chosen from the lower wards, one from the middle, and one from the remoter areas. (The latter two may be considered mechanic wards.) Only 1819 lists give journeyman-master differentials. Because this was a time of economic recession, the results may be somewhat skewed. But it is unlikely that the differences between masters and journeymen would have been much different a few years earlier. The figure for all journeymen with less than $150 personal property in the Sixth Ward was 97.6 percent (272) and in the Fourth Ward, 94.0 percent (579).

7. Journal Mss., Elisha Blossom, Cabinetmaker, July 10, 1811, New York Historical Society.

8. Ibid., March 7, 1812, June 20, 1812.

9. Ibid., February 27, 1813.

10. Ibid., February 1, 1814.

11. Ibid., May 22, 1813.

12. John Bradford, *The Poetical Vagaries of a Knight of the Folding Stick of PASTE CASTLE, to which is annexed the History of the Garrett, &c. Translated from the Hieroglyphics of the Society by a Member of the Order of the Blue String* (New York, 1813), p. 9.

13. Ibid., p. 11.

14. Ibid., p. 3.

15. Ibid., pp. 18-19.

16. Ibid., p. 50.

17. Four constitutions of New York journeymen societies are extant: "Constitution of the New York Typographical Society," in George A. Stevens, *New York Typographical Union Number Six* (Albany, 1912), pp. 42-47; *Constitution of the New York Journeymen Shipwrights Society, Adopted January 5, 1804* (New York, 1805); Constitution of the New York Society of Journeymen Shipwrights and Caulkers, 1816, New York Public Library; "Constitution of the New York Society of Journeymen Cordwainers," in John R. Commons et al., *A Documentary History of American Industrial Society*, 10 vols. (Cleveland, 1910-1911), vol 3, pp. 364-370. (This is taken from the 1809 cordwainers conspiracy trial transcript, *People v. Melvin*, in Commons, et al., *A Documentary History.*)

18. Stevens, *New York Typographical Union Number Six*, p. 47. The 1816 New York Society of Journeymen Shipwrights and Caulkers required all members to work only for shipwrights who had been "at the business" three years. Any member violating this rule was "considered to have forfeited all claim as a shipwright" and could no longer belong to the society. Consitution of the New York Society of Journeymen Shipwrights and Caulkers. The 1804 Shipwrights Society's constitution was more moderate, with no rules requiring a member to quit a shop in which an underpaid hand was employed. However, Article XX did state that any member who instructed or "otherwise assist[ed]" any men who intruded on the "regular business and underwork the established wages" would be expelled. *Constitution of the New York Journeymen Shipwrights Society*, pp. 9-10.

19. *Revised Constitution and Rules of Order of the New York Society of Cabinetmakers* (New York, 1810), p. 3. The standing committee would make an independent judgment of the value of a journeyman's product and report it back to the society.

20. Stevens, *New York Typographical Union Number Six*, pp. 51-57.

21. George Barnett, "The Printers, A Study in Trade Unionism," *American Economic Association Quarterly*, 3d. ser., 10 (1909), 160, 282-3.

22. Ibid., 162-163.

23. *Evening Post*, November 24, 1804.

24. *Columbian*, December 9, 1813.

25. Barnett, "The Printers," p. 287. Similarly, the 1804 Shipwrights Society constitution had no enforcement measure other than expulsion of errant members. They obviously felt that social pressure would keep fellow journeymen in line.

26. *American Citizen,* December 22, 1802; *Morning Chronicle,* January 1, 1803.

27. *Evening Post,* April 10, 1805.

28. *National Advocate,* May 14, 1819. The tailors also employed this tactic. *Evening Post,* July 13, 1819.

29. *People v. Melvin* pp. 369-371.

30. *Washington Republican,* November 4, 1809.

31. *American Citizen,* May 23, 1810.

32. *Evening Post,* May 27, 1819.

33. The Cordwainers Society levied heavy fines on any member not reporting the presence of a nonmember working for his employer, on any journeyman failing to "come forward" and join the society within two months of his arrival in New York, on any apprentice who did not request membership upon the completion of his indentures, and on any member absent without cause from three consecutive meetings. Every journeyman belonging to the society was also required to keep the secretary informed of his current address. *People v. Melvin,* pp. 365-368.

34. For an account of other events leading up to this and to an earlier Philadelphia trial in 1805, see Ian M. G. Quimby, "The Cordwainers' Protest: A Crisis in American Labor Relations," *Winterthur Portfolio,* 3 (1967), pp. 83-101; *People v. Melvin,* pp. 369-371.

35. *People v. Melvin,* pp. 252-256.

36. *People v. Melvin,* pp. 371-372, 382-385; for legal analysis and perspective on the trial see Leonard W. Levy, *The Law of the Commonwealth and Chief Justice Shaw* (Cambridge, 1957), pp. 183-185; Marjorie S. Turner, *The Early American Conspiracy Cases, Their Place in Labor Law: A Reinterpretation* (San Diego, 1967), pp. 172-175.

37. *People v. Melvin,* p. 385; Minutes of the Board of Directors Meeting, New York Typographical Society, March 31, 1810, in Barnett, "The Printers," p. 358. After defeating a motion for support of the cordwainers, the society referred the question to a committee. Fearing that the cordwainers might be in violation of the law, the printers were hesitant to aid them. This failure to give support indicates a lack of intertrade unity among the journeymen.

38. *People v. Melvin,* p. 371.

39. *American Citizen,* May 23, 1810.

40. *Evening Post,* April 10, 1805.

41. *Commercial Advertiser,* April 20, 1801.

42. Barnett, "The Printers," p. 18.

43. In one case the New York Society conducted an investigation of a man whose name appeared on a blacklist sent by the Albany society. Stevens, *New York Typographical Union Number Six,* p. 60. The tailors also were careful to warn other journeymen to beware of accepting jobs in other cities that might be available due to a strike. *Columbian,* April 24, 1815.

44. *American Citizen,* June 6, 1810.

45. Richard B. Morris, *Government and Labor in Early America* (New York, 1946) p. 206, and Walter Nelles, "The First American Labor Case," *Yale Law Journal,* 165 (1913), 165-200, see the conspiracy trials as depicting Republican support for the journeymen's cause and Federalist backing of the masters. However, the Republicans supported the masters; their outlook was at variance with that of the journeymen.

46. *Evening Post,* October 24, 1808. The only known incident of labor violence occurred in 1810 when angry carpenters broke the windows of the offices of unsympathetic newspapers and of the homes of master builders. *American Citizen,* May 3, 23, 31, 1810, June 12, 1810.

47. Edmund S. Morgan, "Slavery and Freedom: The American Paradox," *Journal of American History,* 52 (1972), 9.

48. *Evening Post,* November 24, 1804.

49. Journeymen Cabinetmakers of New York, *Book of Prices* (New York, 1796), p. 3. *Evening Post,* April 10, 1805.

50. Ibid., May 14, 1809.

51. Ibid., July 13, 1819.

52. *American Citizen,* December 22, 1802, May 23, 1810; *Evening Post,* January 30, 1815, February 4, 1815, March 20, 1819, July 13, 1819.

53. *American Citizen,* April 10, 1809, June 23, 1810.

54. *People v. Melvin* pp. 279, 300.

55. *American Citizen,* May 23, 1810.

56. *Evening Post,* May 22, 27, 1819, June 7, 1819; *American Citizen,* May 23, 1810.

57. Barnett, "The Printers," p. 363.

58. *Morning Chronicle,* December 31, 1802; *American Citizen,* May 23, 1810.

59. Letter of John McComb to Building Committee of the New York City Hall, John McComb mss. n.d. (New York Historical Society).

60. *American Citizen,* June 2, 1810.

61. *People v. Melvin,* pp 310-311, 319, 328-329

62. The New York Typographical Society, formed after the demise of

the Franklin Typographical Society, became unwilling to enforce its regulations, lost membership, and then lapsed into a purely benevolent society solely for the purpose of extending welfare benefits to charter members. Stevens, *New York Typographical Union Number Six,* pp. 75-78. The Journeymen Shipwright and Caulkers Society, finding its membership dwindling from a peak of 161 in June 1816 to only 23 in January 1818, was forced into bankruptcy and dissolution. Changing economic conditions after the War of 1812 may have made the society less useful to the shipwrights. Little is known of the other societies, though few seem to have survived much beyond their more strident actions.

63. Turner, *Early American Conspiracy Cases,* pp. 2-3; Joseph Dorfman, *The Economic Mind in American Civilization,* 2 vols. (New York, 1946), vol. 1, p. 314, and in David Gilchrist, ed., *The Growth of the Seaport Cities, 1790-1815* (Charlottesville, 1967), p. 154.

64. For the discussion of the influence of mercantilism see William A. Williams, *The Contours of American History* (Cleveland, 1961), pp. 212-213 and 17-223 passim.

65. This is apparent in a satirical ad placed by the striking journeymen carpenters in response to the earlier announcement seeking out-of-town strikebreakers:

Wanted instantaneously from five hundred to one thousand Country Bosses, particularly such as have been employeed in building Houses and Indian WIGWAMS for the purpose of constructing the droves of country carpenters now on their way to the city of New York.

N.B. No monopolising bosses will be employed, but such as are willing that journeymen should have an existence as well as themselves.

"WIGWAMS" was the well-known symbol of the Tammany Society, a prominent Republican political club. *American Citizen,* June 23, 1810.

66. Richard Twomey, "Jacobins and Jeffersonians: Anglo-American Radicalism in the United States, 1790-1820," Ph. D. diss. (Northern Illinois University, 1974), p. 208, and "Jeffersonian Ideology and Mechanic Consciousness: The Response to the First American Labor Conspiracy Cases, 1806-1809," paper delivered at AHA Convention, December, 1976; Edmund P. Willis, "Social Origins of Political Leadership in New York City from the Revolution to 1815," Ph. D. diss. (Berkeley, 1967), pp. 249, 254.

67. Federalists related journeymen's labor unrest and the entire mechanic class's attack on deference as forebodings of a revolutionary mob.

Linda K. Kerber, *Federalists in Dissent, Imagery and Ideology in Jeffersonian America* (Ithaca, 1970), pp. 173-216; David H. Fischer, *The Revolution of American Conservatism: The Federalist Party in the Era of Jeffersonian Democracy* (New York, 1965), pp. 1-49.

68. See Chapter 7, pp. 197-199.

Chapter 11

WORK AND MORALITY

The growth of modern quantity-oriented production within a number of major mechanic crafts affected more than just the organization of the workshop. It had significant impact on artisans' work culture and moral outlook as well. The evidence indicates that an ethic stressing discipline, piety, moderation, and sobriety— a lifestyle compatible with new efficient methods of operation— was now competing with the preindustrial workshop traditions. The two attitudes coexisted in a tense and sometimes conflicting relationship; neither was dominant, though the trend of financial development did point to the eventual demise of the premodern way of life. Material about these lifestyles is difficult to acquire, and this analysis is meant only to suggest patterns of behavior and their probable origins.

The best source for the nature of preindustrial work habits and values are the fine studies that have been made of seventeenth- and early-eighteenth-century English labor history. As E. P. Thompson and others have shown, work in the premodern period was not oriented to the clock. Craftsmen, usually laboring in their own home or garret—but even in workshops—generally set their own rate. A journeyman shoemaker, for example, might spend Monday and Tuesday in drinking and sport only to toil at a rapid pace the rest of the week (through Saturday) to make enough to support his family. That is, work was task-oriented rather than time-oriented. (Many artisans, in fact, did not even own a watch.) Labor patterns were irregular, varying enormously from shop to shop, from trade to trade, and from week to week.[1]

This pace and orientation was also found among American craftsmen, most commonly in crafts still operating in traditional ways. However, such patterns were not unknown in trades under the influence of mercantile management. For even in the conflict trades, inclement weather, problems in the transportation of goods, and varying tempos of demand produced periods of considerable unemployment and underemployment. Nor was all labor in these crafts performed in large workshops, particularly in the shoemaking and tailoring professions, a factor allowing for flexibility in work patterns.[2]

The most notable symbol of premodern work patterns was the venerable Saint Monday. This was the common practice of craftsmen taking each Monday (and sometimes Tuesday) off for relaxation in a neighborhood tavern, excursions to the country, or other leisurely activities. Upon their return to work, artisans, both highly skilled and less skilled, continued to take extended breaks from their shops, garrets, and homes, usually for draughts of beer or a shot of gin. There was little that employers could do to prevent this work pattern other than hope that the tradesmen would make up the work by the end of the week.[3]

Actual evidence of traditional work culture for this period is scarce; only a few examples remain. Politician Thurlow Weed, recalling his years as a journeyman printer in New York, remembered that at eleven every morning in the printing shop the journeymen would invariably pause to "jeff" for beer, often mortgaging "a large share of their weekly earnings to the local grocery." Herbert G. Gutman also has noted a Massachusetts shipyard in which many men actually quit their jobs in 1817 when the owner refused to continue their "grog privileges." Furthermore, Gutman describes other examples of premodern behavior two or three decades later that were likely common in the early national period. At the New York shipyards, a workman recalled, mechanics would invariably cease working for a quarter hour at 8:30 A.M. for a snack of doughnuts or biscuits, and again at 10:30 A.M. for candy bought from an English vendor. Then at eleven, many shipwrights would go for a drink at a nearby "grog shop." Some men, in fact, went to the shop ten times a day. The afternoon was marked by two more breaks for candy and cakes.[4]

Central to these preindustrial customs were alcoholic spirits, either beer, gin, or rum. There is no lack of evidence as to the popularity of drinking in Jeffersonian New York. The bottle flowed freely. In 1810 the Humane Society reported that one out of every seven families (2,000) supported themselves by selling "poison" to the rest. In 1811, for example, 1,300 groceries and 160 taverns had licenses to sell "strong drink." By 1817, the number of licenses exceeded 2,000 and was blamed for "the deplorable and unexampled number and suffering of the poor." In the outer mechanic wards, these licenses were granted to small groceries who sold liquor by the drink, "a good glass for three cents," and by the bottle with a quart of brandy going for three shillings and a gallon for $1.25 (a day's pay). The spirits were commonly known as "grog" and its sellers, who one historian claims were mainly Irish, could make a handsome profit.[5] Poet Thomas Eaton described the scene:

> The taverns many, but the stores,
> Now groc'ries call'd are many scores,
> Where thousands are maintain'd in style,
> The poor maintaining them the while.
> Who buy their goods in dublets small,
> And pay large profits on them all.[6]

It was in such taverns and groceries, of course, that the city's artisans celebrated Saint Monday and took their various breaks from the workshop.

The city's medical journal, the noted *Medical Repository*, ever alert to local health problems, did a two-part series on the problem of intoxication in New York. The second issue detailed what the analyst considered to be a typical day's consumption by a local tradesman. The laborer began his day with a small glass (half a gill or eighth of a pint) of "bitters, gin, or something of the sort," at the first grog shop he came upon. Then, before he commenced work he

A local grocery (1813) where liquor was readily available. Next door is a boardinghouse where young and unmarried journeymen often lived. In the foreground is the "Dog Killer and Cart." Museum of the City of New York.

took another half gill. On his way home for breakfast, he drank two more small glasses at the grocery. Thus, "a half pint is disposed of before eight o'clock A.M." After breakfast a full gill was consumed, another at middle of forenoon and then again at dinner. During the afternoon and evening another three gills were imbibed, totaling for the day a full quart of spirits. What was remarkable, according to the medical correspondent, was that "the greater part of them can still keep about, and do their work, without being actually drunk." Although eventually the liquor did take its toll, both in illness and expense (the cost of such excess was a half dollar a day, or enough to buy "bread, butter and sweetenings" for the family), there were yet "hundreds of men who go on as long as their health and money hold out." [7]

Along with drinking, tradesmen celebrated Saint Monday by participating in shooting matches, country excursions, and gambling. Games of chance, especially in the city, were plentiful. Mechanics could be seen wagering at horseraces, cockfights, bil-

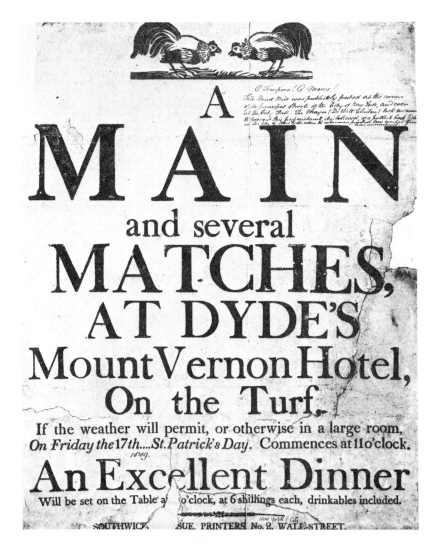

Cockfight broadside, 1809. This was one form of traditional entertainment and gambling. Courtesy, New York Historical Society, New York City.

liards, shuffleboard dice, and cards as well as at bull-baiting contests for which a special rink seating two thousand spectators was constructed. Many lamented the resources squandered at these events. An 1812 Common Council report, for example, condemned poor tradesmen who sacrificed their "small pittance" obtained from a day's labour "in order to imitate, as much as possible, the example of what they may deem the accomplished gentlemen . . . and thereby leave their helpless children in a state of starvation." The brisk business of the city's pawnshops was proof of the popularity of such sport.[8]

Another aspect of mechanics' lives that was likely linked to premodern culture was a common resort to violence. The minutes of the Mayor's Court are replete with cases of assault and battery among craftsmen, their families, and employees. One incident, for example, involved a baker whose wife claimed that she was thrashed by her husband with horsewhips, while a second concerned an indentured lad who sued for release on the grounds that his master beat him excessively. The frustrations of maintaining social and economic standing within a rapidly changing society certainly contributed to the frequent use of force and the large amount of litigation. But the propensity to violence and slander that was a part of preindustrial society was also a factor.[9]

There were, clearly, detrimental aspects to premodern work cultures. As its English historians have pointed out, it could be "intellectually vacant," indolent, brutal, and destructive.[10] But from a more positive viewpoint, it did afford craftsmen time for themselves, time for selective leisure away from work. Moreover, Saint Monday and its attendant customs gave mechanics some control over their work lives. Decisions about how and when they would accomplish their various tasks were in their hands, not those of an industrial boss or his ever present clock. The importance of this is clear in the two examples of traditional journeymen that we have examined. Cabinetmaker Elisha Blossom, it will be remembered, took a job as clerk in 1814 for a bookseller at a good salary. Yet he quickly gave it up because "it was too confining." [11] He wanted the traditional freedom of working at his choice in a task-oriented manner. So, too, journeyman bookbinder Bradford well described the importance of the ability to set his own hours in a poem he wrote entitled "A Song for the Tenth of March: The

Night on Which Journeymen Mechanics Cease Working by Candlelight." According to its author, this was sung, to the tune of "Yankee Doodle," one evening at "PASTE CASTLE":

> The candle-light embargo we've
> Resolved to raise tonight, sirs,
> Until October from this eve,
> No more we'll strike a light, sirs.
>
> Let the masters say what they may,
> And look as grim as can be,
> We'll do't in spite of what they say
> To it—Yankee Doodle Dandy.
>
> For five months every night we were
> Obliged to work till eight, sirs,
> But lamp and candlesticks now are
> Till October out of date, sirs.
>
> Though if at night to work we stay
> You know as well as can be,
> For each hour we'll get the pay,
> Yankee Doodle Dandy.
>
> Now let's be jovial, douse the glim;
> Extinguish every light, sir,
> Tis seven months ere again we'll trim
> Our lamps to work by night, sirs.
>
> Then lay your candle sticks away,
> Where they'll be always handy,
> And jovially we'll end the day,
> With Yankee Doodle Dandy.[12]

As well as depicting the traditional aspiration of a craftsman to set his own hours, Bradford's verse also reveals the inroads of a stricter work code in a trade still chiefly governed by premodern modes of production. For set hours had been established at the bindery for indoor work at certain times of year, and all work in this trade had to be done in the workshop. As described in the preceding chapter, the city's major mechanic trades were undergoing change toward stricter, efficient, quantity production with a stricter regard for work discipline, including attention to work hours. Together with this different pattern of work, a very different moral outlook was also prominent within the city's artisan community, one that emphasized the moderation, integrity, industry, and overall superior moral traits of the active and involved mechanic citizen.

The best source for this ideology is the *Independent Mechanic*, the weekly newspaper appearing for eighteen months in 1811 and 1812. The purpose of his business venture, declared young printer and publisher, Joseph Harmer, was to give his family "sustenance" and to "improve the heart and strengthen the mind" of his tradesmen subscribers. Noting that merchants and lawyers, with greater means and more leisure, could read daily newspapers, while mechanics, with less money and longer hours, could not, Harmer offered his paper as a viable alternative. Now the weary craftsman would have his own journal—free of political intrigue—which he and his "careful and attentive family" could review each Saturday night. Along with a news summary ("Passing Times"); practical advice on such topics as how to move a log, raise sheep, or what underwear to use ("Progress of the Arts"); serialized romantic stories; poetry; and miscellaneous articles, the *Independent Mechanic* ran many essays on what did and what did not constitute proper behavior. From these various offerings, a rough outline of a moral universe emerges.[13]

The most telling contrast between the premodern moral standards and those described in the *Mechanic* can be found in the newspaper's constant attack on the habit of drinking. Spokesmen continually condemned the effect of "taverns and beerhouses." "Censor," scornfully reporting a pathetic knife fight on Fair Street between two drunken "wretches" in which one man's skull was broken, condemned the "multitude of tippling shops" as "dens of iniquity" and "sinks of sin." Taverns were described as the "nurseries of vice and receptacles of the abandoned" for both sexes. Investigations, he declared, were needed of all those who received liquor licenses.[14]

Other writers also attempted to persuade mechanics of the

dangers of alcohol. "Leon" wrote the *Independent Mechanic* to disclose a letter he had received from a youth accused of being a drunkard. The young man denied the charge, but in so doing carefully described the effects of alcohol. A drunk "sacrifices his youth and health, his prospects and his fame." He brings "grey hairs" to his parents, dishonors his family, and loses all friends. He stands alone, a "mark for scorn to point her finger at." In another communication, "Censor" told of a young sailor who, falling in with the "bloods," took up drinking only to be forced to resign from the navy. Soon he turned to burglary and finally committed suicide in disgrace. "TLS," lamenting that intoxication was "so common," named it as the origin of all vices, an evil that turns children into "vagabonds." These and other articles, including one from "Dr. Franklin's File," again and again lamented the perils of liquor, the "parent of idleness and extravagance," and the certain "forerunner of poverty." [15]

Strictures against "gaming" were often included with the articles describing the perils of drunkenness. One writer, calling the vice "very prevalent" in the city, demanded the "interposition of the magistracy." Nothing, he claimed, corrupted tradesmen more than this, the "meanest human passion." Another moralist asserted that no state of mind was more to be pitied than that of the gambler. This "sinful practice" perverted the "understanding" and became a most "laborious" calling, one that did not allow even "that remission which the laws, both of God and Man, have provided for the meanest mechanic."[16]

As well as condemning major elements of preindustrial artisan culture, the *Independent Mechanic* also put forward its conception of mechanics' proper values and behavior. Central to such conduct was a controlled, moderate lifestyle. Correspondent "Misery" cautioned tradesmen to live a quiet, honest, and industrious life. Craftsmen desiring to defeat poverty would do well not to promise customers what they could not deliver, but to contract only for what they could produce. Another columnist, "Robert the Scribe," illustrated this point with the example of Titus Thornbury, an unfortunate farmer who in his zeal to expand his profits, bought extensively on credit, only to find himself in constant fear of the dun. Mechanics, "Robert" warned, should neither buy what they did not need nor purchase on credit what they could do without.[17]

A consequence of greed even more dangerous than financial embarrassment was mental anguish. As a contributor to the *Independent Mechanic* described, "A man whose greatest anxiety is to amass wealth can never be a happy man." Such a being quickly became a slave to riches and appetite and to a desire to copy "the absurd and vicious fashions of a gay, thoughtless, and licentious people." Soon he was confined by the "reproaches of conscience" to a "personal hell." [18] Far more content was a tradesman who pursued a plain life, in search of the "sublime world of nature," and a "more intimate acquaintance with himself." Likely in accord with the agrarian backgrounds of many of the city's craftsmen, the *Mechanic* published many contemplative pastoral pieces describing trips to the country and such sites as Passaic Falls. One point of these essays was that in nature's grandeur, "my neighbor's splendid room, high rank and riches ... beget in me no envy." True happiness was not dependent on wealth but on a clear conscience, a "mind void of guilt or free from any intentional errors." Truly a "sturdy son of industry" who had earned his bread honestly by the "sweat of his brow," avoiding the depths of poverty, could look upon his life with "serene relief." [19]

Together with a mature sense of perspective, mechanics desiring a life of rectitude and peace were well advised to seek and cherish a harmonious family life. For by the hearth the tradesman was the center of his world, equal to anyone in society and likely to achieve a sense of tranquility absent in the homes of more prominent individuals. The importance of domestic joy was well described in a poem written by a "Journeyman Mechanic" and entitled "Saturday Night":

> Now wife and children let's be gay,
> My work is done, and here's the pity;
> 'Twas hard to earn, but never mind it,
> Hope rear's the sheaf, and peace shall bind it.
>
> Six days I've toil'd and now we meet
> To share the welcome weekly treat,
> Of toast and tea, of rest and joy,
> Which, gain'd by labour, cannot cloy.

Come ye who form my dear fireside,
My care, my comfort and my pride;
Come, now, and let us close the night
In harmless sports of fond delight.

To-morrow's dawn brings blessed peace,
And each domestic joy's increase,
To him who honestly maintains
That course of life which heaven ordains.

Of rich and poor, the difference what?—
In working or in working not,
Why then on Sunday we're as great
As those who own some vast estate.

For on to-morrow's happy day
We shall work less, perhaps, than they;
And though no dainties it afford,
What's sweet and clean will grace our board.

This known, for every blessing given
Thankful we'll bow our head to heaven;
At God's own house our voices raise,
With grateful notes of prayer and praise!

Such duties will not interfere,
Nor cloud my brow with thoughts severe;
But still leave time enough to spend,
To take a walk or see a friend.

Sweet the serenity of heart,
That public worship does impart;
And sweet the field and sweet the road,
To him whose conscience is not dead!

Thus shall the day, as God designed,
Improve my health, unbend my mind.
And Monday morning, free of pain,
Cheerful I'll go to work again,

Come ye who form my dear friends,
My care, my comfort, and my pride;
Come, now, and let us close the night
In harmless sports of fond delight.[20]

Vital to this loving home was a good relationship between spouses. Many an article was devoted to domestic difficulties and their solution. Women were commonly seen as the source of trouble, often because of a poor upbringing. Mechanics were well advised to look to the nurture of their daughters. They had to guard them carefully against the snares of the city, as the streets of New York, with a prostitute population of between twelve hundred and seven thousand, had lured away all too many of the offspring of neglectful parents.[21] Of equal importance, they were to rear them to be faithful and obedient mates, attuned to the happiness of the home. As "Robert the Scribe" noted, young women were not to seek to become "belles of the town" surrounded by foolish admirers and betraying flippant manners. Rather, they were to learn to bear a meek and modest deportment, that they might appreciate "substance" and "solid acquirement." Of foremost concern was their ability to discern the true intentions of a man and to be "domestic." Fortunately, "Robert" concluded, "given a solid moral education, women will prefer the home, their proper abode." [22]

A letter received from a reader of the *Mechanic,* "A Tradesman," discussed the problem of a wife who strayed from proper behavior. Describing himself as a mechanic, a "good workman" able to find employment and to earn an adequate salary, he asked that his communication be printed since his wife read the paper and might be led to understand his misery. When he was single, "Tradesman" relates, he saved his money and looked for a neat, respectable spouse who was neither extravagant in dress nor fond of "company keeping." He then met his wife, they married three months later, and all was well at first. Soon, however, she made certain female acquaintances at tea parties. From them, unfortunately, she developed a strong "discontent" with her present possessions, and a taste for extravagance "unfitting for a mechanic's wife." The rag carpet was a "disgrace," as Mrs.——— had a fine Turkish carpet. The chairs were "not fit" compared with Mrs.———'s painted rush bottom." Their calico curtain should be burned in view of Mrs.———'s "white muslin." And the furniture was "too common." At first complying, "Tradesman" bought her new goods, only to have her call them "old fashioned" when they were "scarcely soiled." Meanwhile, her friends' husbands were steadily going bankrupt. Finally he cracked down, locked up the money, and forbade her to run up a debt. Enraged, his wife let her appearance become "careless and sloppy," refusing to leave home since she could "not appear like a Christian." His plight was difficult. Like most mechanics, he looked forward to coming home to a "smiling wife" but instead he found only a "frown and slovenly neglect" from a woman who cared neither for his opinion nor that of the world.[23]

Women, too, wrote to the *Independent Mechanic*. Their responses did not contradict the staunch moralistic position of the paper's male correspondents. On the other hand, while remaining within the fold of righteousness, they asserted their rights with considerable skill.

"Sara Touchstone," for example, presented a defense of women's ability to raise their offspring. Her arguments were given in reply to "A FRIEND TO FEMALES," a correspondent who advised women against taking their children to church, since their "naked bosoms," exposed to "gaping men," together with the cries of their infants, caused inattentiveness. Mrs. Touchstone answered that she herself had a strong need for church. After her devotions she felt "as if I had something very heavy taken from my breast." Nor did her son, "God bless his little dimpled cheek," disturb the congregation. Women's responsibilities in raising their children required their attendance along with their sons and daughters, particularly considering the profligate youth at large in the city. Nor, finally, would sincere churchgoers be distracted by exposed breasts and crying infants. A moral mother had a right and duty to lead her children to worship each Sunday.[24]

Winter Scene in the Sixth Ward. The large building on the right is the "Old Methodist Meetinghouse." Also pictured (left to right) are the dwellings of a bedstead maker and wood inspector, and the "Working Womans Home." Museum of the City of New York.

As "Journeyman Mechanic's" verses depicting the "serenity of heart" that "public worship" afforded, and "Sarah Touchstone's" description of the importance of church to her peace of mind imply, religion was also a major force in the moral life of the mechanic family. Indeed, a "belief in an overruling Providence" was deemed essential to proper conduct. "Monitorial" claimed that religious faith and diligent church attendance were necessary to ward off "depravity." Attention to the pulpit provided the guidance necessary for a true "recognition of holiness." "Scripturus," moreover, declared that a true understanding of the Bible, with its "satisfactory account of everlasting being," afforded insights for genuine happiness regardless of the "vicissitudes of life"— even "poverty and affliction." Finally, "The Gleaner" related a story about a young girl who, through great personal sacrifice, cared for her Aunt Eunice and her two young children. Only the "benign" influence of religion could account for her benevolent behavior.[25]

In making its case for a moderate, sober, religious, and family-centered outlook, the *Independent Mechanic* often contrasted this ideal artisan conduct with descriptions of the pernicious values it associated with the upper and lower classes of the city. The wanton behavior of idleness and debauchery that it describes for New York's elite and meaner elements, coupled with its similar condemnation of premodern mechanic customs, strongly suggests that the editor saw a connection between the two lifestyles.

The parallel is evident in a description of one lamentable member of the city's gentry. A sad "slave to sensual gratification," this man rose each morning after eleven with "grog beaten eyes," and, after many attempts, barely managed to dress himself. Then it was off to his place of business, the tavern, where he consumed in good style a pot of ale and many "segars." This toil lasted from three to eight when it was time for supper: "four pounds of beef, eighteen oysters, thirty pots of beer and a shoulder of mutton—topped by a bucket of brandy." After a little more wine and six additional portions of beef, this poor wretch, assisted by the watchman, finally stumbled home.[26]

The vices of idleness and disdain for work were singled out in descriptions of the empty, meaningless lives of the children of the wealthy. A number of writers described the hours wasted by affluent young ladies as they scorned mechanic suitors in preference to young men who, more than likely, turned out to be empty "fops." [27] Treated with even greater contempt were the city's upstart beaux," the sons of the elite. Aping the fashions of European cities and considering themselves a "superior class," they passed those of lesser callings with "cheeks swollen with arrogance and pride." One such group, the "bloods," youthful miscreants without occupation, walked through the thoroughfares, their arms linked, shoving aside pedestrians and shouting the *"most gross"* obscenities at passing women. Others spent their days pretending to read important correspondence which usually consisted of five lines of nothing. Indeed, how much more praiseworthy was the "honest, blunt and unaffected manners of a young mechanic" than the "pedantic foppish airs of a would-be gentleman." [28]

Original watercolor drawing by   *Broadway - gatan och Rådhuset i New York*   *Baron Klinchowström*

Broadway at City Hall in 1819. Notice the gentry elegantly parading on the sidewalks and in carriages. It was this ostentatious display, and especially that of the wealthy youth, that provoked much of the ridicule in the *Independent Mechanic*. Museum of the City of New York.

The habits of the lower class, too, received harsh judgment. Their generally miserable condition was seen as the result of their unwillingness to work. In one article discussing the "cure for poverty," a contributor wrote that "industry" was the only remedy. Begging, unfortunately, had become a very popular profession in the city, and the only viable solution to this difficult problem was a tough, disciplined *"work house."* Similarly, "Censor" called for the strict enforcement of ordinances against vagrants, those intoxicated "filthy wretches" who wandered and slept in the public streets "half naked, and apparently covered with vermin." It was sad, indeed, he lamented, to compare the pleasure that the "industrious mechanic" gained from a day "well spent" with the listlessness and languor" of the "unoccupied idle." Since opportunity was plentiful in "this happy country," there was no excuse for the wasted lives of these vagrants.[29]

In summary, the *Independent Mechanic* drew a strong case for the life of the humble artisan as the noblest and most righteous existence. The craftsman was ideally pictured as a moderate, decent, honest, religious man, a good parent, and a responsible citizen. He cared more for nature and self-contentment than for the fleeting glory of wealth and renown. This was in stark contrast to the dissipated and wasteful life of those both above and below him in social standing. Providing he forsook the pursuit of drink and gambling, the craftsman's lot was one of profound satisfaction.

There is considerable evidence that the moral code outlined in the *Independent Mechanic* had a significant following within the artisan community. Examples of scorn for the values and life-styles of the upper and lower classes were certainly common. Disdain of the city's gentry is clearly evident in the pointed political attacks against those who held contemptuous attitudes toward mechanics or who endeavored to restrict their political freedom. So, too, in the marketplace craftsmen resented the scorn with which merchant bankers treated artisan entrepreneurs, and the avarice of their attempts to establish monopolistic firms within the mechanic trades.

Contempt for the moral habits and culture of those of inferior social standing was also plentiful. The lack of sympathy for those to be aided by Livingston's public workshops, for the poor unable to afford increases in the price of bread, and for the Irish cartmen wanting to retain their jobs reflects this attitude. Two further perceptive examples of mechanics' disregard for the life-style of the lower class are attempts by artisans to prevent the erection of schools for blacks and immigrants in their neighborhoods. In 1812 residents of the Sixth Ward near William and Duane streets asked the city not to allow a lot near them to be used as a site for a proposed African Free School. Not only was the location far from the homes of most Africans, but it was also valuable property that would increase in worth. Surely, they reasoned, "where a good is attainable as well by a small sacrifice of public property, as by a large sacrifice, there the small sacrifice ought to be made." By choosing a public lot in a more suitable area, fewer people would be hurt and their families not disturbed from the "noise, confusion and uproar" of the youth, "especially of those who belong to the lower class of society." This "remonstrance" was similiar to a petition two years earlier from residents near Augustus Street that protested a proposed site for an "Economical Free School" for the children of French and Spanish immigrants. Once again the inhabitants complained of the noise, confusion, and loss of property value, all of which amounted to "no small grievance." [30]

There is also significant evidence that a considerable portion of the mechanic community valued an honest, balanced life centered around the family and religion. Sailmaker Stephen Allen, later mayor of New York, in reflecting upon his career, agreed with those advising tradesmen against extensive reliance on credit or overextension. A key to his success, Allen declared, was the maxim "not to be in debt and if possible to avoid it." For, he warned, "in a large majority of cases, when the means are wanting to supply the comforts of life, independent of obligation to others, there is little or no happiness." A mechanic was to labor with "industry and full attention to business." Hard work, "good faith and candour towards all" were more likely to succeed than fanciful diversions. An artisan ought to work diligently and honestly at what he knew best, remaining within his own means.[31]

The sense that the mechanic leading an upright life had peace of mind and a clear conscience, a common topic in the *Independent Mechanic*, was evident in a ditty introducing the listing of the city's masons in *Longworth's Directory*.

> ———I pay my debts,
> I steal from no man; would not cut a throat
> to gain admission to a great man's purse,
> or a whore's bed; I'd not betray a friend
> to get his place of fortune; I scorn to
> flatter a blown up fool above me or crush
> the wretch below me.[32]

So, too, contentment of nature, particularly in bucolic scenes reminiscent of agrarian childhoods, appeared in the poems of typographer Samuel Woodworth. A stanza of one of his more well-known verses illustrates this theme:

How dear to this heart are the scenes of my childhood,
  When fond recollection presents them to view!
The orchard, the meadow, the deep tangled wildwood,
  And every loved spot which my infancy knew!
The wide-spreading pond, and the mill that stood by it,
  The bridge, and the rick where the cataract fell,
The cot of my father, the dairyhouse nigh it,
  And e'en the rude bucket, that hung in the well—
The old oaken bucket, the iron-bound bucket,
The moss covered bucket which hung in the well.[33]

The Mechanics Society was also concerned with the subject of morality. Indeed at one of its annual New Year's meetings it toasted "Religion and Morality" as the "necessary and indispensable props of our freedom." The society was especially cognizant of deficiencies in the moral training of the children within the mechanic community. For, as the organization's leaders were well aware, the formal education of many offspring of tradesmen was limited and sporadic. Quite a few did attend either a charity or an inexpensive pay school for at least a few years before they took their indentures. This was enough to acquire the rudiments of arithmetic and reading, and for children of more prosperous craftsmen, who went longer, a somewhat more refined background. But this schooling was also subject to constant interruption by domestic need or the father's lack of interest or employment. During apprenticeship, education, generally confined to evening classes and subject to the discretion and funds of the master, was also erratic.[34]

Responding to the numerous gaps in the minds of youthful artisans, in 1820 the General Society of Mechanics and Tradesmen proudly opened an Apprentices Library, an institution from which, they noted, "all pernicious and immoral works" were excluded. At the institution's dedication, Mechanics Society President Thomas Mercein explained that a major purpose of the new library was to protect New York from "crimes and atrocities" and the "moral contagion, that stalks throughout many of the older cities of the world like a wasting pestilence." Only "the general effect of early education" could direct onto "the peaceful paths of virtue and

industry" youths who otherwise would "pursue the walks of ignorance and depravity, until vice had sealed their hearts against
repentance and prepared them for crimes of the most atrocious
character."

Addressing the assembly of apprentices who had come together
for the dedication along with the students of the society's own
school, Mercein admonished:

> Cherish, I beseech you, a deep-rooted abhorrence of the
> alluring but fatal paths of vice and dissipation. You there
> gather the poisonous leaves of the Upas, and not the laurel of
> renown. Industry, ardour, sobriety and perseverance in your
> different pursuits, will lead to successful competition in the
> world: these will enable you to be useful in your generation,
> and in old age, to look back with delight on the bright season
> of your youthful days, when the foundation of your prosperity
> was securely laid.[35]

Appreciative of this message, the students replied with gratitude.
Their spokesman, Daniel Lowber, called on his fellow scholars to
repay their parents' solicitude by "strictest diligence in the path of
our duty," and by respecting their instructors, "who labour to
improve our minds and form our characters to usefulness." The
apprentice respondent, John Post, noted that while most of his
fellow apprentices were acquainted by their work with the difference between rude material and fine craftsmanship, yet "when we
turn our eyes to the moral world, few, alas! very few of our number
have any adequate perception of the immeasurable distance between the cultivated and the neglected human mind." Unfortunately, because masters, despite their good intentions, often put
their business ahead of their better judgment and failed to encourage their charges to better themselves, "a paternal care and cir-
cumspect watchfulness ... of moral and intellectual education"
was "seldom compatible with an apprenticed condition." Consequently, Post asked the society's elders to become the special
patrons of the city's eight thousand apprentices, though specifying
that the apprentices sought "not the higher walks of literature"
which their "lot of labour" precluded, but only "that simple

THIS INDENTURE

WITNESSETH, That *Charles Andrew aged Fifteen years and six months* Hath put himself, and by these Presents, with the consent and approbation of two of ~~the Aldermen of the City of New-York, and of~~ the Commissioners of the Alms-House of the said City, ~~doth voluntarily,~~ and of his own free will and accord, put himself Apprentice to *Robert Lambert* to learn the Art, Trade and Mystery of *a Cordwainer* and after the manner of an Apprentice to serve from the day of the date hereof, for and during, the full end and term of *Five years and six months* next ensuing: During all which time, the said Apprentice his Master faithfully shall serve, his secrets keep, his lawful commands every where readily obey: He shall do no damage to his said Master, nor see it done by others, without letting or giving notice thereof to his said Master: He shall not waste his said Master's goods, nor lend them unlawfully to any: He shall not commit fornication, nor contract matrimony within the said term: at cards, dice, or any other unlaw-ful game he shall not play, whereby his said Master may have damage: with his own goods, nor the goods of others, without licence from his said Master, he shall neither buy nor sell: He shall not absent himself day nor night from his said Master's ser-vice, without his leave; nor haunt ale-houses, taverns, nor play-houses; but in all things behave himself as a faithful Apprentice ought to do, during the said term. And the said Master shall use the utmost of his endeavour to teach, or cause to be taught or instructed, the said Apprentice, in the Trade or Mystery of *a cordwainer* And procure and provide for him sufficient meat, drink, apparel, lodging, and washing, fitting for an apprentice, during the said term of *Five years and six months, teach him to read write and cypher to the Rule of Three, give him a suit of new cleathes, and a new Bible at the expiration of the Term.*

AND for the true performance of all and singular the Covenants and Agreements afore-said, the said parties bind themselves each unto the other firmly by these Presents. IN WITNESS whereof, the said parties have interchangably set their hands and seals hereunto. Dated the *Seventh* day of *August* in the *Thirty fourth* year of the Independence of the United States of America, and in the year of our Lord One Thousand Eight Hundred and *Nine*.

Sealed and Delivered }
in the Presence of }

John H. Sichels　　*Robt. Lambert*

James Tillery

Apprentice's Indenture, 1809. Notice the concern for the moral, religious, and secular education of the youth. Museum of the City of New York.

mental food, which imparts content to the mind and health to the morals." [36]

The Mechanics Society, as noted in its New Year's Day toast, placed religion on an equal plane with morality. Spokesman M. M. Noah instructed his fellow society members to "be religious; no community ever yet prospered without religion and morality," while student spokesman Lowber, too, asked his classmates to "look to the great God of heaven for direction" in life, whatever their destinies.[37]

These statements, together with those in the *Independent Mechanic*, are indicative that, along with other Americans, artisans were deeply touched by the nationwide revival or "second Great Awakening" that swept through the country beginning at the turn of the century. Decisively defeating the appeal of Deism, a movement that had an impact upon artisans in the 1790s, its local influence could be seen in the numerous revival meetings, missionary societies, pietistic articles and sermons, and in the growth of new congregations. Between 1800 and 1825 New York was home to ninety-three churches, including twenty-one Presbyterian, eighteen Episcopal, fourteen Methodist, and thirteen Dutch Reformed and Baptist parishes. The noted minister Timothy Dwight, visiting New York in the early nineteenth century, observed that the number of citizens believed to be religious was "not small." Many of the churches were "regularly filled," and frequency of attendance was on the rise. The city's clergy were "highly esteemed," and indeed, "everything of a religious nature" was regarded with "reverence by a great proportion of the citizens." [38]

In the outer mechanic wards many new congregations were formed, such as that of the Zion Episcopal Church of the Sixth Ward in which, the minister reported, the membership consisted of "respectable mechanics . . . not in opulent circumstances." Such religious allegiance and appeal was not new, of course. Clergymen had long been attuned to the modern aspirations of the mechanic community. From the 1790s through this era, mechanic Independence Day celebrations had culminated with an oration in one of the city's churches, sometimes delivered by a minister. Stressing belief in a personal divine presence and the power of faith in the fulfillment of an individual life, religion was an important part of the lives of many mechanic families.[39]

(1) The righteous, moral outlook common among Jeffersonian tradesmen drew on a number of sources. One of consequence was the early eighteenth-century English work ethic, based primarily upon Puritan doctrine, but also influenced by benevolism, opposition politics and mercantilism. This ideal valued work that was undertaken not for selfish gain and luxury, but rather in a spirit of industry and frugality (diligence and contentedness) oriented to ths common good.[40] Significantly, the most notable American spokesman for and example of this tradition, indeed, its "apotheosis," was an artisan, printer Benjamin Franklin. In the 1750s Franklin, in various editions of his noted *Poor Richard's Almanac*, preached the same values and modes of behavior that the *Independent Mechanic* detailed seventy years later. This Yankee-bred Philadelphian, who could never condone preindustrial customs, saw his career as a lesson to mechanics (and the entire middling classes of the United States) in how to better themselves and their nation through the practice of sober and conscientious work habits. Many mechanics responded to his achievements and advice. The various artisan societies of the early national era looked to this most famous typographer as a symbol of the opportunity and of the just rewards that came of hard, industrious work performed within the boundaries of an upright standard of conduct.[41]

(2) A second important source of this strict moral outlook was the revolutionary pride of the city's tradesmen. The same quest for dignity and esteem that characterized craftsmen's patriotic celebrations was apparent in their statements of moral value. As the mechanic was the key to maintaining a free, equalitarian, libertarian, and republican government, so too, it was the artisan who alone could set the proper moral direction for the nation. Neither the licentious aristocracy nor the idle lower classes (nor tradesmen still largely under the influence of premodern traditions) were capable of such leadership. The hard working, honest, moderate middle class of tradesmen (and farmers) were the true guardians of republican virtue. Only in their hands could the American experiment be trusted.

(3) A third source of this moral stance was the modern marketplace. By the early nineteenth century an important sector of the mechanic community, the journeymen working in the conflict trades, possessed at least an awareness of the coming industrial age. They

Two engravings describing Franklin's ideals in practice. Taken from a broadside entitled, *Poor Richard Illustrated: Lessons for the Young and Old on Industry, Temperance, Frugality &c.* Courtesy, Yale University Library.

understood that self-control and self-reliance were necessary if they were to prove effective against the considerable capital resources of the masters and merchants. The strict bylaws of the more militant societies demanded this kind of behavior, allowing the journeymen a degree of leverage despite judicial and public hostility. This standard of conduct foreshadowed that held by Jacksonian trades-men in their struggles against factory owners.[42]

The moral outlook of the *Independent Mechanic* was in obvious conflict with the traditional customs common to preindustrial life. But this is not to say that tradesmen could not display patterns of both cultures. The same artisans who listened attentively to Independence Day orations proclaiming the importance of a responsible, educated, and disciplined citizenry, and who formed associations capable of contending forcibly in the modern marketplace, also participated in evenings of drink, merriment, and ceremony that were part of longstanding premodern traditions.[43] This was clearly an age of transition. For, while the growing economy and political system pointed toward a greater acceptance, voluntary or not, of modern work habits and values, new immigrants, entering the city at an increasing pace, strengthened the power of old traditions and cultures. It would be many generations before the ethics and patterns of the capitalist world became fully dominant.

NOTES

1. E. P. Thompson, "Time, Work-Discipline and Industrial Capitalism," *Past and Present*, 38 (1967), 58-97; Douglas Reid, "The Decline of Saint Monday," *Past and Present*, 71 (1976), 75-101.

2. For a discussion of preindustrial life-styles and work habits in America see Bruce Laurie, "Nothing on Impulse: Life Styles of Philadelphia Artisans, 1820-1850," *Labor History*, 15 (1974), 337-366; Eric Foner, *Tom Paine and Revolutionary America* (New York, 1976), pp. 48-56; Herbert G. Gutman, "Work, Culture and Society in Industrializing America, 1815-1919," *American Historical Review*, 78 (1973), 533-588; *Independent Mechanic*, June 13, 1812; *American Citizen*, July 4, 1805; Sidney I. Pomerantz, *New York: An American City, 1783-1803* (New York, 1938), pp. 485-488, 497-501.

3. Reid, "Decline of Saint Monday."

4. Thurlow Weed, *The Autobiography of Thurlow Weed*, ed. Harriet Weed

(Boston, 1883), p. 54. Gutman, "Work, Culture and Society," pp. 544, 556-557.

5. *Evening Post,* January 9, 1810; Rocellus Guernsey, *New York City During the War of 1812* (New York, 1889), p. 73; Report of Committee of the Common Council, City Clerk Filed Papers (hereafter referred to as CC), Box 3181 March 8, 1816; John W. Degraw, *Recollections of Early New York* (New York, 1882); Michael and Ariane Battenberg, *On the Town: A History of Eating, Drinking and Entertainments from 1776 to the Present* (New York, 1973), p. 43.

6. Thomas Eaton, *Review of New York, or Rambles Through the City: Original Poems; Moral, Religious, Sarcastic and Descriptive* (New York, 1813), p. 24.

7. *Medical Repository,* 2d ser., 1 (1804), 333-334.

8. New York City Common Council, *Report of the Committee on the Means to Carry into Effect the Provisions of the "Act for Suppressing Immorality"* (New York, 1812), p. 4. Pomerantz, *New York: An American City,* pp. 485-488, 497-501; David T. Valentine, ed., *Manuals of the Corporation of New York City* (New York, 1842-1868), vol. 5, p. 162; *Independent Mechanic,* June 13, 1812; *American Citizen,* July 4, 1805.

9. For cases see *Evening Post,* January 20, 1806; *American Citizen,* October 19, 1809; *Morning Post,* December 6, 1811; *City Hall Recorder,* 1816, 1817; Mayor's Court Minutes, mss., Historical Documents Collection, Queens College, City University of New York.

10. Thompson, "Time, Work-Discipline and Industrial Capitalism," p. 93.

11. Journal mss., Elisha Blossom, Cabinetmaker, February 1, 1814, New York Historical Society.

12. John Bradford, *The Poetical Vagaries of a Knight of the Folding Stick of PASTE CASTLE, to which is annexed the History of the Garret &, Translated from the Hieroglyphics of the Society by a Member of the Order of the Blue String* (New York, 1813), p. 50.

13. *Independent Mechanic,* April 6, 1811. Harmer's efforts did not succeed in bringing solvency to his project and he soon sold the paper to George Asbridge. Unfortunately, he too could not make ends meet, and the paper folded in October 1812.

14. Ibid., August 10, 1811.

15. Ibid., September 7, 1811, August 17, 31, 1811, April 6, 1811, February 29, 1812.

16. Ibid., November 30, 1811; July 27, 1811.

17. Ibid., November 30, 1811, June 1, 1811, September 7, 1811, October 12, 1811, April 11, 1812.

18. Ibid., November 23, 1811.

19. Ibid., April 6, 1811, May 11, 1811, June 1, 1811, November 9, 1811.

20. Ibid., June 15, 1811. See also March 21, 1812.

21. Ibid., November 23, 1811; Raymond A. Mohl, *Poverty in New York 1783-1825* (New York, 1971), p. 31; *Medical Repository*, 2d. ser., 1 (1804), 91.

22. *Independent Mechanic*, March 21, 1812, September 14, 1811; Nancy McClelland, *Duncan Phyfe and the English Regency, 1795-1830* (New York, 1939), p. 123.

23. *Independent Mechanic*, July 21, 1811.

24. Ibid., December 21, 28, 1811. See also January 4, 1812.

25. Ibid., October 12, 1811, June 8, 1811, November 16, 1811. See also April 20, 27, 1811, June 4, 1811.

26. Ibid., February 15, 1812. See also June 15, 1811, September 5, 1812.

27. Ibid., June 15, 1811, December 28, 1811, January 4, 1812, September 5, 1812, November 30, 1811.

28. Ibid., May, 11, 18, 23, 1811, October 5, 1811.

29. Ibid., August 3, 1811, May 30, 1812.

30. Petition of Inhabitants at and near the Intersection of William and Duane Streets, CC Box 3181, March 8, 1813. Remonstrance against granting a Lot for the Economical Free School, CC Box 3174, July 24, 1810.

31. James C. Travis, ed., "The Memoirs of Stephen Allen, 1767-1852; Sometimes Mayor of New York City, Chairman of the Croton Water Commission, etc." (New York, 1927), p. 93 (typescript at New York Historical Society).

32. *Longworth's New York Directory* (New York, 1806).

33. George A. Stevens, *Typographical Union Number Six* (Albany, 1912), p. 83.

34. Karl E. Kaestle, *The Evolution of an Urban School System: New York City, 1750-1850* (Cambridge, 1973), chap. 2; Thomas Earle and Charles T. Congdon, eds., *Annals of the General Society of Mechanics and Tradesmen* (New York, 1882), p. 21.

35. Thomas Mercein, *An Address upon the Opening of the Apprentices Library* (New York, 1820), pp. 10, 12, 13; M. M. Noah, *An Address upon the Opening of the Mechanics Institute* (New York, 1822).

36. Mercein, *An Address*, pp. 15-18.

37. Noah, *An Address*, p. 11; Mercein, *An Address, p. 17.*

38. Timothy Dwight, *Travels in New England and New York* (New York, 1823), pp. 452-453.

39. Carrol Smith Rosenberg, *Religion and the Rise of the American City: The New York City Mission Movement, 1812-1870* (Ithaca, 1971), pp. 41-69; Hugh Macatamney, *Cradle Days of New York, 1609-1825* (New York, 1909), p. 146; Gordon Wood in Bernard Bailyn et. al., *The Great Republic: A*

History of the American People (Lexington, 1976), p. 409; Carol Groneman Pernicone, " 'The Bloody Ould Sixth': A Social Analysis of a New York City Working-Class Community in the Mid-Nineteenth Century," Ph. D. diss. (University of Rochester, 1973), p. 24.

40. J. E. Crowley, *This Sheba, Self: The Conceptualization of Economic Life in Eighteenth-Century America* (Baltimore, 1974).

41. Ibid., pp. 83-84. For some pertinent examples of Franklin's writing, see L. Jesse Lemisch, ed., *Benjamin Franklin: The Autobiography and Other Writings* (New York, 1961), pp. 92-104, 185-200, and Adrienne Koch, ed., *The American Enlightenment* (New York, 1965), pp. 133-138.

42. Paul Faler, "Cultural Aspects of the Industrial Revolution: Lynn, Massachusetts Shoemakers and Industrial Morality, 1826-1860," *Labor History*, 15 (1974), 367-394; Paul Faler and Alan Dawley, "Working Class Culture and Politics in the Industrial Revolution: Sources of Loyalism and Rebellion," *Journal of Social History*, 9 (1976), 466-471; Laurie, "Nothing on Impulse," pp. 341-350. There were, of course, differences between the outlook of journeymen in the early national era and in the Jacksonian and ante-bellum periods. Jacksonian workingmen saw their employers as equally determined and restrained, while Jeffersonian tradesmen often reviled the upper classes as a useless, gluttonous gentry. Too, the meaning of moral standards differed. "Industry," for example, in the early nineteenth century still referred to diligent hard work, whereas toward midcentury it denoted a "devotion to methodical work routine."

43. See Robert Sean Wilentz, "Artisan Cultural Life in Jacksonian New York," paper delivered at annual meeting of the Organization of American Historians, New York, 1978.

CONCLUSION

Mechanics in the Jeffersonian era achieved significant gains. In the marketplace, within traditionally organized crafts, enterprising masters attained notable financial success, inspiring ambition and pride among fellow mechanics. Furthermore, artisans in individual trades (masters and journeymen) proved worthy lobbyists for tariff protection; if they were not always successful, their petitions were respectfully treated and fully answered. Too, the chartering of the Mechanics Bank, with the largest capitalization of any local financial institution to that date, is telling evidence of the ability of the artisan population to effectively wield its influence. Equally impressive were tradesmen's efforts against potential monopolistic institutions such as the proposed Livingston workshop. In this case, most of the backers of the plan, including many of the city's most prominent merchants and attorneys, quickly recanted their support when they learned of the general concern of the metropolis's craftsmen. Licensed mechanics, as well, were vocal with their demands, gaining a degree of leverage within the Common Council.

In the conflict trades, masters also proved adept at harnessing the growing market for sizable profits. Whether in liaison with mercantile outlets or in efforts to make it on their own, they took advantage of the rapidly expanding economy. Perhaps of even greater consequence were the actions taken by the city's journeymen against masters' attempts to cut labor costs and enforce impersonal, disciplined methods. Forming vibrant, militant trade associations, they battled the masters with a variety of well-planned measures, including boycotts, the establishment of journeymen-owned stores, and both limited and general (by trade) walkouts. In the execution of these actions, they developed and articulated many of the tactics and ideals that would inform labor movements in the following generations. Masters' responses, too, carried critical significance. Their use of the courts, of strike-breakers, and of joint action against rebellious journeymen would continue prominent as management tactics in American labor conflict.

In politics, it will be remembered, the mechanic community also achieved meaningful gains. Building on their considerable electoral experience during the revolutionary era and in the 1790s, they afforded the Democratic-Republicans the votes necessary to overcome the opposition Federalists. In return, mechanics received about one-fourth of the nominations for assembly and charter offices, and at least that many actual positions. It is true that most of these candidacies went to the mechanic elite, the eminent proprietors of sailmaking, coachmaking, and other well-established manufactories. But they still represented the artisan consituency's quest for greater recognition. Moreover, most mechanics could vote, and in defeating the Federalists with their ballots, they were subduing that element in the community which questioned their political abilities, coerced their votes, and threatened to restore an aristocratic society. Even during the embargo and War of 1812, when Jeffersonian and Madisonian foreign policy was costing artisans dearly in loss of work and steeply inflated prices, the mechanic constituency for the most part remained loyal to the Republicans. The battle against those who would bring back an English way of life in which tradesmen were once again but a subservient class was yet deserving of the sacrifice that had been given in '76.

As they participated, year after year, in New York's various elections, mechanics achieved an enduring political influence. After three decades of activity in electoral contests, they were no longer political novices in an age of experiment and uncertainty, but seasoned veterans at a time of established procedure and organization. With the Federalists languishing without their support, it was clear that any party hoping to gain and hold power in the city would have to orient its slate, its appeal, and its program to take into account the needs and aspirations of tradesmen. They were a part of the system. This attainment of a recognized and continuing role in American government was both a major achievement and a source of pride to the mechanic community.

These economic and political accomplishments of Jeffersonian mechanics were most significant, influencing American workingmen for generations. But it must be pointed out that there was also considerable reason for concern. In the marketplace, the outlook, especially for the journeymen, was uncertain at best. Despite the growth of trade associations and the execution of well-organized and sometimes effective walkouts, there was little change in the stark economic inequities—which were, in fact, becoming greater— that threatened to turn journeymen's egalitarian assertions into empty rhetoric.[1] For the masters, too, there was cause for concern. While they may have been successful in preventing publicly owned monopolies, there was little they could do in the growing capitalist market to thwart the rise of factory-like establishments such as the New York Bread Company, enterprises that endangered the business of many an artisan entrepreneur. Furthermore, the entry of mercantile capital into the mechanic trades threatened to turn the master's role into that of a wage-earning foreman, just a step above journeyman standing.

In politics, too, there was cause for worry. Journeymen, particularly, stood little chance of gaining assistance. Their position was incompatible with the ideologies of both the Republicans and the Federalists, and with the economic interests of the merchants and masters who occupied leadership roles in the two major parties. Even the masters, however, other than in exceptional circumstances, could not expect the dominant mercantile elements to support a stand limiting the possibilities of investment and expansion by restricting the private formation of large and potentially monopolistic operations. Furthermore, evidence of the willingness of the Republicans, and particularly dissident factions, to manipulate the interests of artisan constituents solely for personal ambition gave mechanics reason to question the ultimate commitment of that party to their cause.

However, despite these serious concerns and misgivings, for the bulk of New York's artisan population the early national period was an era not of disaffection, but of cautious optimism. For if they could not command the nation's political and economic destinies, tradesmen yet held great hope for the future. Assuredly, masters were troubled over the entry of monopolistic factories, and about the potential mercantile domination of their crafts. The seemingly unlimited promise of the open market, however, remained a stronger force. Journeymen, too, were apprehensive about the increasingly inegalitarian society emerging from the capitalist economy. Still, the congratulatory spirit of their societies' toasts, parades, and speeches, and the proud tone of their marketplace demands, displayed considerable faith about their place in the new republic. The mechanic constituency as a whole, threatened by Federalist elitism and Republican factionalism, also had cause for disquietude. But for the majority of mechanics this was insufficient reason for surrendering either their faith in the Jeffersonian movement or the optimism generated by the accomplishment of '76. Unlike their English counterparts, subject to severe governmental repression, New York's mechanics were heirs to a revolution. The country they lived in was their creation. Their confidence in the victory of American republicanism, and of the enduring and central position of the artisan in that triumph, remained predominant.

NOTES

1. Edmund P. Willis, "Social Origins and Political Leadership in New York City from the Revolution to 1815," Ph. D. diss. (Berkeley, 1967), pp. 113-119.

BIBLIOGRAPHICAL ESSAY

Local New York City newspapers are the basic sources for evidence of mechanics' activities in labor conflicts and in politics. The two most helpful papers, both dailies, are the Republican *American Citizen* (1800-1810) and the Federalist *Evening Post* (1801-1820 +). The New York Historical Society has nearly complete files of both papers. Supplementing these volumes are the *Columbian* (1809-1820 +) for the Clintonian view, the *National Advocate* (1812-1820 +) for the Madisonian position, and the *Morning Chronicle* (1802-1807) for the Burrite stance. The Federalist *Commercial Advertiser* (1797-1820 +) and *Mercantile Advertiser* (1801-1820 +) are less politically oriented but still helpful, as is the Republican *Morning Post* (1810-1812) and the *Public Advertiser* (1807-1813). The Federalist *Washington Republican*, a weekly published for six months in 1809, is valuable as an example of a political newspaper aimed specifically at the mechanic. The *Independent Mechanic* (1811-1812), also a weekly directed at workingmen, was decidedly nonpolitical, but is important for its wealth of evidence on social and moral values. All of the above public prints are available at the New York Historical Society. Occasional missing issues can often be found at the New York Public Library. The political broadsides available in both of these institutions provide important supplements to the newspapers.

A number of valuable quantitative sources exist for the study of the New York City workingman in the early republic. Various account books for masons, carpenters, bakers, and day laborers are available in the manuscript collections of the New York Historical Society, the New York Public Library, and the Henry F. Du Pont Winterthur Library in Wilmington, Delaware. Even more valuable than these unassimilated and scattered records are the New York City Jury Lists for 1816 and 1819 located in the Historical Documents Collection at Queens College, New York City. These documents contain by ward a census of male inhabitants over twenty-one, including age; the number of children, women, servants, and slaves in each household; the location and number of inhabitants of each dwelling; the occupational status (including trade and whether the resident is a journeyman); racial category; and general wealth and property-holding classifications. The Historical Documents Collection also contains helpful rent receipts, will libers, and will inventories along with Mayor's Court records and documents. *Longworth's New York Directory* for the years of this study, available at the New York Historical Society, is valuable for identifying occupational status of political candidates. Newspapers provide lists of candidates and voting results. Finally, the manuscript collection of the New York Historical Society contains the membership list of the Washington Benevolent Society, a Federalist political club which had many mechanic members.

Manuscript sources have been only occasionally helpful. Useful information was found in the papers of Matthew Davis and James McComb at the New York Historical Society. The papers of De Witt Clinton (Columbia University and New York Historical Society) and Richard Varick (New York Public Library and New York Historical Society) along with Peter Van Zandt (New York Public Library) were also consulted and were occasionally helpful. References to workingmen are infrequently scattered throughout the papers of major figures of this era, but to collect such references would be a gargantuan task and one which, in the end, might reveal little valuable information. More helpful are such items as the Shipwrights Society Constitution at the New York Public

Library, the typescript of the minutes of the General Society of Mechanics and Tradesmen located at the society's library in New York City, and the typescript of the life of Stephen Allen, located at the New York Historical Society.

If manuscripts of public figures are of limited assistance, this gap is more than made up for in the uncatalogued collection of letters, petitions, memorials, and public documents available at the library of the New York City Municipal Archives on Park Row in New York City. The manuscript records of decisions of committees of the Common Council are located there, along with the many requests for employment, remission of fines, tax relief, removal of public nuisances, and any other type of communication a resident might send to his elected officials. Many of the everyday problems of workingmen are depicted in the handwritten messages lying in the archive's boxes, as well as invaluable information on the problems of the regulated tradesmen.

Published primary sources are also of considerable help. Various issues of the *Laws and Ordinances Ordained and Established by the Mayor, Aldermen, and Commonalty of the City of New York* (New York, 1799, 1801, 1803, 1807, 1812) along with *Minutes of the Common Council of the City of New York, 1784-1831,* 21 vols. (New York, 1917-1930) are essential in understanding the working conditions of regulated tradesmen. For unregulated mechanics, George Barnett, "The Printers, A Study in Trade Unionism," *American Economic Association Quarterly,* 3d ser., 10 (1909), and George A. Stevens, *Typographical Union Number Six* (Albany, 1912), contain constitutions, labor agreements, minutes, and occasional letters of the New York Typographical Society. Volume 3 of John R. Commons et al., *A Documentary History of American Industrial Society,* 10 vols. (New York, 1909-1911) contains the important transcript of the New York cordwainers conspiracy trial in 1809. This includes testimony and arguments over labor practices as well as the constitution of the Cordwainers Society and a helpful introduction. Of further assistance among published sources are the various Fourth of July orations made to the Washington Benevolent Society and to the General Society of Mechanics and Tradesmen assembled with other craft and fraternal associations. These give both political and moral clues about the values of workingmen. Finally, the political satire in Washington Irving's *Salmagundi* (New York, 1904) gives perceptive insights into both the Federalist attitude toward mechanics and into the vagaries of popular politics at the local level.

Secondary accounts of the mechanic at work are few. The best labor history of the early national era is still the first volume of John R. Commons et al., *History of Labor in the United States,* 4 vols. (New York, 1926-1935), supplemented by the impressive archival volume by Richard B. Morris, *Government and Labor in Early America* (New York, 1946). For helpful if impressionistic treatments of the American craftsman prior to this period, Carl Bridenbaugh, *The Colonial Craftsman* (New York, 1950), supplemented by Jackson Turner Main, *The Social Structure of Revolutionary America* (Princeton, 1965); Eric Foner, *Tom Paine and Revolutionary America* (New York, 1976); and Charles S. Olton, *Artisans for Independence: Philadelphia Mechanics and the American Revolution* (Syracuse, 1975) are available. David T. Gilchrist. ed., *The Growth of Seaport Cities 1790-1875* (Charlottesville, 1967), contains recent and pertinent data and interpretations on the port cities, including New York, for this period. Concerning conditions in New York, two important works are at hand. Sidney I. Pomerantz, *New York: An American City, 1783-1803* (New York, 1938), provides a wealth of information and bibliographic material on early national New York. Edmund P. Willis's excellent computer-oriented study, "Social Origins of Political Leadership in New York City from the Revolution to 1815," Ph. D. diss. (Berkeley, 1967), gives details on the economic and class structure of New York along with a myriad of information concerning the histories of those men elected to state and high local office from the city.

Antique books abound for early American crafts. Since this work has not been concerned with the craftsman as artist, few of these volumes have been helpful. However Charles F. Montgomery's fine book, *American Furniture: The Federal Period 1788-1825* (New York, 1966), is a notable exception. Brook Hindle's small volume, *Technology in Early America* (Chapel Hill, 1966) gives a very useful biblographic essay on the development of the different crafts during this period.

A number of books have been published on the early development of political parties in America, including the fine work by

Alfred F. Young, *The Democratic Republicans of New York* (Durham, 1967). Fortunately Young includes in his book (which takes the party to 1797) a good deal of material on the activity and the importance of the mechanics. Supplementing this volume is his article, "The Mechanics and the Jeffersonians: New York, 1789-1801," *Labor History*, 5 (1964), 247-276. Staughton Lynd's article in the same issue, "The Mechanics in New York City Politics 1774-1785," *Labor History*, 5 (1964), 215-246, is also helpful for background information. For a recent view of local and state politics, Jerome Mushkat, *Tammany, the Evolution of a Political Machine, 1789-1865* (Syracuse, 1971) provides some help. There is not, however, any work for New York or any other city or state on the political role of the mechanic after the election of Jefferson. Much has been said of the Age of Jackson, yet the period of Republican domination during the early national era was a time of fundamental importance in the development of a politically conscious artisan class. Hopefully, this work will encourage similar studies for other areas.

INDEX

127404